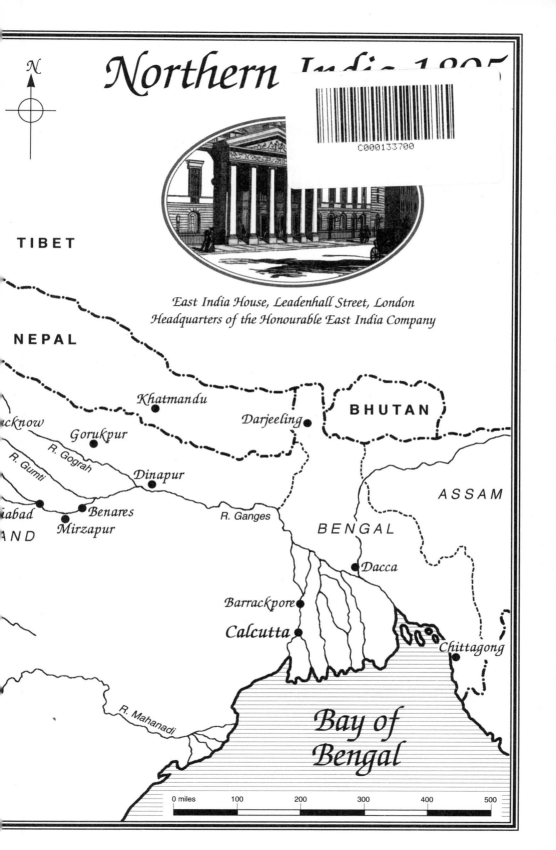

# Northern India 1805

C000133700

East India House, Leadenhall Street, London
Headquarters of the Honourable East India Company

**TIBET**

**NEPAL**

**BHUTAN**

cknow

Khatmandu

Darjeeling

Gorukpur

R. Gograh

R. Gumti

Dinapur

**ASSAM**

abad

Benares

R. Ganges

**BENGAL**

Mirzapur

AND

Dacca

Barrackpore

Calcutta

Chittagong

R. Mahanadi

*Bay of Bengal*

0 miles    100    200    300    400    500

# SOLDIER OF THE RAJ

The Reverend Richard Fortescue Purvis LL.B (Cantab.)
Vicar of Whitsbury, Magistrate for the Counties of Hampshire and Wiltshire
and formerly Captain, Bengal Native Infantry, Honourable East India Company.
*(Reproduced by kind permission of Mrs. C.G.F. Purvis.)*

# SOLDIER OF THE RAJ

IN MEMORY OF
CATHERINE PURVIS (*née* SOWERS)
WHO DIED AT WICKHAM, HAMPSHIRE
ON 3RD FEBRUARY 1789, AGED 31,
ONE MONTH AFTER THE BIRTH OF
HER SECOND SON
RICHARD FORTESCUE PURVIS
WHOSE STORY THIS IS.

# Contents

## PART 3 — HOLY ORDERS

### APPENDIX 1

### APPENDIX 2

### APPENDIX 3

# Plates

**Between pages 80/81:**

(i)     H.M.S. *London (© National Maritime Museum).*
Royal Naval Academy *(© Royal Naval Museum).*

(ii)     Blackbrook Cottage, Fareham.
A Russian cannon-ball from Fort Kinburn.
The Napoleonic Willow.
Blackbrook House.

(iii)     George Purvis R.N. and his wife Renira
*(© Jane Austen Memorial Trust).*
The Purvis Chest.
The Arms of Captain G.T.M. Purvis R.N.
*(Ronald Dunning Esq.).*

(iv)     Letter to Mary-Jane Austen from her father
*(© Jane Austen Memorial Trust).*
Admiral of the Fleet Sir Francis Austen.

**Between pages 160/161:**

(i)     A Sergeant and Grenadier Sepoy c.1812
*(© National Army Museum).*

(ii)     A Grenadier Sepoy of the 30th B.N.I.
*(© National Army Museum).*
Darsham House, Suffolk
*(Mrs. Olive Reeve).*

(iii)     The Children of Edward Holden Cruttenden
*(from a painting by Sir Joshua Reynolds,
Museum of Art, São Paulo, Brazil).*
Lieutenant-Colonel Charles Purvis of Darsham
*(C.J.M. Purvis Esq.).*

(iv)     H.M.S. *Magicienne* leaving Trincomalee
*(© National Maritime Museum).*
Vice-Admiral John Brett Purvis in old age
*(Mrs. W.H.A. Purvis).*
Bury Hall, Gosport *(© British Library).*

**Between pages 240/241:**

# Maps, Plans, etc.

# Conventions

The spelling of Indian place names in the early 19th century was widely inconsistent, often appearing in four different forms in as many documents. In particular, the hard "a", pronounced as "u" in India (Gandhi is pronounced Gundhi) was usually rendered phonetically. Thus, Fatehghur may appear as Futteghur, Futteghar, Futtegur or even Futte Ghur. I have tried, as far as possible, to standardise on the forms used by the Geographical Institute in the late 1920s, by which time a discipline, of sorts, appears to have emerged. I have not, however, altered spellings in letter extracts where the meaning is clear.

I have made some alterations to punctuation in the letters but only where, in their original form, they were unclear or difficult to read. Similarly, I have altered spellings only for the same reasons and have avoided the persistent use of *"sic"* which I feel tends to spoil the rhythm of text when it appears too frequently.

.  .  .    *indicates a passage intentionally omitted.*

[...]    *indicates a word or passage which is illegible.*

[word]    *A* [word] *or* [several words] *in square parentheses indicates my best guess or a considered link to make sense of a passage.*

Regiments of the British Army in India (as opposed to the Armies of the East India Company and, from 1858, the British Indian Army) are distinguished by the prefix H.M. Ships of the Royal Navy are distinguished in the Index by the prefix H.M.S. although this was seldom used in the early 19th century.

Officers' entries in the Index show the rank which they ultimately achieved. In the few cases where I have been unable to identify an officer, I have included him with whatever information is implied within the correspondence. Thus Monckter, who from his despatches from Kamonah was clearly a serving officer, though I have been unable to find any record of him in the India Office archives, is simply listed as — "Monckter, Bengal Army".

# Prologue

One summer afternoon in the late 1950s, I forget the exact year, we were invited to tea with my wife's Great Aunt May Purvis who lived in a big house at Burghfield Common, near Reading in Berkshire.

When we arrived, the old lady was clearly in some distress: her housekeeper had gone down with influenza and she had no idea of how to make the tea herself. She had located the kitchen and identified what she believed to be a kettle but, beyond that, the transaction was a mystery to her. My wife told her not to worry and soon had things under control.

After tea Great Aunt May began to talk about her late husband's family, the Purvises, and encouraged by our attentiveness and obvious interest, confided in us that there was a matter which was causing her much concern: her husband had started life in the Royal Navy and had transferred to the Egyptian Coastguard Service in 1890, becoming its Director-General in 1918. He had retired in 1922, with the rank of Miralai and Pasha, and had died some twenty years previously in 1936. He came from a long line of Admirals, she told us, his family having been prominent in the Navy for over 200 years, and he had inherited many historical letters and documents from his illustrious forebears. It was these that were causing her such concern — she and her husband had had no children themselves and both her husband's younger brothers had died young in the Indian Army. Those documents she had herself identified as valuable, including letters from Lord Nelson, Lord St. Vincent, Lord Collingwood and the Duke of Wellington, she had already presented to the National Maritime Museum at Greenwich. There also appeared to be some connection with the Austen family as there were various other items she had placed in the care of the Jane Austen Memorial Trust.

There was a distant cousin, she told us, who was the "Black Sheep of the Family" and had served a prison sentence for fraud (I shall not identify him). It was imperative that none of her remaining

Purvis treasures should fall into his hands on her death as he would promptly sell them to the highest bidder as he had already done with such heirlooms as he had inherited. She now wished to ensure that all remaining items of family or historical importance were either specified in her Will or were clearly earmarked to pass on to someone who would appreciate their significance and would look after them properly.

She showed us round her house pointing out various objects and pictures but, sadly, we took in only a fraction of what she told us. In Purvis Pasha's study the blinds were drawn. She had honoured her late husband in the same way as Queen Victoria had honoured hers, having left the room untouched, apart from cleaning, since the day in 1936 when he had died. His pen lay beside an unfinished letter and a copy of *The Times* lay folded and unread upon the desk. In the window bay stood a small, brass-bound, leather trunk about two feet long by one foot deep and one foot high. It was a Midshipman's chest, she said, which had belonged to one of her husband's ancestors and had been aboard the *Victory* at the Battle of Trafalgar. We also understood her to say, though we might have remembered incorrectly — she told us so many things that day — that this ancestor had been a friend of one of Jane Austen's brothers who was also a Midshipman in the Navy.

While my wife was shown round upstairs I had to remain in the drawing room — gentlemen were not allowed upstairs — and when she came down she had a bundle of family papers from which, she explained, she had already extracted anything of obvious value and was now uncertain what to do with the remainder. She did not want them to be burned after her death as she had often seen done when houses were being cleared. Knowing that I wrote articles on military history, she wondered if I would be interested in them and could be trusted to keep them safe. I promised her I would.

Great Aunt May died a few years later and my wife inherited certain of her possessions including a small chair, carved by Purvis Pasha, whose absorbing interest in his retirement had been carpentry; a picture of an Admiral which we assumed to be one of the Purvises; three small engravings of Lords Howe, St. Vincent and Nelson; two rather crude watercolours of Nelson's funeral, painted by one of the

Purvises; and the little brass-bound chest which we had seen in Purvis Pasha's study.

For the next thirty-five years the Purvis Chest stood in the window of a spare bedroom in our house and, when asked, we would tell curious visitors what we knew of it: — it was a Midshipman's chest which had belonged to one of the Purvis family and had been aboard the *Victory* at Trafalgar; we believed, moreover, that this Midshipman had been a friend of one of Jane Austen's brothers.

We told the same story to the representative of one of our leading antique auction houses (which I shall not identify either) when he came to undertake the periodic insurance valuation of our house contents. He was not impressed. It smelled all wrong, he told us, the wood was too new to be of the period we believed. The Phillips representative who did the next valuation, some years later, was more astute. Yes, he said, someone had restored it within the last hundred years; the outside shell was clearly late 18th century but the feet had been added and much of the interior wooden carcass had been replaced. Remembering Purvis Pasha's passion for woodwork and his beautifully-equipped carpentry workshop in the grounds of his house, all became clear.

Some years after her death, Great Aunt May's house at Burghfield Common was demolished to make way for a housing estate.

In July 1996, some friends of ours, Geoffrey and Hazel Holt, came to lunch with us. Hazel is Barbara Pym's biographer and literary executor as well as being a very successful author of detective stories. They had an American friend staying with them at the time, Dr. Jan Fergus, and asked if they could bring her with them. Jan is an eminent scholar and Jane Austen expert, with a much-respected published work on the subject to her credit, so we naturally showed her the Chest and told her of the tenuous Austen connection. She was intrigued and insisted that I should investigate the matter and establish its full provenance before she returned to England the following year. On her way out, Jan spotted the picture which we believed to be a Purvis Admiral and immediately identified it as Admiral of the Fleet Sir Francis Austen, the elder of Jane Austen's two sailor brothers.

The next day I took down Aunt May's bundle of papers and, from the hundreds of records of births, marriages and deaths, began to prepare a family tree. Before long I came upon an entry:

Captain George Thomas Maitland Purvis, Royal Navy; born 10th June 1802 at Blackbrook Cottage, Fareham; died October 1883 at Newton Abbot (or Paignton), Devon; married firstly 10th June 1827, at Chawton, Hampshire, Mary-Jane Austen, daughter of Admiral Sir Francis Austen K.C.B. of Portsdown Lodge and niece of Jane Austen the author; married secondly Esther North Harrison, daughter of Revd. W. Harrison, Vicar of Fareham and Canon of Winchester Cathedral. There was issue by the first marriage . . .

So here was the Austen connection; and the name Esther North Purvis, with the date 1846, was the pencil-written inscription inside the Chest which Purvis Pasha had taken care not to obscure when he painted the edges with black lacquer. And so started a burning interest, which would soon develop into obsession, which was to absorb me for the next four years and, I have to admit, still does. Great Aunt May's papers had provided the framework of a vast historical jigsaw puzzle which I now felt compelled to complete. This branch of the family seemed to stem from the younger son of a younger son of a Scottish Borders baronet who had emigrated to England in the 17th century. He had bought an estate in Suffolk at a place called Darsham. Did the house still stand, I wondered? Was there a church with family memorials? I wrote to the Bishop of St. Edmundsbury and Ipswich and his Chaplain, the Revd. Canon Colin Bevington, responded immediately and enthusiastically to my request providing me with full details of the churches which might be of interest to me and alerting the clergy concerned. The County of Suffolk has an enlightened system of appointing Local History Recorders throughout the county and the Vicar of Darsham immediately put me in touch with Mrs. Olive Reeve, the Recorder for Darsham. She was a mine of information. Yes, she knew of the Purvis family connection, there were several memorials in the Parish Church; Darsham House was still standing and she could arrange with the owner for me to see over it. A few days later, a dossier arrived in the post with, not only all the information she had gained over the years on the Purvis family, but also with colour photographs of the Purvis hatchments and stained glass windows in the church. Here was an ally indeed and the quest was on.

Over the next year, my patient wife and our saintly friend and business partner of thirty years standing, Natalie Gilbert, toured the country with me visiting every cold church and colder churchyard with a Purvis connection, searching rows of almost-illegible headstones and reading thousands of dusty documents in libraries, museums and county records offices. Slowly but steadily the jigsaw puzzle started to come together.

I knew that Purvis Pasha's direct male line had died out with him in 1936 but I believed there must be another extant branch of the Darsham family somewhere. I wrote to every Purvis in the telephone directory in each area of England with which I knew the family to have been associated. Most of them replied and were anxious to help but it was clear that they were not of the Purvis branch in which I was interested. Then one morning I received a telephone call from a Mrs. Ros Purvis of Lee-on-the-Solent. Yes, she recognised all the names and dates I had quoted. Her husband had died recently and had left a box full of Purvis family papers which she would allow me to examine if they would be of interest. It had been her late husband's retirement ambition to get them all sorted out but he had, sadly, been thwarted by illness and her son, an international corporate lawyer, did not have the free time at this point in his career to do anything with them.

On the first day I spent with Ros Purvis at Lee she kindly agreed that I should take her papers away in tranches, to examine them in detail and cross-check the information they contained with my own records. Before I left she produced a small leather suitcase which contained old letters; would they be of any interest to me, she wondered. I opened the case and inside there were several bundles tied up with pink ribbon. I opened one and unfolded a letter. It was dated 8th September 1807 and was written by Admiral John Child Purvis from his Flagship *Atlas*, off Cadiz, to his son, Lieutenant Richard Fortescue Purvis who was in India serving in the Honourable East India Company's Bengal Army. The Admiral was castigating his son for being in debt:

I very much fear you have been gaming for without having done so I cannot account for your being in debt for having had much conversation with those who have relatives in your situation I had every reason to think after the complete outfit you had and afterwards on your arrival in India £125 in hand, would have placed you comfortably and easy; I have no money to spare; what little I have I have saved in the course of a long and fatiguing service; I derived no riches from my parents, and they never paid a quarter as much for me in my whole life as I have already done for you . . .

Only those who have had the good fortune to experience the electric thrill of discovery, of one sort or another, will know how I felt at that moment; — the archaeologist whose brush unexpectedly exposes some long-sought artefact; the chemist, or mathematician, who stumbles by chance upon the link in the formula which has baffled him for years. I already knew exactly who Admiral John Child Purvis was, and his son Richard, and had researched and recorded every significant event in their lives; but here, in this suitcase, was the material which could add flesh to their skeletons and bring them to life as real people with human strengths and weaknesses, who felt fear, love, joy and grief just as we do. I cannot describe the excitement I felt at that moment and the excitement I felt throughout the following two years as, one by one, I read, transcribed and catalogued these amazing letters. There were about 300 of them, the earliest dated 10th April 1710. Many were very difficult to read as they were "cross-hatched" — the writer having written again, at right angles, over the original script, thereby doubling the amount which could be got on the paper; a few were so faded or eroded with age that they were almost impossible to decipher. Having been fortunate enough to have handled historic documents for much of my working life, I was already familiar with the little quirks of early 19th century style which are initially confusing to the beginner — the double "s" where the second character is written with a long descender like an "f"; the occasional use of "ye" instead of "the"; the undisciplined hyphenation of words at line endings in order to save paper; and the very different style of punctuation and use of initial capitals and, in some cases, the complete absence of any punctuation at all.

Each letter contributed a little more to the Purvis story and each revealed a little more about the correspondents until they became so familiar to me that I could often surmise what they would say next, as sometimes happens with a close friend, and found myself increasingly in tune with their thought processes and idiom.

One morning, I took the next letter from the bundle I was working

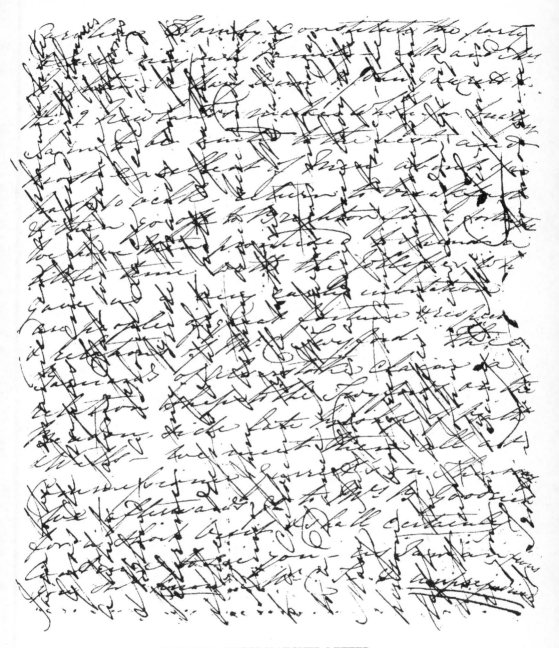

A PAGE OF A CROSS-HATCHED LETTER.
*(Georgina Purvis at Blackbrook to her aunt, Mrs. Timms, at Colchester, 13th January 1828.)*

Merton April 27th 1802

My Dear Mr. Matcham

The contents of your
letter did not surprize me, I was waiting
impatiently for the Post to tell it me, a
Better man never left the world, this must
be our consolation, He is to be buried at
Burnham where I of course shall attend, and
I would have the furnishing of the funeral
from the Parsonage House at Thorpe given
to Mr. Kerrison the Shopkeeper who has always
been attentive to our Dear Father, but
more of this, my heart is too full to set
any I expect William tomorrow & he shall
go to Bath and settle every thing with You
give my kind love to my Sister and
Believe me Ever Your affectionate Brother
Nelson & Bronte

I thank Mr. Bolton for his kind assistance
& I am not sure it would be right for me to attend
on such a distressing occasion —

*Lord Nelson's letter to his brother-in-law, George Matcham,*
*27th April 1802.*

on and discovered, with a spine-tingling thrill, that it was from Nelson. It was written in a clear and characterful hand which at first confused me. The previous year I had examined letters from Nelson to George Purvis, which Aunt May had given to the National Maritime Museum, which were written in a hand so rough and shaky that they were hardly legible. Then it dawned upon me: Aunt May's letters had been written in 1797/98 shortly after the great man had lost his arm at Tenerife and were early attempts to write with his left hand. This letter before me now was written in 1802 by which time he had perfected the art. It was written to his brother-in-law, George Matcham, who was married to Nelson's sister, Catherine, on the day after the death of his father, Revd. Edmund Nelson, who had been Rector of Burnham Thorpe in Norfolk. Though it has no direct relevance to our story, I shall reproduce it here as it has never before been seen outside the Purvis family. Lord Nelson had just heard of his father's death from George Matcham:

To: George Matcham Esq., Kennington Place, Bath

Merton, April 27th 1802

My dear Mr. Matcham, — The contents of your letter did not surprize me. I was waiting impatiently for the post to tell it me. A Better Man never left the world, this must be our consolation. He is to be buried at Burnham where I of course shall attend*, and I would have the furnishing of the funeral from the Parsonage House at Thorpe given to Mr. Kerrison the shopkeeper who has always been attentive to our Dear Father, but more of this my heart is too full to get out. I expect William tomorrow and he shall go to Bath and settle every thing with you. Give my kind love to my Sister and Believe me ever your affectionate Brother, Nelson & Bronte.

I thank Mr. Bolton for his kind assistance.

* I am not sure it would be right for me to attend on such a distressing occasion.

As my work progressed, I came to realise that the story of the Darsham Purvises could now be told on a more intimate level than I had originally envisaged and that it must be modelled around the life of Richard, the son who was in debt, who started life in Nelson's Navy, then spent fifteen years in the Bengal Army before taking Holy Orders and settling down to forty-four years as a country parson. — An eventful life by any standard and one which was enriched for its first thirty-six years by the monolithic presence of his father, Admiral John Child Purvis, and the severe yet loving relationship they enjoyed.

Much of the correspondence, (the "Indian Letters" as I have catalogued them), was between Richard and his brother officers in the Bengal Army. It was necessary to find out something about these young men whose ethos and humour so closely resembled that of any similar group of young men in our time. Here, my old friend, John Brain, generously came to my assistance spending several weeks during the summer of 1999 in the British Library, searching the archives of the Honourable East India Company and sharing with me the thrill of bringing history to life.

There are people I must thank for helping me in what to me has been a great adventure: the staff of the numerous museums, libraries and record offices who daily answer inane questions from people like me and point us, with professional good nature, in the right direction; in particular I would mention the staff of the Caird Library and manuscript archives at the National Maritime Museum, Greenwich. Then there were the clergymen who opened their churches for me when they were rushing somewhere else to undertake the much more important business of marrying the living or burying the dead; Olive Reeve, the Darsham Local History Recorder; John Purvis, a direct descendant of the Darsham line, and his wife Jan for their enthusiastic help and provision of some of the illustrations and, likewise, Ronald Dunning, a Blackbrook descendant through the female line; Hazel and Geoffrey Holt for their unfailing interest and encouragement; Jan Fergus for getting the whole thing started; John Brain for giving me so much of his time and for indulging my feverish demands with such good humour; my family for putting up with me for four years when half of my mind was palpably not in the present; but my deepest debt of gratitude must be to Ros Purvis and her son John for entrusting me with their priceless family letters and without whose confidence and support I would not have this story to tell.

IAIN GORDON
BARNSTAPLE, DEVON, JUNE 2001

# PART 1

# Sailing
# Orders

# 1. The Channel Fleet

*Southwick, near Portsmouth, Hampshire.*
*20th January 1800.*

Daniel Garrett, a kindly man of sixty-three years, reflected upon the circumstances of his son-in-law as he prepared to write to him. Captain John Child Purvis, Royal Navy, had taken Mary Garrett, Daniel's daughter, as his second wife in 1790. She had borne him two children, both of whom had died young, and had been a caring stepmother to her husband's two young sons by his first marriage. Poor Mary, who was not of a strong constitution, had died eighteen months previously leaving the two boys in the care of their old nurse, Ann Porter who, at the age of sixty-five and with her charges' father at sea, could not be expected to provide the discipline required by two high-spirited boys destined for the King's service.

John Brett Purvis, the elder, had been eleven years old at the time of Mary's death. This was the youngest age at which the son of a serving officer could, officially, go to sea in a man-of-war. Daniel's son, Captain Henry Garrett R.N., had at the time been commanding the *Alecto,* fireship, and on 5th January 1799 young John had been sent to sea in his custody. Later in the year he had transferred to the *Queen Charlotte,* of 100 guns, and now he was aboard the *London,* commanded by his own father. Young John had already made a good start in the Navy before he ever smelled salt air. He had been carried on the books of the *Victory,* Admiral Sir John Jervis's Flagship, from December 1795 to October 1796 thereby acquiring ten months of theoretical seatime. This was the practice of the age where a vacant berth existed and a boy had the influence to have his name included in a ship's complement. Young John had this influence as his uncle, George Purvis, was serving in *Victory* at the time as Admiral Jervis's secretary.

The younger son, Richard Fortescue Purvis, had been only nine years old at the time of Mary's death and had remained in the care of Ann Porter until his eleventh birthday, a fortnight ago. Now, his father had written to Daniel Garrett advising him of his intention to take Richard aboard the *London* with him, there being no vacancy at present in the Royal Naval Academy in Portsmouth Dockyard, explaining his difficult situation and seeking his father-in-law's endorsement of his decision.

How could Daniel Garrett do otherwise? Captain Purvis was a man of exceptional ability and strength of character and the two young boys could not be placed under the influence of a finer patron at this impressionable stage of their development. Was this not the officer who in 1778, as a Lieutenant in the *Invincible* on the American Station, was put in sole charge of the young Prince William, Duke of Clarence, the King's third son? What better testimonial of a man's character could one seek? Then, more recently, his appointment to command the *London* which had been at the core of the Spithead Mutinies three years earlier. There had been fighting between the mutineers and the marines with one seaman killed and several injured. Lieutenant Peter Bover, First Lieutenant of the *London,* had almost been hanged by the ship's company who were in violent revolt. When the worst of the trouble had subsided and the Captain and the unpopular Admiral Colpoys had left the ship, the Admiralty knew that a commander of the highest calibre was required to handle the crew, which was still in a state of open insubordination, and to work the ship back to a proper state of discipline and efficiency; a commander of indisputable professional ability; a man of strong character, diplomacy and manifest fairness; an officer with whom the crew would know exactly where they stood. Captain Purvis had been appointed.

Yes, thought Daniel Garrett, young Richard could not be in better hands than those of his own father. Though he had some doubts about the standard of academic instruction available from the *London's* schoolmaster, compared with that he would receive at the Academy, such deficiency would be more than compensated for by his father's ready moral guidance and professional instruction. He must write immediately and reassure his son-in-law of his approval:

To: Capt. Purvis, His Majesty's Ship The London, Spithead.

Southwick, 20 Jany. 1800

My dear Friend, — Both Mrs. Garrett and myself sincerely wish our young friend Richard health to prosecute his new sort of life with every success you and he can desire. I perfectly coincide with you that as you have now masters of every sort to teach every branch of learning to your sons, that Richard being with you will be of service to him in every respect and particularly in that of his time going on in the Service. This will not I apprehend preclude you if you choose it putting him into the Academy when a vacancy offers for him. Under your own eye, both John and Richard will I am sure improve in all those requisites for their situations. Drawing I hope may also be taught them.

He must also know, thought Daniel Garrett, that there is no question of my interest and friendship being withdrawn from him and his sons now that poor Mary is dead. He must know that I am here to help him in any way I can and should he decide to remarry, which I sincerely hope he will, I shall be the first to offer him my blessing.

Indeed, my good and worthy friend, you only express my daily feelings when you deplore the loss of our dear and beloved Mary – a loss to me irreparable. To you I hope it may not be so – for when the war is over I trust I shall see you again happily settled in your sweet cottage with some worthy and good woman as your companion and wife who will make as affectionate a friend to you as did our much lamented and beloved Mary. You are deserving of domestic happiness and we trust and hope that by and by you will again enjoy it. You have both Mrs. Garrett's and my sincerest wishes that you may do so. God only knows when this war will end. To what ever part of the world you may be ordered to, you will have our warmest and heartfelt prayers for your health, happiness and good fortune.

He must have no worries ashore. His cottage at Wickham is only a few miles from Southwick. I will visit it regularly and watch out for damages and necessary repairs. His servants at Wickham must know that they can turn to me if they have any questions or difficulties. They must not bother him when he has a ship to run and a war to fight.

I suppose yet you have no intelligence to what station you may go – whether to the Channel Fleet or to Lord Keith. I must confess, my dear Sir, that I am glad that you have resolved not to lett your house – I hope that your servants will remain in your service, they are good and honest souls and I respect them. Martin and Dinah will I hope not yet think of marrying.

  Depend upon it that Mrs. Garrett and I will do every thing for you in our power at Wickham during your absence and I hope that by and by we shall get the better of our forbearance in going there . . .

Nor must he have any financial worries. I will attend to his investments and taxes and pay his servants' wages.

I desired George to give you Mr. Neary's letter wherein he had enclosed me your half years Divds. due the 5th Inst. amounting to fifty seven pounds 2/3 and to know whether I should pay it to yourself or to credit your [account] therewith. By the last count I sent you with the vouchers, I had then in my hands of your money ninety two pounds 16/6 which added to the above sum 57.2.3 make together £149.19.1 – now this sum is much more than I can want to pay your servants their wages or for taxes of every sort – there being only two more instalments of the Income Tax and the Customary Taxes paid at Lady Day for windows, home and land taxes to be paid. Before, I shall in April next receive from Mr. Neary another half years Divd. of yours and which will be due the 5 of April next. As you may be suddenly ordered to Sea, and I may not have the pleasure to see you – be so good as to direct me what to do in these matters: but I hope to see you before you sail as I would come on purpose down to Portsmouth to say to you – God bless you. Have you your Orders? Are you [intended] for foreign service? Dinah is I hear at Portsmouth – I hope she lives at my house. Can Mrs. Garrett be of any service to Richard in his fitting out? I am sure Mrs. George will do every thing in her power and so will Mary Paffard. Assure yourself, my dear friend, of all our best services to you and yours. Mrs. Garrett unites with me in affectionate regards to you and to John and Richard. While my heart beats with life I shall remain, my dear friend, Most faithfully yours, Dl. Garrett.

Whatever trials and dangers lay ahead of him, Captain Purvis must know that he has the support of a staunch friend ashore, one who will mobilise the resources of the influential Garrett family in his service, and that of his sons, at any time and on any pretext, as if they were his own blood relatives.

\* \* \*

*H.M.S. London, at anchor in Spithead.*
*30th January 1800.*

Captain John Child Purvis sat in his spacious but plainly-furnished day cabin in the stern of the *London* reflecting upon the inequitable lot of younger sons of younger sons who seldom enjoyed any prospect of even modest inheritance. His great-grandfather, Captain George Purves, had been a younger son of a younger son of a Scottish baronet with lands and significant influence in the Borders. George, with five elder brothers and several paternal uncles, had no illusions of a life of leisure and had, around the year 1670, taken the high road that leads to England in search of opportunity and fortune. He had gone to sea and prospered and in 1712 had bought the estate and recently-built mansion house of Darsham in Suffolk. His eldest son, Captain George Purvis R.N. (they had since adopted the anglicised spelling of their surname) had become a Commissioner of the Royal Navy and MP for Aldeburgh in Suffolk. His eldest son, Rear-Admiral Charles Wager Purvis, inherited the Darsham Estates whereas John Child's father George, a younger son, had to work hard for his living as an Admiralty official. He had, however, married well and his wife, Mary Oadham, had inherited the estates of Porters, Essex, and Beckenden Grange, Warwickshire, from her cousin Lady Clifton.

John Child's elder brother, Captain Richard Purvis R.N., had in turn inherited these estates and his father's property in Hampshire. John Child, younger son of a younger son, had gone to sea at the age of fourteen and, in financial terms, now had little to show for his forty years of hard service. Lacking active patronage, he had had to wait until the age of thirty-one for his Lieutenant's Commission. Then on 19th August 1782 his luck had changed. Commanding the *Duc de Chartres,* a sloop of 16 guns and 125 men, on the American Station, he had engaged and captured the French corvette *L'Aigle,* of 22 guns, in a smart action off Cape Henry, Virginia. Twelve French were killed, including their commander, and thirteen wounded; there were no British casualties. As a result of this action, Commander Purvis was made Post (promoted to Captain R.N.) on 1st September 1782.

Then came peace and ten years ashore on half pay. On 11th October 1784 he had married Catherine Sowers, daughter of John Sowers, Clerk of the Cheque of the mighty Portsmouth Dockyard. Between 1785 and 1789, Catherine had borne him four children of which only John and Richard had survived. Catherine herself died a month after Richard's birth and the following year he married Mary Garrett.

In 1793 on the outbreak of war with Revolutionary France, Captain Purvis returned to sea initially in command of the *Amphitrite,* frigate, then his first battleship the *Princess Royal,* a second-rate, of 98 guns, which he commanded for three years in the Mediterranean. As Flagship of Rear-Admiral Granston Goodall,

*Princess Royal* had been badly mauled, with many killed and wounded, in the heavy action against the Revolutionary shore defences in Toulon directed by an up-and-coming young Major of Artillery — Napoleon Buonaparte. In Admiral Hotham's action off Genoa in March 1795, *Princess Royal,* commanded by Captain Purvis, sailed into action fourth ship in the van. The ship astern of him was the *Agamemnon,* commanded by Captain Horatio Nelson.

Then came the Spithead Mutinies and his command of the *London,* the most notoriously disaffected ship in the Fleet. His had been the task of working her back to a proper state of discipline and efficiency. It had taken time and patience but now, nearly three years later, he was confident that his ship could respond to whatever demands were made of it and it was certainly now a better place for his two young sons to serve the early days of their apprenticeship than it had been in those dark days following the Mutiny.

He had not yet received a reply from Daniel Garrett to the letter he had written him regarding his plans for Richard who had been aboard since the beginning of the month. Yet he was confident of his father-in-law's assent. Good Mr. Garrett was a true friend on whose support he could depend in any circumstances, even since Mary's death; a finer and more decent man had never lived. He would have preferred to have enrolled young Richard in the Academy since, even at the age of eleven, he was showing signs of a very good mind and would, his father thought, have benefited from the superior standard of tuition. But there had been no place available so he had had no alternative than to take Richard to sea with him for the moment, pending a vacancy.

Yes, thought Captain Purvis, he himself had had to work hard for the little he possessed in the world. As a younger son of a younger son he had had to make his way in life with little patronage or good fortune. At least, as the Captain of a ship of the line, he could do better for his sons. He was not in a position to subsidise their income but could, and would, use his experience and his influence to push them on in the Navy to the very best of his ability. And, he thought, if fortune should favour him during the course of this war, he would ultimately divide whatever he might have to leave equally between his two sons. He did not wish young Richard to be blighted with the misfortune of a younger son of a younger son.

Meanwhile, cramped in his hammock on the lower gun deck of the ship, with not an inch to spare between the hammocks of the boisterous and evil smelling boys on either side of him, young Richard was having less sanguine thoughts of his career in the Royal Navy.

The floating world he had entered four weeks previously would defy description to any landsman. Seven hundred and thirty-eight men and boys — English, Scots, Welsh and Irish with a sprinkling of Scandinavians, Dutch, Portuguese, Germans, Americans and even a few French — crammed into a great self-sufficient macrocosm of wood, iron, canvas and cordage measuring 152 feet long x 43 feet wide x 21 feet deep. He assumed that the seeming chaos of the ship's routine — the constant, sickening movement, the noise, the cold, the damp, the overcrowding, the lack of proper sleep and any semblance of peace or privacy — had some sort of purpose and control. He thanked God that during that first dreadful month his brother John was there to shake him by the shoulders and push him in the right direction at the right time. Occasionally he would catch sight of his father, the wind tearing at his boat cloak and the driving rain and spray lashing at his weathered face as he stood immobile and godlike at the quarterdeck rail. It is he, thought Richard in sudden awe, who directs this terrible realm.

The previous week the Commissioner had come aboard the ship at Spithead to pay the crew. With money in their pockets for the first time in many months, the temptation to smuggle liquor aboard had proved too great for some and, two days earlier, Richard had been mustered on deck with the rest of the crew to witness punishment — his first experience of the harsh discipline of the Royal Navy. Henry Long and John Cotter had each received twelve lashes for neglect of duty; Joseph Chittenden and Thomas Langley twelve lashes each for bringing liquor into the ship without lease; Christopher Basterfield had compounded the same offence by being insolent to the officer of the boat when discovered and had received eighteen lashes for his imprudence. The defaulters were tied to a grating on the upper deck, stripped to the waist and flogged by a burly boatswain's mate with a knotted, leather-thonged "cat-o'-nine-tails" until the blood ran freely down their backs.

Richard was to witness many more such punishments during his time in the *London;* the following day nine further seamen were flogged for neglect of duty, disobedience of orders and contempt. A week later Joseph Jeffs received two dozen lashes for theft — the one crime, Richard was to learn, for which the offender would receive no sympathy, then as now, from his messmates.

Slowly but steadily he began to adjust to life in his strange new world. Most boys seeking careers as sea officers in the Georgian Navy (they were not to be known as naval officers until much later), went to sea rated as Captains' Servants. Sea officers were entitled to one servant each and the Captain of a man-of-war to four servants for every 100 men in his ship's authorised complement. In practice, of course, no Captain required anything approaching such a personal staff and most of his entitlement was taken up by young gentlemen rated as servants but actually, under his patronage and moral guidance, learning the profession of sea officers. A Captain with vacant servants' berths in his ship therefore had a valuable commodity in his gift and was seldom without requests and pressure from relatives, friends and brother officers to take certain boys under his care.

There was no such thing as officer entry and little formality in the progression of a potential officer's early career. According to the requirements of the ship, more senior boys could be rated as Able Seamen, aged perhaps twelve, and then back to Servant to redress the balance of the ship's company before, ultimately, being advanced to Midshipmen or Master's Mates in either of which rating they would have to serve a further two years to qualify for consideration for a Lieutenant's commission. Richard therefore had at least six hard years ahead of him before he could hope to enjoy the relative comfort of an officer's life. Whether rated as Servants, Volunteers or Able Seamen, the boys' duties remained exactly the same. They would work the ship and learn the ropes under the guidance and care of the petty officers and senior rates, their "sea daddies", and would be instructed in navigation and ship's business by the Lieutenants or the Master or, in larger men-of-war such as the *London,* by a qualified schoolmaster who would also advance their general education.

Ever mindful of the importance of education, Captain Purvis had taken things a step further and had written to the Admiralty in November for permission to take a French prisoner-of-war into his ship to teach the French language to the boys. Their Lordships had given their answer on 29th December 1799:

... I have their Lordships' commands to acquaint you that they have no objection thereto, taking it for granted you will fix upon a person from whose principles no mischief will be likely to happen. †

As far as their moral, and in most cases Christian, welfare was concerned, these boys remained the charges of the Captain by whose interest they had obtained their berth. It was a responsibility not lightly undertaken. The relationship between a Captain and his young charges was one of mutual loyalty and interdependence. They had to rely upon him for introductions, recommendation and advancement, and he upon them to do well and justify his interest and, at the same time, enhance his reputation for bringing up good, sound officers. When a Captain changed his command he would take his boys (and often many of his officers and private men) with him. If he was killed, prematurely retired or, as in a few cases, disgraced, he would leave them like deserted fledglings, frantically seeking an opening with another senior officer.

In his first year in the *London,* Richard was to experience the most arduous form of seafaring that the Royal Navy could offer at the time. The work of the Channel Fleet was always hard — keeping station off Ushant and weathering the violent winter storms and seas in the Channel and the Bay of Biscay — but on 22nd April 1800 *London* rejoined the Flag of Lord St. Vincent whose culture of discipline and inflexible efficiency was legendary. No longer could the ships blockading Brest stand well out to sea to observe the enemy. Lord St. Vincent ordered that they must patrol close inshore at all times, day and night, which demanded impeccable navigation and pilotage from the officers and continuous sail drill and work on deck for the men and boys. Frigates and cutters had to keep station in the very harbour mouth, just out of range of the enemy's shore batteries. Time and again the blockading fleet would be scattered by violent storms and would then return to its hazardous duties among

---

† N.M.M. Ref: PRV37, *Loose Papers,* MS.55/029

the jagged reefs, surf-beaten islets and treacherous currents close inshore. Three times while the *London* patrolled off Brest, contingents of the enemy fleet tried to break out and three times they were driven back by the British warships. In May a tremendous storm scattered the blockading fleet far and wide. Three British sloops-of-war were lost with all hands and Richard watched as the lower yards of the *London* dipped below water and the ship's carpenters stood by the masts with axes in case she could not right herself. The instant the storm abated the blockade was resumed.

In August, *London* took part in the abortive landing at the Spanish port of Ferrol. Eight thousand soldiers and sixteen field guns were landed by the boats of the *London* and the other ten ships in the force. The following day they were all re-embarked, the General in command having decided, after a couple of minor skirmishes, that the enemy fortifications were too strong for him to achieve his objectives. Three days later, a squadron of twenty boats from the force, operating under the batteries of Vigo Bay, successfully cut out the privateer *La Guepe* after a furious fight lasting fifteen minutes during which twenty-nine were killed and over sixty wounded. A young shipmate of Richard's, fifteen year-old Midshipman John Scott, played a gallant part in this action for which he later received a Commendation.

In September another violent storm drove the *London* and most of the Channel Fleet back to Torbay and, once again, as soon as it had abated they were back on station off Brest. And so it went on. Richard's introduction to naval life had been no soft option and by his twelfth birthday on 4th January 1801 he was well on the way to becoming a man.

# 2. The Academy

The famous "Signal 39" which Nelson pretended not to see, by looking through his telescope with his blind eye, was actually flown from the masthead of the *London* when she was Admiral Sir Hyde Parker's Flagship at the Battle of Copenhagen. Early in 1801, *London,* "in consequence of her easy draught of water", was selected as part of the force which was assembling for the expedition to the shallow waters of the Baltic which was to culminate in that renowned battle.

Captain Purvis was given command of the historic *Royal George,* of 100 guns, and the transfer took place at sea, off Ushant, on Tuesday 10th February. Admiral Sir Hyde Parker and the *London's* new Captain, Captain Olway, together with six Lieutenants, the Master, boys and several Petty Officers transferred to the *London* while Captain Purvis, his Master, five Lieutenants, boys and Petty Officers took over the *Royal George.* The boats of both ships were employed throughout the day in ferrying the Admiral's and the two Captains' furniture from one ship to the other. As soon as the changeover was complete, Captain Purvis resumed blockading duties with the Channel Fleet where he remained until October when hostilities with Revolutionary France ceased and a brief eighteen-month period of peace commenced.

Peace, however, brought no relaxation of discipline or vigilance in the Channel Fleet. The standards which had been set by Lord St. Vincent, who had become First Lord of the Admiralty earlier in the year, were still maintained, often causing deep resentment among the officers of the Fleet and their wives and families ashore: Captains were required always to sleep aboard their ships while lying at an anchorage and were forbidden to travel outside a given radius when ashore. While at anchor, a Lieutenant was expected to be on deck at all times — a regulation which was apparently tested by the officers of the *Royal George* invoking the following directive from Captain Purvis:

5th November 1801. The deck having been often left without a Lieutenant contrary to the Standing Orders of the Commander-in-Chief and myself, I deem it necessary to direct that the strictest obedience may in future be paid to this essential part of the officers' duty. †

In April 1802 the *Royal George* was put out of commission and a vacancy became available for Richard at the Royal Naval Academy.

It is easy to imagine his feelings of frustration on being placed in a controlled academic environment having spent the last two years of his life at sea. It is also easy to understand his feelings of resentment and superiority to his fellow pupils who would gain two years remission of qualifying seatime on completion of their course and would go to sea rated as Midshipmen with the duties and pay of Able Seamen. Their parents, it must be said, had paid handsomely for the preferment: the fees at the Academy were much the same as for Eton but the King had insisted that fifteen of the forty available places should be reserved for sons of sea officers, to be educated at public expense, and it was one of these places which Richard obtained. With two years seatime behind him, Richard no doubt knew more of the Navy and the seaman's art than all his classmates put together and he naturally found the regime restrictive after the active life he had been leading. He would later describe his time at the Academy as "a protracted confinement within the Dockyard walls of Portsmouth".

By the end of his first year at the Academy he had approached his father and begged him to consider the possibility of a different career. The options at the time for the sons of gentlemen of limited means were not great; he realised that his father could not afford to purchase a commission for him in an infantry or cavalry regiment of the King's Army and a commission in the artillery or engineers would require further academic study, which would be as bad as staying at the Academy; the Law, the Church, Medicine, or any other profession fitting for a gentleman's son, would require both money and further academic study. Any form of trade or commerce, at the time, was out of the question for the son of a gentleman which really left the Military Service of the Honourable East India Company, where a cadetship could be obtained without premium,

---

† N.M.M. Ref: PRV24, *Orders Issued,* MS.59/076

by recommendation and interview, and was an honourable career which many younger sons of younger sons seemed to be choosing at the time.

Captain Purvis was initially outraged by his son's stupidity in wishing to abandon a career in which he had already served three years of a hard apprenticeship and in which his prospects were bound to be enhanced by the interest of his own father. However, he soon realised that Richard was determined in his wish to leave the Navy and agreed, at least, to examine the possibilities:

Brentwood, 15th May 1803

My dear Richard, — I have just received your letter of the 11th Inst. and am sorry I cannot yet give you a full answer to your questions. That I have been mindful of your interest you can have no doubt, and I trust you will be as much so in respect to the advice I gave you the day before I left Hants. I will again repeat my earnest desire that you will pay the strictest attention to your business at the Academy for should we not succeed in the pursuit of our new plan, we may at least have the pleasing reflection that no time was lost in the former one. . . . I cannot, my dear boy, too often remind you how very necessary it is that you should be always very circumspect in your behaviour and conduct, never on any account do anything which your own Mind and Conscience tells you is wrong – a fair and honourable character is the greatest recommendation a young man can possibly have, and you can easily judge how dreadful must be that person's case (as well as all those connected with him) who has by his vices lost all claim to so great a happiness; but the latter I trust will never be your case, or that of your brother. Accept my best affections and believe me, my dear Richard, Your truly loving Father, Jhn. Chd. Purvis.

Any hopes that Captain Purvis may have entertained of being able to personally guide Richard through this crisis in his career were soon shattered. The following day, 16th May 1803, war was declared with France and Britain was to be engaged in the fight against the tyranny of Napoleon Bonaparte for the next twelve years. Captain Purvis was recalled for sea service, this time in command of the *Dreadnought,* 98 guns, under orders of Admiral Cornwallis in the Channel. Committed once again to continuous and arduous sea service, he turned to his stalwart friend Mr. Garrett to prevail upon Richard to change his mind; but with little avail:

To: John Child Purvis Esq., Commander of His Majesty's Ship Dreadnought, off Brest to the care of Mr. Glencross, Dock Plymouth

Portsmouth, 22d. Septr. 1803

My dear Sir, — I have had to day a conversation with my young Friend Richard on the subject of his going to India or to continue in the Navy: – he is decidedly determined in his preference to the former provided it meets with your perfect approbation. He says he has given the subject his frequent consideration and wishes to take his lot to India. He does not hesitate in making this declaration and hopes with your coincidence.

The East India Company had three armies in India — Bengal, Madras and Bombay. Of these, Bengal was, at the time, thought to offer the best prospects to a young man. Captain Purvis's cousin, Charles Purvis, proprietor of the Darsham Estates and High Sheriff and Deputy Lieutenant of Suffolk, had married Elizabeth Cruttenden, daughter of a former Director of the Company in Bengal. Daniel Garrett felt that Captain Purvis should solicit his cousin's influence in getting Richard into the Bengal Army:

I hope your Friend Mr. Chas. Purvis will be able to prevail on Mr. Roberts to send him to the Bengal Establishment. I do most sincerely hope it will turn out for the Benefit of Richard. In any way that I, or any of my family can be serviceable to you or to Richard you will I trust command us.

Meanwhile, thought Mr. Garrett, there was the question of the delightful Mrs. Barwell who hoped to obtain a place for her son in Captain Purvis's ship:

More than three weeks ago William wrote you a letter directed to you at Plymouth to request you would take one of Mr. Barwell's sons (his third son – a fine youth) into your Ship and under your care. Mrs. Barwell herself came to solicit this favor of William – and I heard her express herself how happy she should be to have her Boy under your care as she was much prepossessed in your favor when she had the pleasure to see you at her house. . . . We have all pledged ourselves that you will not object to take this young Gentleman – which we trust you will be so good to acquiesce in and let one of us know when and how this young Gentn. may be sent and how accoutred etc. I never saw Mrs. Barwell before – and I was in love with her manners and conversation.

Even some gentle flattery and a smile from a pretty woman could be enough to invoke the rolling process of patronage!

. . . I am glad to find that you have a good man for a Steward. Martin, Dinah and Jerry go on very well. I have not yet met with a purchaser for your horse; I intend to advertise him in Motleys Paper – he will do for the Yeoman Cavalry extremely well . . . The News Papers tell us that we may expect Bonaparte upon our Coasts in a week or two – I think it is impossible and at present I feel no alarm: and yet I feel we ought to have more Ships on the Coast – and we also ought to attack all their Sea Ports – at least, that we may alarm them.

By 7th October Richard had showed no change of heart and the civil population in the south of England were mobilising against Bonaparte's imminently-expected invasion. Daniel Garrett wrote again to his son-in-law:

My dear Sir, — If report is true, you will be an Admiral in a few days — however I risk this letter though you may have quitted your Dreadnought before it reaches you . . . I have [seen] young Richard [since] my last Lr. to you and he still continues resolved to try his fortune in the East. Every thing goes on well at your pretty cottage at Wickham. You have received I hope a letter from your son John, which was forwarded to you a fortnight ago. He is Richard tells me, in a Sloop. William met Captn. [Oughton] the other day in London. He gives a most excellent character of my young friend John your son, both as an officer, seaman and good young man. You must push him on with Lord St. Vincent as, without his Lordship's orders, Captn. [Oughton] says he will not perhaps be made a Lieut. . . . We are told by the Ministers etc. that we are to expect Bonaparte in 10 or 12 days — let him come from the shores of France — I hope and trust he will never put his foot in England nor in France again. Your Brother is Gazetted — he is now Captain George Purvis . . .

Acting upon Mr. Garrett's advice, Captain Purvis wrote to his cousin Charles to ask for his help in getting Richard placed in the Bengal Establishment. Charles Purvis, the current representative of the senior Darsham branch of the family, had long since let the great house at Darsham and had moved with his wife and daughter to the more congenial ambience of Bath. His two sons were both serving officers in the King's Army — Charles in the 1st Royal Dragoons and Edward in the 4th Regiment of Foot. Captain Purvis had stayed with his cousin in Bath when he was last ashore and the dashing Captain had clearly been a great favourite with the ladies. In the tit-for-tat convention of patronage, Captain Purvis had offered his cousin a place in his ship for a boy of his choosing in return for his help with Richard's appointment. Charles Purvis replied from Bath on 17th October 1803:

Better late than never is an old proverb, my dear John, that many a lazy fellow has taken shelter under and perhaps you will be good natured enough to admit it in behalf of your Old Friend. – To any man but yourself what a contrast would it appear from singing, laughing and playing with a parcel of good humored girls in a few hours to be rolling and tumbling about the Chops of the Channel serenaded occasionally with the shrill pipes of the Boatswains Mates or the more sonorous sound of the Quartermaster on duty . . . Our party, my dear John, regretted your departure amazingly and the Girls were quite disconsolate; what you have done to them I can not conceive; I only know they have ever since sworn by their agreeable Captain – but you, young fellow, seem not aware of the mischief you make . . . I want to talk to you likewise about your Son – you know what my opinion is on the subject and I have not since had any reason to alter it. Leman called here a day or two ago and said so much more in favor of it that I wished to know what fresh motives he had to be so well satisfied with the destination of his Nephew. He had been, he said, at Cheltenham where he had seen and conversed with several East Indians who had confirmed him in his previous opinions. . . . I tell you only what I learn – I fear to advise. If you make up your mind to your son's going, inform me immediately that I may remind Cruttenden to apply again for a Bengal appointment. . . . We have nothing but the threats of Bonaparte; thank God this Country never was so unanimous and there are certainly very many people who calculating even for the Horrible Carnage that must ensue, that wish he would attempt to put his threats in execution and ease their minds from the irritation they now suffer. . . . I am, my dear John, Your sincere Friend and Cousin, C. Purvis.

P.S. I am exceedingly obliged to you for your offer. At present I have not any young man to trouble you with

By now, Captain Purvis was more or less reconciled to his son's determination to go to India although he had not entirely given up hope of dissuading him. Richard's ambition had, to some extent, been influenced by the affluent and comfortable lifestyle enjoyed by certain of their neighbours in Wickham whose service in the East Indies had been during a period of greater personal opportunity and who had retired, seemingly as minor nabobs, from the Company's military service. Yet all the intelligence Captain Purvis had gathered from friends and relatives suggested that present opportunities for a young man in India were not what they had been. He urged Richard to speak to Major Budden, an ex-East India friend from whom he was confident his son would receive candid advice.

Dreadnought, off Ushant 2d. Novemb. 1803

My dear Richard, — Your letter of the 4th of last month I have only just received, and had I not got one at the same time from Mr. Garrett, wherein he mentions your continuing in the same determination of wishing to go to India, I should not at this moment have known it for you promised me you would have some conversation with Major Budden and then would let me know how your inclination stood. You may be assured, my dear boy, it is one of the first wishes of my heart that, whatever line of life you make choice of, that success and every possible good should follow. I wish I could be with you at this particular time for many reasons, but that cannot be. Our good friends the Garretts will I am sure stand in my stead and give you every assistance and advice you may stand in need of. I have written to Mr. Roberts requesting he would appoint you to the Bengal Establishment and have begd. Mr. Charles Purvis to back the application with another letter, therefore as you are to go, I trust it will be to that part of India which is most likely to prove beneficial to you. In the event of your being fitted out, there may be many things recommended, which may be of little or no use, therefore I would have you take such things only as may be approved by Mr. Garrett. I would have you take the earliest opportunity of seeing your Uncle George and with my love to him, tell him I shall be obliged to him to procure an account of the things your Cousin Leman carried out with him. This Mr. Charles Purvis told me there were many that were needless and this he had from Mr. Leman at Bath. I wish you to have everything that is proper and comfortable, but as I have not been much in Fortune's way, it will be necessary to be somewhat economical. As I am now more in the way of getting letters regularly than I was whilst off Rochefort, I beg you will frequently write to me, and let me know everything which you may judge interesting for me to hear respecting yourself. Mr. Garrett will have the goodness to point out to you everything that you have to do if this plan of going to India should take place, but as many disappointments happen when least expected, you must not be too sanguine. The Academy must not be given up, nor must your attention slacken there till all the matter is settled by Mr. Roberts, whose address is John Street, Bedford Row, London, which you should tell Mr. Garrett in case he should think it necessary to write to him. I hope my dear Richard you do not neglect Blackbrook for I do not find you have been there a long time, your Uncle and Aunt I am sure will always be glad to see you. Remember me to them all and tell your Uncle I wrote to him whilst I was off Rochefort. Give my love to all Mr. Garrett's family and tell Mr. Garrett I have written to him this morning. Accept my love yourself and be assured I am, and ever shall be, my dear Richard, Your Affectionate Father, Jhn. Chd. Purvis.

Your Brother is extremely well and desires his love to you. He went into the Driver at the particular desire of Capt. Compton who was the Admiral's 1st Lieutenant, and also with the approbation of Sir Andrew Mitchell. I was much disappointed to find he has not yet received his Box with his Journals and Certificates. Ask Mr. George Garrett how they went, or I will thank Mr. G. G. if he will write a note in my name to Mr. [Rothery] requesting he will let me know how the box went as John has not received it - adieu -

Captain Purvis's elder brother, Captain Richard Purvis R.N., had died the previous year at the age of fifty-nine leaving a widow, four sons and two daughters. The eldest son, Richard Oadham Purvis, was a naval Lieutenant serving in the West Indies. The second son, John Leman Purvis (known in the family as Leman), had recently gone to India in the Company's Military Service and Captain Purvis, anxious that Richard should have all he needed but to avoid unnecessary extravagance which he could ill afford, wrote to his brother George asking him to obtain details of the items which Leman had taken out with him. Unable to supervise Richard's kitting out himself, he once again turned to his good friend Mr. Garrett asking if he would pay for Richard's purchases and expenses and send him an account when everything was complete. Mr. Garrett replied on 13th November:

My dear Sir, — With great pleasure I received your letter of the 2nd Novr. Inst. . . . Respecting my young Friend Richard your Son: he still continues firm in his wishes to go to India but from what I hear of the Military line of Service in India, it is not so good a one as it used to be. Lord Wellesley has made so many Regulations that the value of the Service is greatly diminished. For these reasons I wish Richard had continued to like the Naval Life, especially as you would by and by, if Providence spared your life, have had it in your power to forward his promotion in the Navy. I saw your Brother on Thursday last at Fareham at a Meeting of the Deputy Lieutenants etc. on the Defence of the Coast. He told me that he had had a letter from you that morning. I mentioned to him my wishes that he would again talk with Richard on the subject of his going to India – which he promised to do next Sunday, as he expected then to see him at his house. I saw Admiral Linzee† the other day who said he had had a letter from you wherein you mention your wishes that he (the Admiral) would hear what Richard had to say on the same subject of his going to India. One would not confront his inclination, or prejudice him against the Service, and I hope that if he goes out he will succeed in it – but it will be tedious, uphill work. However, let me assure you, my dear Friend, that every thing that I, my wife and any of my Family can do for his service and your wishes shall be readily and cheerfully done – and respecting the money matter you allude to – all shall be complied with agreeable to your desire and I beg you will assure yourself that it will not be in the least way inconvenient to me.

If Richard goes out this year, your application to Mr. Charles Purvis and to Mr. Roberts should not, I think, be deferred – and by all means get him on the Bengal Establishment which I have always understood as the best, but herein don't take my opinion . . .

I do suppose that you see the News Papers – therefore I shall say but little on Public Matters – we are in daily expectation of hearing that Bonaparte's Troops are embarked for the invasion of this Country – I hope our Defence is equal to withstand all danger – but the Papers are full of the danger. The anxiety however is great – and the expense and inconvenience supremely so. . . . With great regard, affection and good wishes I remain, my dear Friend, Yours most faithfully, D. Garrett.

---

† Vice-Admiral Linzee was a neighbour of the Purvises in Wickham. Captain Purvis, when commanding the *Princess Royal* in the Mediterranean Fleet in 1796, had served in Admiral Linzee's Division.

Both Mrs. G. and I will follow any directions we may receive respecting Richard's outfit – from your Brother or any other quarter for you're please to observe that we are both perfectly ignorant in these matters . . . We all rejoice to find that you have received pleasing accounts of our young Friend John – and hope to hear soon of his being an Officer. You must jog Lord St. V. on this subject – for without, perhaps, Sir A. he may not be able to promote John – push him on – and be not too nice in writing to his Lordship; excuse me, but I am and always was so for Henry – anxious to get on.†

Mr. Leman of Wenhaston in Suffolk, a brother of Captain Richard Purvis's widow, was assisting his recently-bereaved sister in placing her remaining three sons in suitable careers — the eldest being already established in the Navy. Mr. Leman had heard that prospects for a young man in India were still good and, consequently, one boy had already been placed as a Cadet in the Bengal Army and the other two would eventually follow him. Apart from Mr. Leman, every relative and friend with a knowledge of India had advised Richard against entering the Company's service at this point in time — particularly as his future in the Navy, where he enjoyed his father's patronage, seemed so soundly assured.

---

† Henry Garrett became a Vice-Admiral and Commissioner of the Navy.

# 3. Appointment

An 18th century Admiral had no "staff" as we know it in the naval and military sense today. He did, however, have a very high-calibre secretary upon whom he relied to a large degree in the administration of his fleet. The eminent naval historian Dr. N.A.M. Rodger describes his role thus:

> An admiral's secretary was less a private amanuensis than the business manager of the squadron. He controlled, drafted, and sometimes even signed the admiral's correspondence; he was heavily involved in victualling (on distant stations like the East Indies he was often himself the agent-victualler); he was usually the admiral's prize agent and often the squadron's as well. This was big business and it demanded ability and experience. A secretary needed extensive connections and good credit in the worlds of business and finance, and he needed to move easily among senior officers afloat and great men ashore. Not surprisingly, secretaries were often members of families already prominent in the Navy or naval administration. †

Such was the case with Captain Purvis's younger brother George who had made his mark, not just as an Admiral's secretary, but as secretary to two of the greatest Admirals in the history of the Royal Navy — Lord Howe and Lord St. Vincent. With the latter, he had been aboard the famous *Victory* at the Battle of Cape St. Vincent in 1797. He had been appointed Prize Agent to Lord Nelson and the other Flag Officers after the Battle of the Nile and was a prominent and well-respected figure in the Navy.

He had retired, a rich man, before he was fifty and had bought the Blackbrook Estate outside Fareham in Hampshire. Disliking the austerity of the existing mansion house, he had built his own amazing *cottage orné* in the grounds — a stately home with gothic windows, fifteen bedrooms, and what is still today the largest thatched roof in Europe, supported at the eaves on one side by rustic timber posts forming a colonnade. He called it "Blackbrook

---

† *The Wooden World, An Anatomy of the Georgian Navy,*
N.A.M. Rodger, Collins 1986.

Cottage" and surrounded it with beautifully landscaped gardens of sweeping lawns, orchards and herbaceous borders.

In 1791, at the age of forty, George Purvis had married nineteen year-old Renira Maitland, a great beauty, daughter of Lieutenant David Maitland R.N. They had two surviving daughters — Renira aged eleven, Georgina aged three and an infant son, George Thomas Maitland Purvis, who had been born at Blackbrook Cottage the previous year. Though now in retirement, George Purvis was a Magistrate for the County of Southampton and, as Mr. Garrett had already advised Captain Purvis, had recently been gazetted Captain in the Militia which had been formed to repel Bonaparte's expected invasion. The two brothers had always been very close, insofar as their Service careers would permit, and George was naturally only too willing to do what he could for Richard:

Blackbrook, 16th Novemb. 1803

My dear John, — To reply most correctly to your letter of the 3rd inst. I think it best to transcribe that part of Mr. Leman's which relates to the subject you wish information about. He says "I paid for his (John Leman's) passage £95 and afterwards more (but I know not for what reason) for the same purpose £40. To Weeks the great shopman for the India House for fitting him out £146. 14s. 0d. To the Bookseller £13. 15s. 6d. (but remember in this article was included what I think rather an unnecessary article, a Persian Dictionary of about 16 guineas but some of his friends thought otherwise). To the Shoemaker £12. 8s. 0d. To the Taylor £9. 12s. 0d. To Mr. Turquand for various expenses attending his going abroad £10. 5s. 6d. besides £5. 5s. 0d. for Pocketmoney at the same time desiring the Captain to advance him anything more which he thought reasonable in case they made any long stay in any port. As for the bills themselves, they are I believe in Mr. Turquand's hands (who is at present absent from London on a tour into the West) or in Mrs. Richard Purvis's, I do not know which. In regard to the necessary articles for fitting him out, any East India Captain will tell you what are the essential articles." So much for Mr. Leman.

If you think I can be useful with respect to Richard's outfit, you may command my best services, yet I think someone in town ought to superintend that part in particular which is provided by Mr. Weeks . . . Mr. [Ives] is very much obliged by your attention to young [Rotton] and hopes he will requite your kindness by good conduct . . . You have a youngster on board by name Harris, he is probably a near relation of our Inspecting Field Officer Col. [Mannock] who reviewed our Exercise and Evolutions last Monday and afterwards dined here, a party of 18, mostly Red Coats. . . . If you can shew civility to the young man I will thank you, as the Colonel seems a worthy little man and well known to your friends at Portsmouth and Leigh. . . . I remain, Dear John, Your faithful affectionate Brother, Geo. Purvis.

Richard was well Sunday sennight. Mr. Leman says the whole expense to him of J. L. P's. outfit was £350. I had poor Achilles shot about three weeks ago, least the chance of war might throw him into other hands.

Richard spent the following weekend with the Garretts at Southwick during which Mr. Garrett again tried to persuade him to change his mind:

Richard came to me here on Saturday and spent Sunday with me; we have had several conversations respecting his going to India as a Cadet. He is, he says, with your permission, determined to go in that Character – and prefers it to continuing in the Navy. I pointed out to him the good prospect he might have of Preferment in the Navy through you – for you must be an Admiral in the course of this War – and that you would push him on as well as his Brother John – and that it was highly probable you would see them both Captains. In vain I said these and other things to Richard – his resolution seems to be firmly taken and resolved on – therefore I do suppose you will not oppose his going to India.

On Saturday I recd. a letter from Mr. Roberts, the India Director, an old correspondent and acquaintance of mine formerly . . . Mr. Roberts tells me that as soon as the arrangements for the Season are made, that he will write me again respecting what settlement he may be able to appoint him . . . I yesterday wrote him a letter saying that I was very much interested in my young Friend Richard's welfare – and that I should be extremely obliged to him to exert his influence and interest to send him to Bengal where he would find many Friends – and that I should also be particularly obliged to recommend him for a Commission in the Company's Troops as soon after his arrival as possible. I said nothing about his being put in the Artillery or in the Troops of the Line. I mention these particulars to you that you may on your arrival at Plymouth give me full instructions how I must act and what I must say to Mr. Roberts in future, and whatever other matters you have to say regarding Richard's voyage etc., etc. In the course of 10 or 12 days Mr. Roberts tells me he hopes to write to me again on this subject.

Now with regard to Richard's equipment I know nothing – I must therefore request you will inform me, somehow or other, what must be done in every respect – before, at, on his voyage and on his arrival in India – I am really ignorant in these matters nor do I know where to apply for information. Every thing in Mrs. Garrett's and my power for his comfort etc. shall be done – but I must entreat to have your full directions as it is a matter of such great importance to Richard to have every thing necessary for such a voyage and not to have unnecessary things.

We are all safe yet from Bonaparte – I hope you'll get a Medal – Ireland is his object – and from Brest the Fleet and Troops must go there – I trust you will prevent that – and send all of them to old England . . . Mrs. Garrett and Betsy join with me in sincere wishes for your health and happiness and I remain most faithfully, Yours, D. Garrett.

P. S. What am I to say or to do if I am asked by Mr. Roberts, or any one else, what age Richard is? Inform me what you have said on this subject to Mr. Roberts, that we may agree. I forget what the necessary age is for a Cadet.

Richard was fourteen years ten months at the time and the minimum age for a cadet in the Company's service was fifteen. It appears, however, that Mr. Garrett thought the age limit was seventeen and was prepared, if necessary, to exercise a little of the subterfuge that has been practised by impatient recruits since time immemorial.

On 26th November Captain Purvis wrote to Richard from Cawsand Bay, where *Dreadnought* was temporarily at anchor, finally advising him that he would no longer withhold his consent and urging him to write better, more frequent and more carefully-considered letters:

My dear Richard, — I have just received your letter of the 23rd and though there is nothing in it which requires a reply, for you have scarcely noticed anything contained in that you acknowledge to have received from me, yet I will not let a post pass without writing to you; Mr. Garrett has told me the event of his conversation with you on the subject of your going to India and, as you appear so very desirous of going, I shall no longer with hold my consent and I hope and trust it will prove in every respect beneficial to you; I wrote your Uncle to have the goodness to get an Account of what your Cousin Leman had provided for him and I think I desired you to ask it of him also, that it might be in readiness to assist in fitting you, when your appointment takes place, and I have requested our Friend Mr. Garrett to act for me on the occasion; I am sorry circumstances have so turned out that I am under the necessity of giving so much trouble; but when that busy time arrives, you must endeavour to do all you can to take the weight off from him, as he will direct in the more material business. I am much obliged to your Aunt George for the present she has made you and you will not forget to tell her so with my love to her. When I left Wickham I delivered the keys of the house to my Friend Mrs. Garrett, and did not calculate on your going there (where there were only Servants) when you had so many Friends who would have been glad to receive you in their houses. When directions are given by Mrs. Garrett about your new shirts, recollect they must be made of Callico. I hope you will take care not to put yourself in the way of catching the Fever, it would be bad at any time, but just now it would be particularly so. Tell Mr. Garrett I received his letter and answered it immediately; do not fail reminding your Uncle of the Account of John Leman's outfit, it will be a great guide to Mr. Garrett and he would not know how to manage without it, and no time is to be lost; I fear you do not refer to a letter received when you are making a reply to it; for I think there were many things in my letter which you would have noticed in your answer, had it been then before you, a custom I recommend you to adopt in future. . . .

Let me know as soon as you have your appointment and how you go on; and I wish you to be something more correct and particular in your letters, the more you write the pleasanter it will grow. Adieu my dear Boy and believe me always, Your truly affectionate Father, Jhn. Chd. Purvis.

Richard spent his Christmas holidays with the Garretts at Southwick during which time there was some confusion as to whether or not he had actually been appointed. Mr Garrett wrote to Captain Purvis on New Year's Day 1804 to explain the situation in ponderous detail:

... By a letter I received the 18 of December from Mr. Charles Purvis of Bath, I was informed that my young Friend Richard was appointed a Cadet in the Bengal Establishment. I waited for a letter from Mr. Roberts, the Deputy Chairman of the India Company, as he promised me to write in this subject when the appointment should take place. In another letter from Mr. Charles Purvis, he recommended Richard going out in the Sir William Bensley, East Indiaman, Capt. Rhode, which would leave Gravesend the 14th or 15th of this month – and though I had not received another letter from Mr. Roberts, I had made up my mind to take Richard to London to morrow – but before I set off I thought I would write to a Friend at the India House (the Deputy Secretary) to enquire into a few particulars concerning Richard appearing before the Directors, or some of their Officers; my Friend wrote me word by return of post, on Friday last, that Richard was not yet appointed – and advised me to postpone my journey to London until I heard that Richard was appointed. I therefore have put off my journey till I do hear more about it – but I immediately wrote to Mr. Charles Purvis informing him of these circumstances – I own I was surprised at what my Friend wrote me, after what Mr. Charles Purvis told me by letter that Richard was appointed. I had got Richard's Certificate of his Baptism from Doctor Thomas and had made him of a proper age viz. 17 – but my Friend sent me an Abstract of the Act of Parliament concerning the age of a Cadet – he must be above 15 and under 22 – so that we are all right in this respect.

It had not been considered prudent to advise the Principals of the Naval Academy of Richard's intended change of career until matters had been finalised. In the meantime, it was neccessary for him to take leave of absence from the Academy for his interview and kitting-out in London.

I hardly knew what to do about taking Richard to London without leave of Mr. Bailey or Sir Chas. Saxton – had we asked leave it might have been necessary to have gone to the Admiralty which time then we could not have spared. When Richard is appointed and we know it to be a certainty we must go with or without leave. Richard continues still inflexible – as he has your permission – he is determined to go to India.

I shall be now in daily expectation of hearing from Mr. Roberts or from Mr. Charles Purvis but if the appointment is delayed we must look out for another ship for Richard's embarkation – the money to be paid to be at the Captain's table will be from £95 to £120 – the India Company paying only about £15.

Thinking that I should set off with Richard to London on Monday, I went to Mr. Goodlad on Thursday last to get letters of recommendation for Richard to [.....] Friends at Calcutta and in Bengal – and also to get a Letter of Credit for Richard that he may be supplied with money when he arrives at Calcutta to supply him with every necessary thing for an Officer which I hope he will be immediately on

his arrival. Mr. Goodlad very kindly promised to do every thing in his power for
Richard – I told him that you would be very much obliged to him and so should
I. . . . I have got the list of necessaries which Mr. J. Leman Purvis your nephew
was supplied with. Mr. George Purvis sent it me and I shall follow it nearly, not
wholly, as some books etc. appear unnecessary and are very expensive.

  As we do not go to London on Monday, Richard will return to the Academy on
that day – every day he can be learning something . . . I have been daily in
Expectation of seeing in the News Papers of your arrival at Plymouth or in
Torbay – thinking that it was impossible for you and the other Ships to keep the
Sea in the midst of storms and hurricanes – and I hope soon to hear that you are
well and have escaped all the dangers which must have surrounded you . . .

  We on Xmas Day drank your health – and so we shall again by and by. Accept
our best regards and affectionate wishes, and believe me to be, my dear Friend,
Most faithfully yours, D. Garrett.

The good news was added as a postscript on the cover of the letter:

Since writing the within, a letter is come to me from Mr. Roberts informing me
that Richard is appointed in the Infantry – we shall leave for London about
Wednesday next.

Captain Purvis in *Dreadnought* had been having a hard winter in his
old patrolling grounds off Ushant beset by some of the most violent
Channel storms in memory. Time and again the squadron was
blown off station and his long experience and outstanding
seamanship had been taxed to the limit. In England, as we have
seen, the civil population was in daily dread of Bonaparte's arrival;
but out at sea, ships like the *Dreadnought,* with commanders like
John Child Purvis, kept their station day and night in almost
insufferable conditions, standing four-square to the tyrant's
challenge and, once again, giving the Nation cause to thank God for
the Royal Navy.

  In spite of the demands of his ship and his men, Captain Purvis
was deeply concerned for Richard's welfare. Having no great
knowledge of any profession other than his own, he felt powerless
to advise his son on the paths and pitfalls of a military career and
realised that he was about to enter a world in which he had neither
influence nor opportunity to serve him. Moreover, he deeply
regretted the fact that active service prevented him from being with
the boy at a time when he was setting out on a strange career, on the
other side of the world, when he would, perhaps, be most in need of
a father's guidance and support.

Some things, however, were always the same, regardless of a man's profession: the importance of a commitment to one's duty; the need for honest, honourable and conscientious behaviour; the maintenance of a good character and a ready submission to the dictates of one's conscience — these were the things of which he wanted his son to be ever mindful.

With the ship set on a course she could comfortably hold for an hour, and seeing a brief lull in the demand for him to be on deck, Captain Purvis went down to his cabin to write what might well be his last letter to Richard before he sailed for India:

Dreadnought, off Ushant. 7th January 1804

My dearest Richard, — I have received your letter of the 25th ulto. and having a prospect of an opportunity of replying to it, I am unwilling to let it pass, for they so very seldom occur. In respect to the choice of which Corps you should be [placed], I am really no judge; whichever you are placed in, I hope will prove the most to your advantage and satisfaction, I therefore can say nothing on that head, because I may chance to be wrong. The sum necessary for your equipment is certainly very large and considering my confined circumstances, more than I can well spare, but as your Cousin John has had a good friend to assist him and thereby has had such advantage, I am unwilling to allow you to be worse off than he has been, trusting that you will as far as lays in your power, avoid any unnecessary expense. You are perfectly right, my dear Richard, in determining to be master of your business, whether as a Sailor or Soldier; your lukewarm Gentry will never get forward, or cut any figure in their profession, and as you have so decidedly fixed on yours, I hope nothing will induce you to swerve from the resolution you appear to have made to acquire the knowledge of a Soldier's duty, this you may be assured will always afford you a comfortable reflection, and make all the points of Service pass pleasantly; steadiness, obedience, perseverance and valour are the grand outlines of a soldier's character and I trust you will not be wanting in them, but remember the admonitions I have so often and so pointedly endeavoured to impress on your mind; the principles of morality and true Religion; without these there can be no inward peace, for there is within us a sort of Monitor or Conscience which never fails to warn us when we are about deciding on a point between right or wrong. Therefore I charge you, as you value my affection, never loose sight of such advantages, but make it a first rule in your future conduct always to act honestly, honourably and conscientiously; by which you will secure to yourself the esteem and affection of all good people, and as you are likely to carry out with you many letters of recommendation to the principle Gentlemen in Bengal, it behoves you in an especial manner to be very correct in every part of your conduct. The families in India are famed for kindness and great hospitality, your business (when your duty will admit of it) will be to cultivate their friendship and pass as much of your time with them, as by their behaviour you have reason to think they wish you. Do not be too hasty in forming friendships with young men you know but little of; civility is due to all and never lose sight of good breeding, that outline of the Gentleman. I should have been glad to have been with you before you go, my dear boy, but as that is not in my power, we must think ourselves fortunate in having such good friends as those who have so kindly undertaken the trouble of fitting you out. I will continue writing to you by the few opportunities which may offer before you go and in the meantime you will assure yourself how sincerely I pray that every good may constantly attend you and that you will never be wanting in your gratitude to that Being whose Blessing will I hope always await you.

Farewell, my dearest Richard, and I repeat again and again how much my happiness is connected with the character you in future support in life; if good, I am sure of hearing it, I will not suppose it can be otherwise. I am and always shall be, my dear boy, Your truly affectionate father, Jhn. Chd. Purvis.

And if not so good, as Richard was to discover, his father would be equally certain to hear of it.

# 4. Passage to India

On Wednesday 4th January 1804, Mr. Garrett and Richard, in company with Mr. Garrett's son William who had business to attend to in town, set out for London. The following day they reported at East India House, the impressive headquarters of the East India Company in Leadenhall Street, for Richard to attend his interview with the Court of Directors and to start the formalities for his enrolment as a military cadet in the Bengal Army.

The Honourable East India Company, known popularly as "John Company", was, at the time, the greatest commercial organisation in the world with a Charter dating from Elizabethan times and an effective monopoly on all trade with India and the Far East. It was directed by a "Court" of Directors or Proprietors, had its own armies in India, its own Civil and Medical Services and its own fleet of armed merchantmen, the Indiamen, which were run very much on Royal Naval lines.

The intimation that Mr. Garrett had received from several of his friends, that the value of the service had been greatly diminished during the Governor-Generalship of Lord Wellesley, had sound foundation. Though the Company had acquired the proportions and responsibilities of a sovereign state, it was still primarily a trading organisation with the object of making profits for its shareholders and a distinct distaste for anything which added to the expense or responsibility of government.

Lord Wellesley, however, had recognised the importance of securing Britain's place as the supreme power in India in view of the Napoleonic threat. His programme of annexations and subsidiary alliances had, to a large extent, achieved this end but at the expense of Company profits. This, the following year, was to lead to his recall, and almost to his impeachment and, in the meantime, had imposed a new culture of penny-pinching economies in both the civil and military services.

As far as individual employees of the Company were concerned, the sole compensation for service in a country where the mortality rate among Europeans offered less than even odds for their return to England, was the chance of making some money. The high-minded ideals of Empire, and of uniting the shattered and warring remnants of Moghul India into a unified and peaceful territory under British protection, were for later generations. Lord Wellesley had, however, already teased the public morality with this concept and the start of great change was now inevitable.

Mr. Garrett and Richard first had to kill time until the following Monday which was a "Court Day". Then, having waited in an ante room for two hours, Mr. Garrett was sent for by Mr. Roberts, the Deputy Chairman, who pointed out the alteration they had made to Richard's Birth Certificate which, had it been spotted by the Court of Directors, would have debarred Richard for ever from any form of employment with the Company. Richard wrote to his father on 16th January with his account of the proceedings:

. . . We have settled all the business now, but after much trouble and vexation: our first rebuff was in not having the Certificate of my age signed by the Church Wardens after having altered it so as to make me old enough so that we could not send it back again to be signed by the Church Wardens but were obliged to send for a new one signed by them. Well, we got that and waited two or three days for a Court day when after having got everything we waited near two hours when Mr. Garrett was sent for by Mr. Roberts who in a very friendly manner pointed out to him an alteration which we made in order to make me old enough from my Baptism and if this Certificate had gone before the Court of Directors and they had found it out I should have been rendered incapable of ever serving the Company in any capacity whatever. The reason why we altered it was because I was not baptised until March when born in January (which you must know) so the only way was to get a new Proper Certificate and both to make Oath that I was more than 15 years of age, which we did besides getting Mr. Maidman and my Uncle to Certify it also; that answered and on Friday I went before the Court of Directors; passed there and paid my Passage Money (i.e. Mr. G. did for me) and in short did every thing that day and on the next set out for Hampshire and got to Leigh in the evening. I did not like London at all but was glad to get out of it as fast as I could. I am going out in the Sir Wm. Bensly. I saw the Captain. He seems to me to be much of the Gentleman and very good natured. I have no doubt but I shall Benefit by the good advice which you so much impress on my mind in your kind letter. Every letter that I have received from you has always contained some good and wholesome advice all of which are kept and I constantly read them over, in which I take great delight. I beg you will write by the very first opportunity as every letter I receive from you I value more than gold. Direct as you did the last to the care of Mr. G. G. as I embark at Portsmouth consequently must get them. Mr. G. has under gone a great deal of trouble and fatigue on my account for which be assured I did not fail to thank him accordingly. . . . I have not yet seen my Uncle George to thank him for his kindness in Certifying my age. You may depend upon it I shall so far endeavour to benefit by your Good Advice as ever to ascribe myself in truth, Your Dutiful and Affectionate Son, Richard Fortescue Purvis.

## The following day Mr. Garrett wrote with his version of their trip to the India House and an update on Richard's arrangements:

My dear Sir, — I have now the pleasure to inform you that I have been in London with my young friend Richard and that every thing at the India House, and concerning his voyage to Bengal, are settled to our satisfaction. Richard goes out a Cadet in the Bengal Infantry and I trust that he will on his arrival at Calcutta be appointed an officer in one of the Company's Regiments – I am told there is no doubt of it. I have taken his passage in a ship agreeable to Mr. Charles Purvis (of Bath's) wishes; – in the Sir Wm. Bensley Captn. Rhode – who will sail by the first convoy from the motherbank – and I expect him to be there (ye motherbank) the latter end of this month. Captn. Rhode's character is good and I like his countenance – before he sails, I hope we shall be better acquainted. I am to give him £95 for Richard's Passage – of course he is to be at the Captain's Table – I hope this you will approve of – at the third mate's mess he could have gone for £55 – but this would not have been look'd upon as so respectable. I have bespoke his [necessaries] at the same Warehouse where his Cousin Leman was fitted – but I have omitted, by the advice of others, some unnecessary articles. Mr. Roberts the Deputy Chairman was very kind and obliging and was very glad to oblige Mr. Charles Purvis and you with Richard's appointment, and which I most ardently hope and wish may turn out to Richard's future happiness and success – I shall certainly give him such advice as I would my own son – and as Richard does not want for understanding – his good sense will I hope lead him always to act as a Gentleman and a good moral man. We were in London 9 days – our stay so long was occasioned by an informality in the Certificate I had of Richard's age and which I could not get over without getting another Certificate signed by the Rector Churchwardens – and as this Certificate was only of his Baptism, not his Birth – he did not appear by it to be 15 years of age – the age at which he must have arrived at to be a Cadet – I was then obliged to send for another Certificate countersigned by your Brother and Mr. Maidman that Richard was bona fide – 15 years old – this ended all our difficulties and apprehensions – and Richard was admitted last Friday a Cadet and received his Commission as a Cadet and he and I went through all the necessary formalities of the different offices at the India House. . . . Tomorrow we go to Portsmouth to have some clothes made for Richard – as we did not order all in London. Agreeable to Mr. Bailey's wishes and directions, I wrote to the Admiralty in your name to say that as Richard was appointed a Cadet to Bengal that he would no more return to the Royal Academy. Richard will go to Mr. Bailey and if necessary to Sir Chas. Saxton to [...] and take his books etc. from his [...] and the School. Some of his time before he sails he will spend with his Uncle at Blackbrook and some with me and be on the spot with my son George when the ship is ordered to sail.
  Respecting his Lr. of Credit – Mr. Goodlad told me that he would probably want

about £100 or £150 to fit him out to join his Regiment – after he has his
Commission as an officer perhaps his pay may enable him to go on without your
assistance – but this depends so much on the disposition and economy of the
young man that nothing can be said to a certainty about it – I shall recommend
economy – and to avoid all societies which may lead to extravagance and
debauchery. Mr. Goodlad is gone to Bath with his wife for 2 or 3 months – I will
write to him for a Letter of Credit and recommendation to his friends – we will
get other letters of recommendation to other Families. After Richard is sailed, I
will send you an Account of every Disbursement I have paid. It will come to a
good deal of money including his Passage paid to Captn. Rhode – this is
unavoidable – and I am sure you would have him appear in every respect as your
Son, and as a Gentleman. Richard continues pleased with his intended voyage
and the situation he is going out in. He is now by my side writing to his brother.
Both he and I have read your letters of the 3 and 7 Inst. and were much rejoiced
to find that you was well and had weathered the storm of Christmas Day – and
indeed other storms between that day and the date of your letter. May you ever
weather every storm you meet with till you get into the haven of an Admiral's
Flag – surely the great man at the Admiralty will think soon of a promotion or has
he totally forgot his own feelings when he was looking up himself to a Flag – but,
he's a strange man.
. . . We are expecting Bonaparte every week – let him come – he will find us
ready to crush him and his Banditti. Adieu, my dear friend . . . and believe me to
be with the greatest sincerity, yours, D. Garrett.

. . . I had almost forgot to say something to you about my young friend John your
son – I hope soon to hear that he is a Lieut. – I was speaking to Daysh about him
and Daysh advises your writing to Lord St. Vincent without loss of time to direct
Sir Andrew to promote him there for there is no promotion at home.

The following week the newspapers announced the arrival of
*Dreadnought* at Plymouth for repair of storm damage and Mr.
Garrett took the opportunity for a quick update:

I congratulate you on having escaped the dangers of the terrible and frequent
storms you have lately met with – I see by the Papers that you are arrived at
Plymouth, somewhat damaged – as you will probably remain there long enough
to receive a letter from me, I write you this short one to inform you that Richard
is appointed a Cadet in the Bengal Infantry, that I have taken his Passage in the
Sir. Wm. Bensley, East Indiaman, commanded by Capt. Rhode – bound for
Madeira, Madras and Bengal. I expect her at Spithead next week. I have bought
and paid for all his necessaries for the voyage, they are received aboard the Sir
Wm. Bensley and that Richard is very well and much pleased with his situation.
He is at present at your Brother's till the ship arrives at Spithead when he goes to
my Son George to wait her sailing. I wrote you all this last week to the care of
Mr. Glencross, which perhaps you may have received . . . but I would not lose a
post in acquainting you something about my young Friend your Son – lest my
former letter of last week might have been sent by Mr. Glencross on board some
ship to join Admiral Cornwallis's Squadron. . .

The repairs in Plymouth having been completed, *Dreadnought* lay at anchor in Torbay awaiting a favourable wind. Captain Purvis, in what was to be his last letter to Richard before he sailed for India, repeated his "Good Advice" to his son and reminded him that he must live on his pay as he could not afford to subsidise him.

My dear Richard, — I received your letter of the 16th on my arrival at this place yesterday, and as the Wind will not admit of your Sailing, I think it probable this will catch you before you go. Mr. Garrett has indeed, my dear Richard, taken uncommon pains and trouble on your account, and as I am well acquainted with his disposition and goodness of heart, I can venture to assure you, that you cannot gratify him in anything so much as scrupulously attending to the good advice he has and will continue to give you as long as you remain within his reach. I have occasionally given you advice since your having decided on the plan of going to India, but as my Mind has been so much employ'd on the business of the Ship and the continual interruptions in consequence of the uncommon bad Weather we have had; I have not been so collected as I would wish to inforce on your mind the very great consequence it is to you to preserve through life a fair and unspoted Character, too much cannot possibly be said on so interesting a subject, and as Mr. Garrett will probably commit some of his thoughts to paper for your future guidance; I intreat you to pay every possible attention to them, preserve them, and read them over frequently and always keep in your mind the pleasure and satisfaction I shall derive from hearing as good accounts of you as I have of your Brother; I have been very much gratified from reports frequently brought me of his good conduct Gentlemanlike behaviour and great attention to his duty, he has met with many friends in a distant country, who are always showing him civilities, tho totally unknown to me; Remember Richard the strong admonitions I have so frequently and forcibly given you in common with the other youngsters on board the London and Royal George, I think they can never be forgot unless the Heart should become so corrupted as not to retain a virtuous sentiment; this my dear Richard I trust will never be your case; God forbid it should; I only wish you clearly to understand how much I am interested in your doing well and always acting uprightly honourably Religiously and honest; never suffer yourself to be led out of the proper path, by any specious deceitful Characters, which you may [chance] to fall in with; civility is due to all, but do not hastily form friendships with those you scarcely [are] acquainted with, you will have the advantage of being recommended to some of the Principal Gentlemen in the Settlements, to them you should look for advice, and their reports of you will give me I hope all the satisfaction I can wish. I come now, my dear Richard, to another matter which I desire you pay the greatest attention to, this is your expenses; the fitting you out is more than I can well afford and therefore the most exact economy on your part is absolutely necessary, the Sum to be paid will reduce my income considerably and I had nothing to spare before; you must make your pay support you in India as others do; your two Uncles as well as myself had no assistance from our Father, and yet pass'd on without ever disgracing our family in any respect whatever; If I could assist you in the early part of your service I would, but this heavy expense of the outfitting will prevent me. Be assured my dear Richard of my best love, and that it may please God to forward your happiness and take you under his protection is the sincere wish of your affectionate Father, Jhn. Chd. Purvis.

The day of Richard's departure approached. Unknown to Mr. Garrett, the East Indiaman *Sir William Bensley* had already left its anchorage in the Downs on 29th January and was making its way down channel to Portsmouth. Captain Rhode had been ill and was not aboard, the ship being commanded by a Mr. Eastfield for her passage from Gravesend to Portsmouth.

Richard was staying with his Uncle and Aunt George at Blackbrook. Though the weather was not suitable for him to enjoy the beauties of the gardens, he spent many happy hours playing with his little cousins, Renira and Georgina. Georgina he was to remember in the years to come as "one of the sweetest children I ever saw".

Meanwhile from Southwick, good Mr. Garrett, determined to leave no stone unturned in his young friend Richard's service, continued to seek introductions and solicit interest and letters of recommendation from every quarter. On 4th February he wrote again to Captain Purvis at anchor in Torbay but, by the time the letter arrived, *Dreadnought* had put to sea and his letter was endorsed "Sailed" and forwarded to Plymouth for transmission through the usual channels:

My dear Sir, — We are all extremely happy to learn, which we do by your letter of the 29th ulto. that you are safe arrived in Torbay after encountering so many violent storms. The weather has been uncommonly tempestuous and rainy – the floods of water here have been higher than I have ever known them since I have resided at Southwick: I hope we may have fine sun shine days in future which are much wanted; – for dry weather is much wanted in the fields and in the gardens. Be assured, my dear Friend, that I receive great pleasure and satisfaction in being useful to you, and to my young Friend your Son. We are now all ready and waiting for Captn. Rhode who I see by the Papers is in the Downs; the first Easterly wind will bring him to the [Motherbank] – how long he may stay there is uncertain, but it is supposed it will not be long. Richard is I believe still at his Uncle's at Blackbrook. I have several Letters of Introduction and Recommendations for him from Mr. Goodlad – both to Military Gentlemen and to others in a Civil Employ at Calcutta and in Bengal, and also from Mr. Goodlad a Letter of Credit for 1,000 Sicca Rupees – which in Sterling money amounts to about £100. I shall instruct Richard not to take up more money than is absolutely necessary – and in the necessity of having any sum he will be instructed by Mr. Goodlad's Military Friends and also by a Gentn., a Military Gentleman also, who Richard will take letters for from a Captn. [Missing] an Acquaintance of your

Brother's. My Son William has got letters from Mr. Barwell to his Friends in Bengal, recommending strongly and kindly Richard to these Friends' notice and attention – these letters are warmly written, and so are Mr. Goodlad's, and I have expressed your and my obligations to him. I wrote a very pressing letter to the Right Honble. George Rose to recommend Richard to the Civil and Military Suite of the Marquis of Wellesley, but the Right Honorable Gentleman has not condescended to give me an answer – which treatment I shall remember. He can ask me for favors and I immediately comply – but Courtiers in and out of place are not to be depended upon. I hope, however, your application in favor of your Son John, to the great man at the Admiralty will be such as we all wish it to be – an order to Sir Andrew Mitchell to promote our young Friend to a Lieutenancy – I hope to live to see him a Captain.

I shall give Richard my advice for the good conduct of himself in India – I trust that the letters he takes out will introduce him to the best Society . . . Richard has good sense – and that will, I trust, lead him to avoid every thing unbecoming the Gentleman and the Officer. I hope that soon after his arrival he will get a Commission as an Officer . . .

I was in great hopes that ere this I should have congratulated you on being an Admiral – what can the great man mean in postponing such a necessary and proper boon to Gentlemen who have so dearly earned and deserved such Promotion. He is not backward in promoting his own creatures and turning out others. However, as I am not in the secret, I may be mistaken in my opinions of men and measures . . .

Bonaparte has not yet crossed the water – he still threatens us, and it is confidently said that he really means to invade us – I trust that we are able to repel him. Henry, by being at Southampton, has escaped many a tough gale – Bonaparte, however, keeps him at his Post . . . I hear of nothing new at Wickham – the Spinsters of Southwick are Spinsters still, and will remain so till some good natured man takes compassion on them.

I suppose you will not remain long in Torbay – the first fair wind will take you back off Brest. You have a great deal of fagging and no Prize Money – nothing but wear and tear! I will write you again when Richard has sailed – I wish with all my heart that you could both meet once more – to take a farewell – but this I fear is not likely . . . God bless you my worthy good Friend – all here join me in best wishes, Most faithfully I remain yours, D. G.

At last, after the months of preparation, Richard embarked on the *Sir William Bensley* on 10th February 1804. Mr. Garrett accompanied him and put in a good word for him with Captain Robert Rhode who had rejoined the ship after his illness. It was to be the last time that Richard saw his good friend Mr. Garrett who had worked so tirelessly in his interests. The following day Mr. Garrett wrote to Richard's father to advise him that he was aboard the Indiaman and that his departure was imminent:

My dear Sir, — I came from Southwick yesterday to see Captn. Rhode of the Sir Wm. Bensley, East Indiaman, in which ship Richard embarked today – the

Convoy is appointed – the Isis, Captn. Lebb. The wind is foul therefore we shall probably see Richard on shore again. He went off in good spirits and seems highly pleased with his new situation. I have strongly recommended Richard to the attention of Captn. Rhode. There are eleven Cadets going out in the same ship. There is a ship in the Downs, the Fame, East Indiaman, which Captn. Rhode says he must wait for. I hope she will be here in a few days.

I have the pleasure to say that I have received a very handsome letter from Mr. Rose – with one enclosed from him to Marquis Wellesley the Governor in Chief in India. The letter to his Lordship was couched in warm terms in favor of Richard and will, I trust, be of great service to him. Richard has a great many letters to very respectable Persons at Calcutta. . . . I hope in God that Richard's expedition to India will turn out to his advantage and to his happiness. I have not time or subject to say much now – I thought it proper to tell you that Richard was gone on board; – I have desired him to write you and to keep letters ready written to put on board any ships they may meet in their Passage. I have given him 20 Dollars on your account for any circumstances which may happen on his voyage. His Letter of Credit from Mr. Goodlad is for 1,000 Sicca Rupees at Calcutta – I have enjoined him to be very economical and not to take at Calcutta any monies unnecessarily. I hope he will meet with Friends to advise him well and that he will on all occasions take their advice. I have given, as you desired I would, a long letter containing Good Advice on all occasions which may occur to him.

Despite Mr. Garrett's prediction, the ship sailed on the same day in company with the frigate *Brilliant* and the Hon. Company's Ship *Fame* which had made a good passage from the Downs. Just before he sailed, Richard received some last-minute advice from his godfather, Captain Fortescue, an old friend of his father's after whom he had received his middle name:

Take care of your health, do not forget your prayers to that Being who has power to conduct your steps, in safety and prosperity, but you must do your duty and which from the excellent precepts and example of your worthy Parent, I am sure you must and will follow . . . As you run down into a low latitude, be abstemious and don't drink but little [beer] or wine and take a dose of salts once a week for three weeks following. I have learnt this from experience as it will save you from any complaint that in general attends people passing from a cold to a warm climate. But your best plan will be to consult the Surgeon and don't [take] your Physick [too] strong, unless you are a strong fellow and require it. . . . Adieu my good young man. †

After two years hard, slogging sea service in the Channel Fleet, the voyage to India must have been like a holiday to Richard. As Mr. Garrett had intimated, there were eleven cadets aboard, five for the Madras Army and six for Bengal. There were also four

---

† N.M.M. MS/73/125 box 2

Midshipmen in the crew with whom Richard no doubt exchanged some salty yarns. Mail was taken off the ship in Cawsand Bay including a letter from Richard to his Father who was displeased with its brevity and the fact that it appeared to have no purpose whatever "but that of recommending a bumboat woman"! Madeira was sighted on 29th March and the ship anchored in Funchal Roads the following day where she remained until 8th April.

On 13th April they parted company with the frigate *Brilliant.* Ceylon was sighted on 24th July and Fort St. George, Madras, three days later. The *Sir William Bensley* and the *Fame,* which had kept company for the whole voyage, anchored in Madras Roads on 28th July where the Madras cadets were disembarked. They sailed again on 12th August and were anchored by the Calcutta pilots on 3rd September 1804, nearly seven months after leaving Portsmouth.

Richard and his fellow Bengal Cadets were boated up the Hooghly River in "paunceways" — native Bengal river craft propelled by six oarsmen. Passengers sat cross-legged on a raised platform beneath a low matted awning to protect them from the sun. At length they came to the Garden Reach and Richard had his first view of the opulence which was John Company's India — the magnificent houses of the senior Company officials with their green and pleasant gardens stretching down to the river shore. Up river, beyond a shimmering expanse of calm water nine miles long by two miles wide, he saw for the first time the massive bulk of Fort William, symbol of British power and permanence; and beyond that the skyline of the mighty city of Calcutta — the greatest trading centre of the East and the gateway to a new life of adventure and opportunity. At that moment he had little doubt that he had made the right decision in rejecting a hard, slogging, predictable career in the Navy for the challenge which now lay before him in this exciting country.

Richard had been appointed Ensign on 18th August, shortly before his arrival in India, and the following month, on 21st September 1804, in line with Mr. Garrett's expectations, he received his Lieutenant's Commission in the Bengal Army. He was then aged fifteen years and eight months.

58

## PART 2

# Marching Orders

# 1. Joining the Regiment

*Wickham, near Portsmouth, Hampshire.*
*21st April 1805.*

The year 1804 had been an eventful one for Captain Purvis. In February his younger son Richard had left the bosom of his patronage and had sailed for what, at best, had to be regarded as an uncertain future in India. Shortly thereafter he had learned of the death of his nephew, Richard Oadham Purvis, in Jamaica. He was a naval Lieutenant and had, ironically, just left his ship, which was returning to England, in the hope of improving his chances for promotion by remaining in the West Indies. He was not yet nineteen and his death had been a bitter blow to his mother who had lost her husband, Captain Richard Purvis R.N., two years earlier and whose happiness was now focussed in the lives of her children. As yet unknown to his family in England, her second son, Lieutenant John Leman, Bengal Native Infantry, one year younger than Oadham, had died in Rangoon the previous month.

On 23rd April 1804, Captain Purvis's forty-three years of hard service had been rewarded with his long-awaited promotion to Rear-Admiral. He had consequently left the *Dreadnought* and come ashore for a time. Then, on 2nd August, he had married his third wife, Elizabeth Dickson.

Elizabeth was the only surviving child and heiress of Admiral Sir Archibald Collingwood Dickson, Bart. who, as a Captain in 1793, had commanded the *Egmont,* 74, when Captain John Child Purvis was commanding the *Princess Royal,* 98, in Lord Hood's Mediterranean Fleet. She was twenty-one years younger than her groom and had been previously married to her cousin, Captain William Dickson of the 22nd Regiment, who had died in San Domingo in 1795. Admiral Dickson had recently died and under the terms of his Will, Elizabeth received £15,000 in 3% Bank Annuities and, after the death or remarriage of her mother, she would inherit the mansion house at Hardingham and the residue of her father's estate. This, coupled with Admiral Purvis's increased pay as a Flag Officer, ensured the couple a comfortable income for the rest of their lives even if Admiral Purvis never received another seagoing appointment. He had written to Richard last November advising him of his promotion and his marriage and assuring him that, in his new stepmother he would always find:

... one sincerely disposed to look on you as a Son, and always inclin'd to render you every possible service.

His elder son, John, was in the sloop *Driver,* on the North American Station and showing due promise in his career. Although he had not yet received his Lieutenant's Commission, he had a promise from Sir Andrew Mitchell that he should have the next vacancy.

Richard, however, was giving him cause for concern. It was now over a year since he had sailed for India and, apart from a brief and mildly impertinent note from Cawsand Bay, he had received not a word from his son. To make matters worse, several of his friends had received letters from Richard although he had apparently not found time to write to his own father. In February the Admiral had purchased two books entitled *"The Military Mentor"* which he felt sure would be of use, as well as pleasing, to his son; but he had reason to believe that they had been shipped aboard the Indiaman *Earl of Abergavenny,* commanded by Captain John Wordsworth, brother of William Wordsworth the poet, which had been lost with 300 passengers and crew in a great storm off Portland at the start of her passage. If this was so, his gift for Richard would be rotting at the bottom of the ocean.

Then there was the question of the money. On his arrival in India, Richard had drawn £100 on his father's account without even a note of explanation or excuse. The Admiral imagined that this had been necessary for his son's regimentals and other setting-up expenses but he felt he should at least have received the courtesy of an explanatory note.

His late brother Richard's third son, George Thomas Purvis, was about to sail for India as a Bengal Army Cadet so he would not lose the opportunity of entrusting him with a letter for Richard which would express his growing displeasure:

Wickham, 21st April 1805

My dear Richard, — As your Cousin George is going to Bengal, I do not like to allow him to take his departure without sending you a letter by him, but I am sorry to say I have none from you to reply to; it is usual for people to write a letter of advice when they draw for Money but tho I have had a Debit on me for £100 you have not given me one line or at least none have I received; I have written you many letters since you sailed, and your good Mother has also sent you two letters, but the last I received from you was from Cawsand Bay and for no purpose whatever but that of recommending a Bumboat Woman. I think a little reflection will shew you this neglect on your part must be very displeasing to me, therefore I trust you will in future act very differently.

   George will make the third of our family who have made choice of a Military life in India and chance has directed them all to the same Presidency. You may easily suppose the friends of the Trio do, and will continue to feel very great anxiety for their welfare and I hope and trust they will all conduct themselves in such a manner as to be respectable to themselves and creditable to their Family. I very much wish you to retain in your memory the advice I have so often and so fervently given you and never allow yourself to forget that you became a soldier by your own particular desire and against my inclination; therefore I cannot too often remind you how much you ought to exert yourself to make yourself master of your Profession and when you are call'd on Real Service, I doubt not you will do your duty in such a manner as will ever after please you, when you reflect on the subject. Most of the letters I have written you have been enclosed to Mr. Lindegeen of Portsmouth therefore do not fail to let me know what you receive; I very much disapprove of letters being given to the care of private hands, the safest and best mode is to put them in a way of going in the Company's Packet, where they are safe and certain. Your Brother I have not heard from since December, he was then very well and desired his best love to you; your Uncle and Aunts with all your Cousins, Mr. English, the Maidmans, Grants, etc. desire their kindest regards. Your Mother joins me in love to you and John Leman and believe me always, My dear Richard, Your affectionate Father, Jhn. Chd. Purvis.

Admiral Purvis had now been ashore for a year during which he had had ample time and opportunity to write several letters to Richard although he had received none in return. In Europe, Bonaparte had been Crowned as Emperor of France and clearly had territorial ambitions which were going to involve Britain in a long and protracted war. If, as he sincerely hoped would be the case, he was to be recalled for sea service, who could tell what the future might hold for him; what was certain was that the duties of an Admiral in a major continental conflict would not allow him the same time for personal correspondence as he presently enjoyed. Moreover, if he were to be posted to a seagoing command, wherever in the world it might be, the lines of communication with his soldier son would inevitably be further dislocated. How he wished that before such a time might arrive, he could be assured that Richard was settling into his chosen career and was living his life in accordance with the "Good Advice" he had so frequently tried to impress upon him.

\* \* \*

*Muttra, India.*
*3rd September 1805.*

Since his arrival in India a year ago, Richard had indeed received several of his father's letters. It was perhaps a wonder that he had received the first, which told him of his father's promotion and remarriage, as it had twice been endorsed "Dead" and returned to Calcutta before eventually being forwarded to the 2nd Battalion 21st Native Infantry to which regiment he had been posted shortly after his arrival.

His brother officers seemed to constitute much the same social mix that he had observed in the wardrooms of the *London* and the *Royal George* – younger sons of mainstream gentry and elder sons of minor gentry; sons of officers who could not afford to purchase a King's Commission for them or whose scions were unable, or unwilling, to undergo the period of specialist further education required for the artillery or engineers; a few sons of socially ambitious tradesmen who had secured the patronage of an influential customer for their son's Cadetship; and a few sons of emigrés who had fled the bloodshed of Revolutionary France for the political serenity of their country's traditional enemy. By and large, they seemed a more relaxed group of young men than the fiercely competitive and professional junior sea officers he had known during his naval service. One thing he did notice was the lack of that sense of tradition which existed in the Navy where many boys were following in the footsteps of several generations of their forebears. The Bengal Army had not had the time to acquire such tradition. In 1760 there were sixty officers on its strength which had increased by the turn of the century to over 2,000 with new regiments being formed every year to service the demands of the Company's expanding activities. The 2/21st had only been raised in 1803 and by the time Richard joined them, early in 1805, two battalions of a further six regiments had been added to the strength. For young Cadets just out from England this was good news as they received their Lieutenants' Commissions almost straight away. Richard and his immediate contemporaries joined their regiments as Lieutenants within months of their arrival in India. A year later, a boy might have to remain as an Ensign, or even a Cadet, for several years after his arrival.

Although in its infancy, the 2/21st had received its baptism-in-arms the previous year in the Second Maratha War. Together with the 2/8th Native Infantry, they had stormed and captured Holkar's great fort at Rampoorah. Four companies of the 2/21st remained to garrison the fort while the other six joined Colonel Monson's force, which had been detached from the main body of General Lake's Grand Army. For fifty-four days the Detachment had fought its way back to Agra from an exposed position near Jaipur, a distance of some 350 miles, suffering appalling casualties and constant harrassment from a greatly superior enemy. The six companies of the year-old 2/21st had played a prominent part in this heroic action which would thereafter be remembered as "Monson's Retreat".

Richard joined the Regiment with two other young officers both of whom had received their Lieutenants' Commissions on the same day as himself. Although, at sixteen years, Richard was the youngest of the three, he had received his Ensign's Commission a few days earlier than the others and therefore joined the Regiment as the senior Lieutenant of the three.

Next was John Home, two years older than Richard, a tall Irishman from Dublin with a slightly bewildered air about him. John Home's father was a portrait painter of some note in Calcutta and his younger brother, Richard, was at the time on his voyage out from England as a Bengal Army Cadet. His father's elder brother, Sir Everard Home Bart., was a Captain in the Navy and represented the senior branch of an old-established Southern-Irish Ascendancy family.

David Charles Livingstone, at twenty-one the eldest of the three though the most junior, was a Scot from Stirling – 9th and youngest son of Sir Alexander Livingstone, Bart. of Westquarter. His elder half-brother, Thomas, was in the Navy and would eventually become an Admiral and the 10th Baronet. David Livingstone had few frills about him but was tough, dependable and clearly cut out as a career soldier.

On their arrival, the three new Lieutenants had been introduced to their Commanding Officer, Captain William Nichol, who had taken over command of the Battalion as both his senior officers, Lieutenant-Colonel Joseph Gascoyne and Major Alexander Morrison, were on furlough. William Nichol was a battle-seasoned senior Captain aged forty-one who enjoyed the universal regard and respect of his officers and men. He had been in India since the age of sixteen and had taken part in almost every major campaign since. For two years he had been attached to a Marine Regiment for the Expedition to Macao in 1801/02 and in the previous year he had led the six companies of the 2/21st which had taken part in Monson's Retreat. At one point, outside the town of Khushalgarh, the retreating British detachment was surrounded by 20,000 of Scindia's horse supported by twenty-five pieces of artillery. As the enemy cavalry bore down on the rear of the column, Captain Nichol had turned the 2/21st to meet them. The Regiment closed its ranks and held its fire until the enemy came within fifty yards of them then, with cool and well-directed file-firing, with almost every shot taking effect, they had held the enemy onslaught at bay for three hours until, their horses intimidated by the steady hail of fire and their riders dispirited with their lack of success, Scindia's men withdrew and the British retreat continued. There was not an officer, NCO or sepoy of the 2/21st who did not venerate Captain Nichol after Khushalgarh. Like so many very brave men, William Nichol was quiet and courteous in his demeanour and had welcomed Richard and his two friends to the Regiment with warmth and hospitality.

Below William Nichol in the hierarchy were three Captains – John Yardley Bradford, aged forty-seven, from London; John Robertson, aged thirty, a Scot from Ross-shire in the Northern Highlands; and James Cock, aged twenty-five, another Scot who had two younger brothers in the Bengal Army. Both Robertson and Cock had been with the 2/21st in Monson's Retreat the previous year and, though friendly enough to the new arrivals, bore that air of detached superiority assumed by men who have recently taken part in great events. James Cock enjoyed another distinction and it was not long before the new officers were party to the favourite element of regimental humour – Cock's search for a wife and his insistence on visiting and inspecting every new female who arrived from England in the district, and sometimes far outwith it.

Then there was a Captain-Lieutenant, John Swinton, 3rd son of Captain William Swinton R.N., proprietor of *"Le Courrier de l'Europe"*. His mother was Félicité Jeanne le Febvre, daughter of an officer of the French Guards who had been guillotined by the revolutionaries. John Swinton had transferred to the Regiment two years earlier having been wounded in the foot during operations in the Jumna Doab. In the Battle of Deig on Christmas Eve 1804 he had been wounded again, this time seriously in the thigh by a cannon ball which lamed him for life. Although on the strength of the 2/21st, Swinton had been commanding the newly-formed Pioneer Corps since 1803 so the regimental officers saw little of him.

There were five Lieutenants senior to Richard and serving with the Regiment when he joined: John Ramsay, aged twenty-five, a Shetland Islander; Jeremiah Martin Johnson who held a particular place in the 2/21st's history as it was he who had raised the Regiment in Cawnpore in July 1803. As was the practice of the time, it had initially been known by his name as *"Jansin-ki-Paltan"* (Johnson's Regiment); next was Charles Russell, aged nineteen, second son of Sir Henry Russell Bart., of Swallowfield in Berkshire, who had been with the Regiment in Monson's Retreat; then came the Adjutant, James Brook Ridge, aged twenty-two, and one place above Richard in seniority – George Hunter, aged twenty-one, another Scot who had joined the Regiment the previous year but had to return to England on sick leave in March 1805 where he remained for two and a half years.

Below Richard, as we have already seen, were Lieutenants John Home and David Livingstone. The regimental officers were well below strength and there were vacancies for two more Lieutenants and five Ensigns. Two months later, one of the Lieutenant's vacancies was filled with the arrival of George Casement, a chubby seventeen year-old Ulsterman from Co. Antrim, 5th and youngest son of a Naval Surgeon. Two of his brothers were also serving in the

Bengal Army. This left them still short of one Lieutenant and five Ensigns and, as a consequence, Richard was given temporary command of the 1st Grenadier Company – a grave responsibility for a boy of sixteen who had been in India for less than a year.

At Cawnpore, on his way from Calcutta to join his Regiment, Richard had written to his father but it seemed he had not received it. He must explain his reasons for having written so infrequently:

Chuttrah. September 3d. 1805

My dear Sir, — I received your letter dated 25 February about a week ago, and am happy in extreme to find that your displeasure has not risen to the degree I expected, on account of my only having written one letter to you since my arrival in this Country which, I suppose had not reached you when you wrote as you do not mention any thing of it. The chief reason of my not having written oftener was the manner in which I have suffered by the villainy of the natives of this part of the Country, but my greatest loss was all my pens, paper, accounts etc. which were the contents of one or two trunks that were slung across a bullock, and the rascal of a driver ran away with the trunks, bullock and all; and at this moment I have not a sheet of Europe paper in my possession which obliges me to write on this Country paper which I beg you will excuse as there is no Europe paper procurable within the distance of a journey of five days; or even if it was to be got here I should not be able to purchase it on account of the scarcity of ready money for we have been most shamefully kept in arrears; we are now going on our seventh month, by which you may judge how much we are distressed tho' we are now in expectation of a payment of two or three months pay.

The books which you were so good as to send have not yet reached me so I must join you in your supposition that they were shipped on board the Abergavenny – I cannot help thinking but that the letter I wrote you from Cawnpore has been lost as all the Posts are frequently robbed; that might have been the fate of every letter. In case the war should not be renewed we shall go into cantonments where I shall make myself comfortable and my knowledge of Camp etc. will enable me to fit myself out in a proper manner then, I flatter myself, nobody in England shall complain of my remissness in writing which, I must own, they have ample reason to do at present. I think it a most idle time in Camp, or at least it is to me at present, for I have not a book to look into; I left them all at Cawnpore on account of the enormous expense, the carriage of them is, for we have no such thing as Baggage Waggons in this Country, we keep our own camels, bullocks etc. and at this rate I thought it best to leave them behind as they would have required an additional camel; I have now only two, and three bullocks which carry wine and every thing I have with me; these, together with two horses and seventeen servants are my establishment – you must not be surprised at the number of servants, for it is the custom of this Country that no servant will do two sorts of business; as a horse requires two men – one to clean him etc. the other to cut grass; the servant who dresses you (called a Bearer) does not attend you at table, neither does he who attends at table lend a hand to cook the dishes and this is the reason we keep so many; tho' be assured this is all done within my pay, which now I have command of a Company, amounts to 300 Rupees a month, the exchange of which is about £37. 10s. monthly and £450 annually, you may suppose how comfortable I can live upon that, but as the Company is not my own right, it only continues as long as the senior Lieutenants are absent. Without the Company it will be only 250 Rupees a month I have the honor to command the 1st Grenadier Company of the 2nd Battalion of the 21st Regiment, and am the fifteenth Lieutenant in the Regiment. I reckon myself to have been extremely fortunate in my time of coming out; had I been a season later I should not have been a Lieutenant at all, but perhaps remained three or four years an Ensign. I suppose you have heard of the death of my Cousin John Leman; how his death and that of my Cousin Richard Oadham must have distressed my Aunt Mrs. R.P–! I am glad to hear my Brother is well; but sorry to find he has not got his commission. I hope his intended letter to me will contain the agreeable news. I long to get hold of a Navy List to see your rank. I received a very kind letter from my good friend Mr. Garrett informing me of several deaths which I was extremely concerned to hear amongst them that of poor Martin. I hope you have got another servant but am sure not one to suit you better than he. You may depend upon my taking an opportunity to write to my Mother . . . This letter from Mr. Garrett contains some [good] advice for which with my love to him [please convey] my most sincere thanks telling him of my intention of writing to him, as also to all my friends as soon as I find myself a little comfortable. I also beg you to mention me to all who I knew and believe [the] most earnest assurances of duty and affection from, my dear Sir, your dutiful Son, Richard Fortescue Purvis.

Remember me to your remaining old servants.

In due course, Richard would regret having painted such a rosy picture of his financial position but, for the moment, his new life gave him no cause for other than optimism and good cheer.

# 2. First Command

*Fort Bijaigarh, near Aligarh, India.*
*27th September 1805.*

The history of Northern India since 1700 BC has been that of a continual succession of invasions by foreign powers each of which established a dynasty, stamping elements of its culture on the region and its inhabitants, and eventually crumbling through internal conflict or defeat at the hands of a new invading power. Aryans, Greeks, Persians, Arabs, Afghans and Turks all battled, with varying degrees of success, for lordship of India.

Then in the 16th century, Mongol hordes from Samarkand, descendants of Genghis Khan and Tamerlaine, swept into India through Afghanistan and founded the mighty, and immensely rich, Moghul Empire which was in place when Europeans started to make their first tentative approaches to trade with the sub-continent. Less than two centuries after its establishment, the Moghul Empire, in turn, began to crumble leaving Northern India in a renewed state of anarchy with former Moghul governors, European powers, foreign adventurers and dispossessed Hindu princes all trying to establish their own independent principalities.

Some thirty-five centuries of almost unabated internal warfare had resulted in every tactical position in what are today Rajasthan and Uttar Pradesh, every mountain pass, hilltop and river crossing, having been made defendable with a fort. These varied in size and magnificence from whole fortified cities, with beautifully engineered stone defensive works, to simple country mud forts commanding less important rural keypoints.

The fort at Bijaigarh, which had been subdued and occupied by the British two years earlier, was of the latter type and was one of two, the other being Anupshahr, the manning and defence of which now fell to the 2/21st Native Infantry stationed at Aligarh which was roughly midway between the two at a distance of some thirty miles from each.

The 2/21st had ten companies of which eight were at Aligarh and one each manning the forts at Bijaigarh and Anupshahr. Each company comprised about ninety privates and ten NCOs and was commanded by a British officer. The periods of duty at these forts were of about six weeks duration but this was frequently extended due to the unavailabilty of a suitable relief or, in the rainy season, because of flooded rivers and unpassable roads.

In September 1805, the month before Trafalgar, Richard, aged sixteen, took up his first command at Bijaigarh with the 1st Grenadier Company of the 2/21st. On the 27th he wrote for the first time to his new stepmother:

This place is a small mud fort the command of which I at present have but expect to be relieved in a day or two by some [more] senior officer who is likely to join the Battalion. I wish it was my lot to retain this command, there are a few little perquisites attached to this office of the Garrison.

The greatest of these was the *Batta* payment. The basic pay of the Company's military officers was shamefully inadequate even for their most essential needs. Debt among junior officers was almost universal while credit was easily obtained thereby exacerbating the problem. Richard was fortunate in having been able to draw on his father for his kitting-out on arrival but few officers of the Bengal Army had recourse to private funds and most had therefore to borrow for this essential expense. On a Lieutenant's pay they could only hope to cover the interest charges on their loan, and the life insurance premiums on which the lenders not unnaturally insisted, and most officers remained deeply in debt until they obtained promotion to Major. *Batta* was paid to officers on active service or detached duties and this amounted to considerably more than their basic pay. Detached commands were therefore popular, despite the loneliness and boredom, and had the added advantage of keeping the officer away from the temptation to spend money.

It is about a mile round and is garrisoned with one Company and about 30 miles from where the Battalion is stationed. . . . The only pleasures I have here at present are my horses and gun, there is a deal of game here and indeed all over India we always have enough [to shoot].

Of the twenty-one months that the 2/21st was to be stationed at Aligarh, Richard was to spend eight in command either at Bijaigarh or Anupshahr. In addition to shooting, he occupied his time by studying the local languages. As the only European in the fort, for several weeks at a time, it was an ideal opportunity and he hoped for a sustained period of peace with the Marathas so he might continue his studies.

Lord Cornwallis here is now dangerously ill and I fear there is little probability of a man of his age recovering† – besides that, he must have a great deal on his mind considering the purpose for which he came to this country. If he dies I suppose we shall have more fighting – Holkar, who was our strongest enemy last year is now reduced almost to nothing and if Scindiah remains quiet we shall be [peaceful] for a few years, it is more my wish to do so than to be campaigning . . . [it requires] about three years before you can get a perfect knowledge of the language, which is a great thing. While I was at Cawnpore I studied the Persian language but have been obliged to give it up for the want of a Moonshee or Master, my last one was a very old man and could not stand the fatigues of a campaign.

His periods of isolated command also gave Richard the chance to get to know the soldiers he was commanding. They were tall, fine looking men — few were less than 5 feet 8 inches — mostly high-caste Brahmins or Rajputs from the province of Oudh who related strongly to individual officers who treated them with kindness and consideration. Their bravery was unquestioned and most were veterans of the recent Maratha War in which there had been numerous instances of great gallantry. Nor was their loyalty to the Company, the *Sirkar,* to be questioned; although their pay was meagre, it was significantly more than they could have earned in civilian life and there was nothing obnoxious to them about being in the service of a foreign power in a country which, since time immemorial, had always been under the rule of one foreign conqueror or another.

The uniform which Richard and his friends wore was based on that of the King's Infantry Regiments — a red tunic, which was worn open, with high collar and, in the case of the 21st, black facings on the collar and cuffs, silver lace and a silver shoulder belt

---

† Lord Cornwallis died nine days later on 5th October 1805, at Ghazipur, and was succeeded by Sir George Barlow.

plate bearing the regimental number. The sword was carried on a
black leather shoulder belt and junior officers wore a single
epaulette on their right shoulder. Beneath their red coats they wore
tight fitting waistcoats and breeches of white linen the outfit being
completed by black leather boots and a bicorn hat.

The sepoys' red tunics were similar to those of their officers.
Privates wore white shorts and sandals *(chapplis),* while senior
NCOs wore breeches and boots. Richard's men, being of a
Grenadier Company, had the distinction of wearing wings at their
shoulders instead of the simple plaited shoulder cords of a normal
company. The thing that distinguished the sepoy of the Bengal
Infantry above all else at this time was his head dress; this was a
flat, circular cap with a little pyramid rising from the centre and was
popularly known as the "sundial cap".

Richard, aged sixteen, with no formal military training and less
than a year's service, must have relied heavily on the experience of
his senior NCOs to guide him in the day-to-day decisions which he
had to make in this his first command. It was the same for his
contemporaries and was the basic difference between young
officers in the King's and the Company's Armies. In the King's
Army there were twice as many officers to the same number of men
and young officers enjoyed a continuous process of professional
education being always in touch with their Captains and Majors
and, because of the greater number of officers, were not called upon
to assume serious responsibility until they were ready for it. In
India, on the other hand, a "Griffin", as new arrivals were known,
could find himself in command of 100 men and in charge of the
treasure for a battalion's payroll, on a route where the possibility of
ambush was great, and with no other European with whom he could
share the burden. To add insult to injury, the Company's officer was
paid very much less than his counterpart in the King's Army.

Alternating between the commands at Bijaigarh, Anupshahr and
battalion duties in Aligarh, Richard soon got into the swing of his
duties as a regimental officer. He was popular with his contemporaries and began to form a particular friendship with John Home
who, if not his equal intellectually, shared his interest in shooting.
Having arrived at Anupshahr for his first command, it was not long
before Home was exploring the moat for fish and wrote to Richard:

Yesterday morning I arrived here (God be thanked) in a whole skin, for I was nearly killed on the road by a black fellow because I wanted him to shew me the road but he seized his Lathi (a great bamboo loaded half way up with iron) and jumped on a bank and told me he would not go, I on my little Tattoo, without anything but a switch in my hand could not attempt force, for he had the upper hand of me entirely so I was obliged to leave him alone as he would not have hesitated knocking my brains out . . .To tell you the truth, I don't think as much of Anoopshir as I expected I should but I have not yet run all its beauties. I was almost drowned yesterday. I made a raft of Kedgerey Pots to get over to the large rock in the nulla, but I no sooner launched than the pots began to break and five of them broke before I got back. I intend making a stronger one tho' in a day or two as there are lots of fish in the nulla, tho' not very large that I have seen. The black fellows swear they saw some two cubits long, I should like to catch some of these. I find the Hookah a very pleasant companion; I smoke two chillums after breakfast; I shall dine at three and then try the fish again and if I prove unsuccessful I shall take my Hookah down on the rocks tomorrow and smoke, read, and fish at the same time.

Back in England, Admiral Purvis was deeply saddened by the death of his good friend Daniel Garrett on 29th November 1805 but cheered by the news that John had received his Lieutenant's Commission in Bermuda in May and of Nelson's great victory at Trafalgar the previous month. By 28th April 1806 he had still not received a letter from Richard and his patience was becoming increasingly strained:

It is now more than two years since I received a letter from you and tho' I have endeavoured to find excuses for this great omission on your part, circumstances are so combined as totally to exclude the possibility of one; you wrote to Mr. Garrett and Mr. Maidman from Madrass telling them you intended to address me on your arrival at Calcutta, when you did get there, you drew two Bills on me without even a letter of advice and in a few months afterwards you drew another Bill with as little ceremony; how you can reconcile all this to your own feelings, I cannot form any judgement, since it is so different from my conduct when I was as far removed from my Father, and also from that of your Brother towards me; I will not however dwell longer on this painful subject than to say that you cannot expect me to write to you if you continue to neglect me, however anxious I am to know every particular respecting you . . .

He also understood that Richard had taken upon himself the duty of winding up the affairs of his cousin Leman who had died at Rangoon in March. Yet he had received no confirmation from Richard and was anxious to be able to reassure his sister-in-law that it was being undertaken in a proper manner.

I had a letter some time ago from Beccles wherein I am asked whether you had taken on you the management of the concerns of poor John Leman. I told your Aunt I had not received any Account whatever from you but that if you have interfered, I had no doubt you would render a just and faithful account of what you had done, and tho' I should be better pleased that some other person had undertaken the business, yet if it was done by you, I desire you write your Aunt all the particulars and how you disposed of the balance.

Unknown to Admiral Purvis at the time, on the same day as he wrote this letter to Richard, Lord Collingwood, who had taken over as Commander-in-Chief Mediterranean after Nelson's death, had written to him to say that he was finding the strain of sole command too great and had urgent need of a second-in-command upon whom he could really depend.† He had written to the Admiralty requesting that his old friend Rear-Admiral Purvis should be sent out in this appointment.

Admiral Purvis, who had been feeling increasingly impotent in his comfortable life ashore as Bonaparte steadily increased his grip on Europe, was fretting for a sea command. He might have been more conciliatory to Richard had he known the contents of the letter Lord Collingwood was, on that same day, writing.

†N.M.M. Ref: AGC/XX111 Ms Letter Lord Collingwood, off Cadiz, to Rear Admiral Purvis 28 April 1806. Presented by Mrs. May Purvis 1946

# 3. Debt

*Aligarh, India.*
*2nd June 1806.*

Despite the two bills he had drawn on his father since his arrival in India, Richard had, in common with all his fellow subalterns, got himself seriously into debt. The *Batta* payments he received for his periods of exile in Bijaigarh and Anupshahr, for which he put himself forward at every opportunity, were simply not sufficient to enable him to service the high interest charges on the debts he had run up during his first year in India.

Nor could he share his friends' relaxed attitude towards debt; John Home, in particular, seemed quite unworried by the position he was in; he simply borrowed money where and when he could with little thought of how it was to be repaid. Some of the "Good Advice" that Richard had received from his father and from Mr. Garrett, however, had obviously made its mark and his attitude to debt was more puritanical than that of his friends. He, himself, had made a very real attempt to live within his income and to put a little of his pay aside. He had tried to persuade John Home to do the same but with little success:

You have had a sample of my saving cash, but by God I can't do it, it is all nonsense talking, if I once get hold of the money I can't keep it . . .

The sale between young officers of horses, dogs and guns was commonplace but every transaction was controlled by what credit could be obtained by the purchaser and granted by the seller. John Home coveted a Turkey horse of Richard's but his ability to buy it would depend upon what terms Richard could offer:

In what manner, or what time will you give me, to pay for your Turkey, I have a liking for him because he is a Turkey, and I have often said that I liked one better than the country horses. I should willingly become the purchaser but you know

the state of my finances will not allow of present payment, and owing to a letter
I had today from the India Gazette man which is really too civil to put him off
any longer, it will be out of my power to pay you for some time. Now to let you
know at once when you may expect the cash, I shall tell you that I can't pay
before the issue of movements pay. If this likes you, [then] I have no more to say
on this subject, but I think you will send the horse over as soon as you like, but
if the terms you have [negotiated] on the Arab one will not admit of your giving
so long credit, why I can only regret the opportunity being lost of my getting a
good, decent animal . . . I know if you had not bought Phosphores you would not
stick on the terms knowing I am always out of cash.

Richard tried hard to discourage his friend's extravagance but John
could not resist a bargain:

I picked up a very neat small medicine chest, the same kind of one that I was
asked 80Rs. for in Calcutta. I got it for 56 which is a great difference considering
the places. I should not have got it so cheap but the man has lately set up in
opposition to another merchant and sells his goods much cheaper on that account.
The box is very complete — ten bottles of medicine in the upper part, the lower,
or drawer, contains the scales and weights, a small glass pestle and mortar, a glass
measure of an ounce and a half, with the different marks for smaller quantities,
two tin boxes of cerate and ointment and some lint. I should have taken it, tho' I
had not the money to pay for it, but it would have been the enormous sum of 4Rs.
dearer. Upon the whole I think you will like it. There is a book of directions given
in a very general style.

As Richard saw his friend sliding deeper and deeper into debt, he
would berate him at length on every foolish deal he made on a horse
or a dog, imploring him to be more astute and less impulsive. When
Richard bought a horse and buggy for transporting him to and from
shooting expeditions, then planned to enhance its performance by
putting his Arab horse "Trim" between the shafts, John saw his
chance to retaliate:

I have just recd. your letter by Cock's bearer who came with bread and cannot
help calling you a d----d a-s indeed I should call any one so who gave 300 for an
old buggy and broken down horse — even tho' he had the money to spare and as
to its being of service in the shooting way, where were your senses not to consider
that the expense of keeping an extra horse for it, besides the repairs it will require
(which I think will be often the case in going over ditches and drains while
shooting) will more than compensate for the small pleasure you will experience
in driving home after perhaps a bad day's sport. Again I must ask where your
senses were when you put Trim in to it, you will find in a short time that Trim is
not a proper horse for sporting — he is not really strong enough for such work
and, when you wish to sell him, it will be greatly against the price you could have
got for him had he remained a riding horse, for I think him much too valuable a

horse to be put to such hard work. Why, Good God, I had rather you had sold Trim and bought an elephant at once. In an elephant you wd. have had all the advantages of a buggy, and five thousand others, that a buggy, especially an old one, can boast of. Had you sold Trim as you might do, or have done, for six hundred which I think he might have fetched, you could then with the 300 that you have thrown away have bought a good elephant. You will say you will not be at so much expense as I think with the buggy, as you may sell one horse and keep but one riding horse — the same advantages you would have had in an elephant. I'll say no more, but am well persuaded you will repent your bargain very shortly — indeed I can scarcely imagine how you could have made it. Now, Dick, I think this may convince you that every man should fool away his money as he likes best. In my opinion, I have as much reason to lecture away on your bargain as you had on mine. You no doubt think that your bargain is as good a one as you could have made. I have exactly the same idea of mine and from what I can judge we have the same of each other so we had better let them alone. Cock sends his love. [As] to your valuable sporting purchases, which he says will prove a noble acquisition to the Corps, he is enjoying in imagination the delightful pleasure he is [in] time to experience in a drive to Poonah, tho' he swears, By God, he would ten thousand times [prefer to] ride home than be driven after having a fatiguing days sport (tit for tat, fair play's a jewel).

James Ridge, the Adjutant, endorsed John Home's view:

You will ruin the Arab to put him in so heavy a buggy. Mine is the exact pattern of it and White [Surrey] is by no means strong enough for it which is the cause of my having left off driving . . . †

Despite John's incurable recklessness with money, his irrepressible good nature made him a great favourite with all his contemporaries and, at the end of the day, Richard could refuse him nothing. His joy in making what he considered to be a good bargain was childlike and infectious. Time and again Richard's attempts to put some money aside against his own debts were frustrated by John's need of a loan to get some pressing creditor off his back or to fulfil a debt of honour. Never did he doubt that he would be repaid — a more honourable man than John did not exist — but his own financial position was beginning to weigh heavily upon his mind.

Towards the end of May 1806 he wrote to his father requesting a loan to enable him to clear his debts. Having sent the letter he realised that, in his haste, he had not mentioned how he proposed to pay it back. On 2nd June he wrote again to explain further:

---

† N.M.M. Ref: PRV/101, *Loose Papers*, MS. 55/009

A few days ago I sat down in great confusion and wrote you a letter begging you would enable me to pay my debts. I was then so much displeased with myself at being under the necessity of imploring your assistance and so intent upon what I was writing that I fear I neglected to mention anything except what was connected with the subject. I should not write twice within such a short space of time but to make up for that one thing I perfectly recollect to have omitted which indeed is connected and which no doubt caused you some surprize, the payment of the sum. I do most honestly promise to pay it within one year after I am promoted to the rank of Captain if it please God that I live until that takes place. You will I know naturally ask how I happened to contract debts to that large amount, in answer to which I only beg you to consider the great mortification it must have been for me to see my Brother Officers with every comfort about them that could make them happy and myself not even able to make any return for those civilities which were occasionally shown me by them. Do not, my dear Sir, attempt to judge of my situation by comparing it with subalterns in the Army in England; it is far different; we have no messes but are our own house keepers in every sense of the word. Bad management contributed greatly to bring me into debt; for this you cannot blame me for where had I experience and can it be expected that the art of management in which hundreds are never perfect during the whole course of their lives should come naturally to me. Every body in my opinion must have a beginning and mine unluckily has been a very bad one, however it has brought me experience and I now find I can live upon my pay but no more my debts must remain increasing at the rate of 12 per cent per annum for some years unless you put a stop to them altogether. It is that interest which makes me so impatient to get them paid was it not for that you know I might as well leave myself indebted. When I am comparing the King's Service to ours again we have not only the expense of the first purchase for our tent but must keep men to take care of and pitch it, cattle to purchase (Bullocks and Camels) to carry it to keep up, and cattle men to take care of them. I believe I must have told you in some of my former letters that no one man will do business of more than one description, thus a horse requires two men, one to clean him the other to cut grass etc. and so on, so that I have now no less than twenty servants. This I do assure you is a small establishment and I cannot do with less. The attempt to give you an account of all the differences between a King's Officer in England and a Company's in India would be far too much for a letter, however I hope that what I have said will induce you to comply with the request.

\* \* \*

### H.M.S. Atlas, off Cadiz.
### 8th January 1807.

The Admiralty having acceded to Lord Collingwood's request, Admiral Purvis had hoisted his Flag in the *Chiffone* in 1806, had transferred it shortly thereafter to the *Atlas,* 74, and was now in command of the Blockade of Cadiz — a sea duty in which he had gained extensive experience with the Channel Fleet off Brest.

He had now received Richard's early letters from India but not that written seven months previously about his debts. For the time being his younger son was back in favour:

Although I am placed in a part of the World where it is difficult to get letters conveyed to India yet I can no longer delay the satisfaction I feel in communicating to you the pleasure I had in reading your letters, I thought indeed they were very long on their way, and I sometime thought you very inattentive, but that now being all done away with will think no more of it.

John, recently back from the West Indies, was due to join *Atlas* at any moment to act temporarily as his father's Flag Lieutenant.

I have not seen him since you did, and therefore expect to find him much alter'd in his Person; his conduct has been uniformly correct and from every account I have had of him, I have great reason to be pleased and am perfectly satisfied that your character, my dear Richard, may be equally good; I have not the smallest reason to question; you both had the advantage of such admonition as I judge proper to give you, when I had you both under my observation and since that time I have communicated to you by letters such advice as I thought might tend to your good as you advance in life. You may easily judge how a Father feels for the welfare of his Sons in general but I think, my dear Richard, you know how much anxiety I have ever expressed for the well doing of all the youngsters I have had under my care and therefore how happy it will make me to have two sons who have never given me any serious uneasiness which I am proud to say has ever been the case, and I trust will ever continue.

Before he had completed his letter, John had arrived on board and added a postscript assuring Richard that their father was no longer displeased with him:

Your Father being kind enough to give me a part of his paper I feel myself much gratified in telling you I am once more with him. I was appointed Lieut. of the Terrible after a short stay of only three days in Hampshire where I had the pleasure of being with my Mother who was extremely attentive and kind and in short thought she could not do enough to make me comfortable and Happy; you cannot think, my dear Richard, what a lively interest she feels in your welfare and what pleasure it gives her to hear from you. I trust you still continue to be pleased with the line of life to which you have changed. The reason your Father was a little displeased was for not writing to him for a twelve month after your arrival in India not for any money you drew on him for. I can only assure you, my dear Richard, I never was master of so much money as you say you drew for at one time yet however I suppose it was necessary – your Father has of course forgot all that and explained.

In September 1807, one year and three months after it had been
written, Admiral Purvis received Richard's letter asking for
assistance in paying off his debts. The Admiral's reply was
predictably severe:

Some time ago your Mother sent me your letter dated 2nd June 1806 the contents
of which gave me great uneasiness for I am indeed more disappointed than I can
find words to express; I had flattered myself I possessed two sons, who had
benefited so essentially by the advice and example of their Friends, that I had no
apprehension that any part of their conduct would occasion in my mind an
unhappy reflection and I can safely say your Brother has in all his conduct
merited my full approbation. You say in your letter you had written another some
short time before, on the subject of your embarrassment, but as that letter has
never been received, I am quite at a loss to find to what extent you have involved
yourself; however as I think it very disgraceful to be in debt, I have made up my
mind to allow you to draw on me for one Hundred Pounds and you are not to
exceed that sum. I very much fear you have been gaming for without having done
so I cannot account for your being in debt for having had much conversation with
those who have relatives in your situation I had every reason to think after the
complete outfit you had and afterwards on your arrival in India £125 in hand,
would have placed you comfortably and easy; I have no money to spare; what
little I have I have saved in the course of a long and fatiguing service; I derived
no riches from my parents, and they never paid a quarter as much for me in my
whole life as I have already done for you; I feel hurt that you should give such
extraordinary reasons for involving yourself; you say your Brother Officers lived
in such a style that you could not find it convenient to make suitable returns
without getting in debt; indeed Richard if such was your reasoning, you did not
exercise that good understanding which I gave you credit for; I again repeat, I
suspect it is a gaming debt which has given you this trouble, and if so you will
never be happy till you have determined to leave it off and never again risk the
inquietude I judge you feel; . . . You told me you had fifteen servants in a former
letter, in this (now before me) you say you have twenty. I know very well what
your Pay is and I also know what the Pay of an Officer in the King's Service is,
and you know I did not advise your going to India, but on the contrary
endeavour'd to prevent it; in short I am at a loss to find out how you came by the
high notions you appear to have adopted, you did not have them from me or any
of your family; you wrote me, if you at any time acted wrong when in India it
must be your own fault, for that no young man had the advantage of better advice
than you had, alluding to that given you by poor Mr. Garrett and myself; you
dwell much on your want of experience, I would ask what experience was
necessary to measure your Expenses by your Income? And how is it that most
other young men get forward with credit and not older than you were, I was much
younger than you were when I began my career and I never had occasion to
reproach myself nor did I ever give my Father uneasiness. . . I must add that I
shall be made much happier by receiving a pleasanter account of you and from
you than the one now before me; whenever a person involves himself in debt, the
most honorable plan he can possibly adopt, is to lessen his expenses immediately
by discharging every unnecessary part of his establishment and not from a false

H.M.S. *London* which Richard joined in January 1800, a few days after his eleventh birthday, and served aboard until February 1801 when he transferred to H.M.S. *Royal George*. Both ships were commanded by his father, Captain John Child Purvis R.N. The *London,* a three-decked, 90-gun ship of the line, was launched at Chatham on Saturday 24th May 1766 and was a sister ship of the famous *Victory*. Her gun deck measured 176 feet 6 inches and more than 4,000 cartloads of timber — oak, elm and fir — were used in her construction. She carried a complement of 738 officers, men and boys.

The Royal Naval Academy (later College) in Portsmouth Dockyard which Richard attended in 1802/03. The fees were much the same as for Eton but, on the King's insistence, fifteen of the available forty places were reserved for the sons of serving sea officers to be educated at public expense.

**Above:** "Blackbrook Cottage", Fareham, built by George Purvis in the 1790s in the grounds of the Blackbrook Estate which he had acquired. The house remained in the family for around 100 years and in 1927 was bought by the Church Commissioners as the Bishop's Palace for the newly-created Diocese of Portsmouth. Renamed "Bishopswood", it remained the Bishop's Palace for seventy years and is now back in private ownership. The house is believed to have the largest thatched roof in Europe.

**Right:** A Russian cannon-ball from Fort Kinburn brought back from the Crimea by Lieutenant (later Rear-Admiral) Francis Reginald Purvis.

**Below left:** A weeping willow grown from a cutting from the tree on Napoleon's grave on St. Helena brought back by Captain George Thomas Maitland Purvis R.N. and planted in the garden at Blackbrook by his wife, Mary-Jane, niece of Jane Austen.

**Below right:** Blackbrook House, today a maternity hospital, the original mansion house of the Estate which George Purvis rejected in favour of his pretty *Cottage Orné*.

**Above:** George Purvis R.N., the builder of "Blackbrook Cottage" and his wife Renira (*née* Maitland). George Purvis, younger brother of Admiral John Child Purvis, served as Secretary to both Lord Howe and Lord St. Vincent and was Nelson's Prize Agent after the Battle of the Nile. After his retirement from the Navy he was a Magistrate for the County of Southampton and was a Captain in the local militia formed to counter the threat of Bonaparte's invasion.

**Right:** The Arms of Captain George Thomas Maitland Purvis R.N. of Blackbrook Cottage.

**Below:** The brass-bound leather chest in which George Purvis R.N. kept his personal belongings. It was with him aboard H.M.S. *Victory,* in which he was serving as Secretary to Sir John Jervis (later Lord St. Vincent), at the Battle of Cape St. Vincent in 1797.

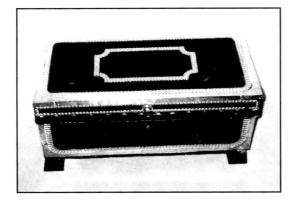

**Above:** The start of an early letter of "Good Advice" from Captain Austen to his daughter, Mary-Jane, for her fifth birthday. Written in a specially-clear hand aboard H.M.S. *Elephant*, which he was commanding in the North Sea, the first page reads:

*My dear Mary Jane — When I wrote a letter to you before in the same sort of hand I am now using it was because your Mamma expressed a wish that I would do so; I now write because you have yourself asked it. I hope my readiness to oblige you on this and all other occasions when I have been able to do anything you wanted done will not be forgotten by you and that it may help to impress on your mind how much it is your duty always to do not only whatever your Mamma or I may desire of you but also anything which you know will contribute to the comfort of your Brothers and all other persons with whom you have intercourse. It is the duty of us all to be kind and obliging to one another . . .*

**Above:** Admiral of the Fleet Sir Francis Austen, the elder of Jane Austen's two sailor brothers. His daughter, Mary-Jane, married Richard's cousin, Captain George Thomas Maitland Purvis R.N., of Blackbrook Cottage.

pride continue the destructive habits which have brought him into so mortifying a dilemma but on the contrary resolve to be as saving as possible; I am not ignorant of the ease with which an Officer in the Company's Military Service may live on his income and therefore it is useless to attempt to persuade me to the contrary; and by your own account you have been in the enjoyment of the pay of a Captain for a considerable time.

Richard did not receive this letter until 20th May 1808 — almost two years since he had written to his father for assistance. In the intervening period he had, ironically, pre-empted his father's advice. He had reduced his establishment to an absolute minimum; he had resisted the blandishments of John Home and his other friends towards an extravagant lifestyle; he had volunteered for every spell of command at the outlying forts, and any other unpopular duties which offered the opportunity of *Batta* payments. Such had been the economies he had instituted that he was not only living within his income and servicing the interest on his loans, but had also started to repay the capital sums he owed.

His father's offer of £100 was followed by an offer of help from his stepmother and even from his brother John. As a result of his retrenchment measures, he was able to decline them all though he felt deep gratitude for the offers having been made and deep shame for his having asked for assistance in the first place. On 21st May he wrote to his father:

I yesterday had the pleasure to receive your letter of 8th of September last . . . [and] lose no time in making a reply, in which I hope to convince you that you still possess two sons who would never willingly cause you an unhappy reflection. My letter of the 6th June 1806 I regret did not meet the same fate with the one I wrote upon the same subject some weeks before. Not a month had elapsed when reflection pointed out my error in having ever addressed you upon the occasion, but I had taken my situation much at heart and by constantly pondering upon, probably aggravated my distress in my own imagination. My mind thus harassed by the most tormenting reflections I only saw the difficulties in which I was involved without deliberating upon the proper methods of extricating myself and I inadvertently fixed upon that path which appeared the easiest and pleasantest, regardless of the longer but more honorable road that was open to me. A very short time, however, with cool consideration made me resolve upon becoming indebted to my own prudence for the state of independence I wished. I therefore immediately reduced my expenses as much as I possibly could and in the course of time had the happiness to see my efforts assisted by peculiar good fortune – I got the command of Bijaigarh in December 1806 and January, April, May part of September and October 1807; by which means and with the plans of economy I had adopted, and to this day continue to pursue, I am enabled to decline acceptance of the sum you have permitted me to draw on you for; and for which kindness, I assure you, I am equally grateful as though I had availed myself of it. What debts now remain, and which I am happy to say are decreasing monthly amount to much less than half the value of the property I at present possess; and as, in case of my decease, nobody would suffer in convenience, I reckon them very trifling. With regard to reasons I gave for being in debt, as that calls in question my knowledge of mankind, which tho' but little is as much as could be reap'd from what experience I have had, I must still maintain they were valid. In the first place with regard to making suitable returns for the kindnesses I received from my brother officers, I have had reason to regret having done so and it may have been of false pride but a pride of which, I have observed, every young man of proper spirit to be susceptible. Now the older officers had received their supplies from Calcutta before the war but I joined the Army without a supply of wine or in fact anything else, and was consequently obliged to purchase [such from] the merchants with the Army at the most exorbitant prices. The only charge I can now remember, altho' they were all equally unreasonable was 27 Rupees a dozen for Beer, (27 Half Crowns about equal to £3.7s.6d.) not to say that I ever bought a drop but I saw that paid by others; liquors which I was obliged to purchase were sold proportionally dear.

It is true, my dear Sir, you were younger at the time you quitted your friends and went to sea than I was when I embarked for India but still I will be bound to say you were placed under the care of some person who had equal influence over you with that which would have been exercised by your Parents – and I will only ask you whether the conduct of the other youngsters (as we were called) aboard the London etc. etc. was not full as much restrained by you as mine was – and my brother. But here I had no such friend – no person to give me an idea or warn me of the perplexities into which I was precipitating. Merchants, instead of surveying me with a suspicious eye, and proceeding with caution, as they would in England, to give me credit for a sixpence, continually exerting every probable means to induce me to add another [pound] to my bill. – Consider these, my good Sir, and I will ask you if a boy of fifteen can be supposed to resist such temptations. It is probable you would have plunged yourself into the same difficulties had you had the same inducements and the same opportunities. Convinced as you appear to be that I had involved myself in gambling, I am somewhat surprised at your having answered my letter – and more astonished at your having consented to relieve me when persuaded that I have been guilty of such unpardonable imprudence – No – when I enter upon a life of such disgrace as that of a gambler, I hope you will disown me for ever. You seem amazed at the number of servants I keep. I can not conceive who you could have conversed with that neglected to explain a circumstance that must appear so extraordinary in the eyes of people in Europe. In this letter, as the chief subject has already made it too long, it must suffice to say that they are indispensably necessary, and without them there would be no existing. Mine is a very small establishment (now reduced) and barely sufficient to keep me comfortable. I have hitherto had no reason to repeat having [regretted] my inclination to come to this country, except that I am apprehensive this disagreeable affair, which otherwise would never have occurred, will cause you in some measure to withdraw from me your affection – I know not in what manner to make atonement for my conduct and to convince the best of Parents that I am still not unworthy of his regard. What ever reason I have given you to suppose to the contrary, permit me to assure you, your advice, and that which Mr. Garrett so kindly gave me has never been inattended to so far as concerns the character of a Gentleman and an Officer – your letters and those of poor Mr. G. are carefully preserved and pointing out to me the path of true happiness. I am still in hopes to profit by them. And I am in hopes never again to have reason to reproach myself, or never more to be so imprudent as to force a [rebuke] from the heart of so kind a Father. My good Mother kindly offered me more cash in case that which you sanctioned should not be sufficient for my purpose. I shall of course express my grateful feelings for her having voluntarily stepped forward to my assistance, in the best manner I can, but may tell her it must come far short of what I really feel.

## And to his stepmother:

As I wrote you on the 7th, I will defer giving a full reply to your kind letter for a week or two longer – suffice it now to say, I could not, however elaborate, give you but an imperfect idea of the gratitude I really feel for the permission you gave me to draw on you. I am happy in saying I require neither my Father's assistance nor that which you so obligingly offer.

## And to John he expressed his gratitude for his offer of help and his concern that there seemed no way of convincing his father that his difficulties had not been brought about by gambling and that he might, as a consequence, have lost his place in his father's affection:

You are no doubt acquainted with the subject of the last letter my Father wrote me – or I mean rather the last I received from him. It has certainly given rise to thousands of unpleasing reflections; but my greatest grief is that I ever gave him cause to write such a letter. I hope what I have written him in answer may wipe the whole circumstance from his remembrance: but I can scarcely bring myself to imagine otherwise than that [he might] almost think me unworthy of the tenderness and anxiety he always before expressed on my account – not that I in any degree acknowledge myself unworthy of it; but from his appearing so firmly persuaded that it was by some disgraceful means I had involved myself – such as gambling etc. and the most tormenting reflection I have is the impossibility of his being undeceived, except by what I myself write, which I fear may not be regarded as sufficient testimony. . . . I cannot give you an idea of the pride which swells my heart at this moment that I reflect upon the happiness of possessing such a Brother as you have proved yourself to me. No, my dear John, I have long overcome my difficulties: – but were they still existing I would not deprive you of a penny of that which was caused by "the sweat of your brow"; however, the gratitude I feel for the offer you have made, I must leave you to imagine, for it is more than I can describe.

# 4. First Blood

*Aligarh, India, 1806.*

In September 1806 the 2/21st's Mess at Aligarh was enlivened by the arrival of a young Ensign, Edward Bowerbank, son of a Yorkshire parson and brother of Revd. Thomas Bowerbank, Vicar of Chiswick. Richard, John Home and David Livingstone, by now old India hands, had much amusement in subjecting him to the usual pranks and indignities with which every new subaltern must be tormented on joining his regiment. Bowerbank, however, was ready to give as good as he got and his high spirits and cheeky manner very soon won the affection of his fellow subalterns — with the exception of George Casement who did not find his rebellious attitude to the Mess rituals endearing.

Even the Regimental Surgeon, Dr. Josiah Ridges, who as a man in his forties was prone to irritation from the Subalterns' behaviour, was charmed by young Bowerbank whom he called the *"Butcha"* [child]. Dr. Ridges had been surgeon on the ill-fated *Earl of Abergavenny,* in which Richard's copies of *"The Military Mentor"* had been lost, then, after a spell in the Indiaman *Canton,* he had transferred from the Maritime to the Military Service of the Company and had been appointed to the 2/21st. Assisted by one native doctor, he was responsible for the health of around 1,000 officers and men. He lived with his Indian mistress, Lutchimar, whom he considered:

. . . a nice wench — a good rough ---- and a fat a--e — an old man like me needs something to stimulate him to action. She will I fear be getting too fast hold of my attachments by and bye but never such a torment as Begum was, this I am determined to guard against.

Richard and his friends held Dr. Ridges in high esteem and had complete faith in his professional skills. As well as his military duties, he was retained to attend certain of the Company's civil servants in the district which carried an additional fee. His consequently above-average income coupled with the congeniality of the 2/21st's Mess led him later to describe his time at Aligarh as:

. . . the best station for a Medical Man I ever was at or perhaps ever shall experience again . . . I shall never again be so happy.

It was, clearly, a happy Mess comprised of a largely compatible group of young men commanded by a senior Captain who enjoyed their universal regard and confidence. James Cock, though a Captain, was only in his mid-twenties and dropped more comfortably into the subalterns' social coterie than that of his fellow Captains some of whom were twenty years older than himself. With a Captain's higher pay, he was also the only one of them who could, at the time, have considered marriage, had he wanted to, which enriched his reputation as the regimental Romeo — a source of constant banter which he took in good part:

I hope you do all in your power to prevent the virtue of the amiable and innocent Captain Cock being ensnared by the Syrenic wishes of the fair Paulina. Hunting, I hope, proves one means of saving him from the dangers he is exposed to in her company.

The Ensign [Bowerbank] intends visiting Camonah under pretence of a day's hunting, but in reality to request an explanation from Captn. C. concerning a report which is in circulation here . . . that the late departure of a certain young lady for Madras was in consequence of her having contracted, or rather expanded, a complaint within the last nine months of her residency in Bengal . . .

In reality, they feared the marriage of any of their number which would erode the social circle of the Mess although John Home considered that James Ridge, the Adjutant, would be no great loss:

. . . to tell the truth, I had rather Ridge was the person to marry for he is as much changed from what he was as it is possible to be, so marrying would not deprive us of a jolly companion, and as I much fear it will in Cock — he'll be a jealous husband I think and then it will be all over with us . . .

Most of their leisure time was spent in shooting and short, local leaves provided the opportunity for organised expeditions with elephants. One such was described to Richard by William Price, a friend in the 2/5th Native Infantry:

I ought to have written you before this but you know I am a damn'd lazy boy. We have had very good sport this month . . . we killed 22 tigers, 5 bears and 81 hay-deer. I never saw such savage tigers in my life, we met with some accidents but none of a serious nature. My elephant (the one I purchased of Ogilvy) got dreadfully wounded in the flank by a tigress that I had mortally wounded on the 16th inst. and he is still very lame. If it does not make him timid hereafter, I care not for the accident; I never saw a better elephant before the accident occurred. Another day, an immense large male tiger (that we supposed was completely disabled) charged Scott's elephant and seized him by the trunk and, had she not thrown herself down upon him, she would have suffered more materially. A tigress a few days after sprung behind Scott and slightly scratched the elephant on the back; she also bit the ladder nearly through. Patton's [Mukna] attacked my small male elephant one day without the least provocation when we were all assembled round a large snake that I had shot. He knocked him over and pounded him in the most horrid manner you can conceive and had it not been for the [Gudda] in all probability would have killed him on the spot but he luckily escaped without any material injury. Steuart of the 1st Cavalry and McDonnell of the 7th Regt. arrived here on the 20th inst. We shall go out again in a few days and should the weather prove favorable I have not the least doubt but we shall meet with great sport . . .

Price added his less important news as a postscript on the cover of his letter:

Remember me to Cock and all my friends in your Corps. If you want to purchase horses, dogs or guns, now is your time — Humbleton wishes to part with all his [possessions], with the exception of his wife. I lost my little boy on the 8th inst. the poor little fellow had been dreadfully ill for some weeks before. I should like to see you very much, for my regard for you is great.

Richard would dearly have liked to have purchased a good gun, to the want of which he attributed his rather unimpressive record as a sportsman, but his self-enforced regime of economy would not permit of such a luxury. John Home, who was an excellent shot, was concerned for him:

. . . you seem to have fallen off terrible; I think it is owing to your firing at too great a distance, and out of your reach, that's my idea, not that you shoot ill for I assure you I have a very good opinion of your shooting — however if you want shooting, I mean practice, I can tell you that there is a very good Snipe Gill on the Anoopshir Road where Cock and I went to last year; that black fellow, what's his name, will shew you to it as he went with us . . .

Yet even Home's success was blighted by his inability to afford a really good gun:

I threw a ball at a deer but with bad success, to tell you the truth, I can make no hand of that little gun and can place no dependence on its carrying at all, sometimes it goes high and sometimes low, altho' I take as fair an aim as ever I did. I took several shots at Geese on the Gill as we passed but had better have kept the balls, for it was only throwing them away, however I have lots with me so it does not signify.

Richard's delight can therefore be imagined when he heard that his godfather Fortescue, now an Admiral, who had given him such "Good Advice" on his health during his voyage out to India, had sent him a present of £10 with which to buy something he really wanted. He wrote to his stepmother with explicit instructions:

My Father desired me to point out to you what I would wish Admiral Fortescue's present to be converted into. Now you must excuse me if I give you a little more trouble than you expected, and I pray you attend <u>very exactly</u> to the instructions. The article I most require is a gun — a fowling piece — and being somewhat of a sportsman, I am desirous of having one of a superior sort. You will therefore oblige me by fixing, amongst your friends or acquaintances, upon a sportsman to purchase it for me. Let it be a single barel'd one and <u>let it be bought from the maker's shop.</u> The makers must be either <u>Nock</u>, <u>Manton</u> or <u>Mortimer</u>, whichever your friend may have the best opinion of. Let it be in a case and as I am particularly anxious to have it <u>Really</u> good, I dare say my Father will have no objection to your adding a guinea or two if requisite. Then, for the conveying of it to me, you must look out for a friend, or a friend's friend aboard an Indiaman to whose charge it must be given with a request to look at it and wipe it now and then during the voyage. It must be delivered in Calcutta to the house of Messrs. Williams & Holker to whom I shall give directions regarding the forwarding of it to me. Let my Crest or Cypher be engraved both on the Gun and the case to prevent its being changed — a thing sometimes practised in these parts and I think there will be some danger when it has to travel from one end of India, almost, to the other. Do, my dear Madam, use all your utmost endeavours to hinder my being disappointed as I have set my heart upon it . . .

If Richard relied upon John Home's help to improve his shooting, John certainly relied upon Richard's more agile mind when it came to the paperwork which it was necessary, even in those days, for a Company Commander to complete and which baffled him entirely:

Damn the Confirmation Rolls! Will you send mine here with some explanation of what is required, I cannot make them out.

Each time he was posted to the command of one of the outpost forts, John would write for Richard's help when the unpleasant time for the paperwork arrived:

I have been, and am now, going to bore you with questions about these Rolls etc. etc.

Building Certificate.
"I do hereby Certify . . ." What else? I can get no farther. Is there also to be something "I do declare" on it? Let me know that — and how many signatures it requires in all.

Artillery and Company.
Do I, or should I, sign twice or three times? Lt. in Charge, 2nd M.G.Offr., any more?

Bildars.
Any Abstract (I believe not)? What signatures, etc. etc.?

Dooley Bearers.
The same as Bildars (Abstract, Signatures, etc.)

Now, my dear Dick, don't delay with the answers, if you can understand the illustrations. I am all ready for sending them off — Abstracts etc., all . . .

Even after Richard's explanations, he had little confidence in his resultant efforts:

I have only to say now that I send by him the Muster Rolls of Artillery, Bildars, Dooley Bearers and return of Public Buildings which I hope may be right tho' I fear the reverse. I send two Rolls of the Artillery, Ridge will shew you which is the best to be sent. My reason for making out two is that he inserted old and new guns in his and you want only the new therefore please yourselves. I have made the certificates out as well as I can, I hope they are right but the one on the buildings I had no idea of wording so I leave it for you — neither do I know if an abstract — (presentation, Rolls, etc.) — should be put to Dooley Bearers and Bildars Rolls — or the Certificate for the [day] — these things, my dear Dick, I have left for you, should they be requisite. My not having ever made out or paid any attention to things of this kind must plead my excuse. Another thing I have left undone in both Rolls of Artillery, is the arrival and departure of the people that relieved and were relieved here. I did not know what to say on the subject — I send copies on China paper which I will thank you to get R. or C. to fill up, agreeing to whatever alterations you may find necessary to make in those I send — which will enable me to make out the others properly. You will say I have left more undone than I have done, I believe I have, but ignorance is the cause. I forgot, let me know about Issued and Received, what it means, how have I to find out when the old things were got in here, and where what and when they want, a [return] on that subject — my arm is quite tired . . .

Nor did he ever seem to learn from Richard's tutorship. Every period of command brought the same plea for help. But his ineptitude, or assumed ineptitude, in such matters was all part of John Home's mercurial charm.

Now how the devil does things go. I have no idea. I send the others I have made out just to shew you and you can get R. or C. to mark out the places where it should be altered and how it should be and return them by my Khitmaghar [table waiter]. Bus! [enough!] J.H.

* * *

In September 1807 a force began to assemble at Aligarh to take punitive action against a *zemindar* [landowner] called Dhundiya Khan who had defied the Government and had barricaded himself with his supporters in the heavily-defended Fort of Kamonah a few miles north of Aligarh. The British force consisted of five battalions of Native Infantry, supported by three companies of Bengal Artillery, two half-squadrons of H.M. 24th Light Dragoons, nine troops of Native Cavalry, two companies of H.M. 17th Regiment of Foot and a Flank Battalion made up of the Grenadier Companies of several regiments of Native Infantry among which were the two Grenadier Companies of the 2/21st.

Speculation and rivalry as to which officers would go with the Grenadier Companies was high. As Richard explained to his father, his own inclusion would depend on when the force marched:

If it happens before the end of this month, I shall go, but if after, I shall have again the command of Anupshahr as I am next for duty.

In the event, the force did not march until October with John Robertson and David Livingstone in command of the 2/21st's Grenadiers. John Swinton was also with them, commanding the Pioneers and John du Feu of the 1/23rd, a friend of Richard's who came from the Channel Island of Guernsey. John du Feu was disappointed to have missed seeing Richard and wrote to him at the end of October:

Many thanks mon bon ami for yours of the 28th and if I mistake not, I am in your debt with respect to the intelligence you received from Ross, I was much in hopes it wd. prove such but alas, not knowing when we may move (the g. being encamp'd near the fort) I am depriv'd of the pleasure of seeing you, not being able to be absent for even two days. . . . The 9th is the only Corps that has yet joined, we expect the Train and the Flank Companies on or about the 5th next

# The Siege of Kamonah
## 18th November 1807

N

**No.1 BATTERY**
2 x 6-pdrs.

Fortified Garden

**GARDEN ASSAULT**
800 rank and file from 1st Brigade
(1/9th, 1/27th and 2/27th BNI).
**Brigadier Duff**

**No.2 BATTERY**
2 x 8"
& 1 x 5.5"
Howitzers

Kamonah Fort

**No.4 BATTERY**
(Breaching)
6 x Iron
18-pdrs.

Kamonah Village

**No.3 BATTERY**
3 x Bronze
12-pdrs.

**No.5 BATTERY**
2 x 5.5"
Mortars

**MAIN INFANTRY ASSAULT**
6 companies HM 17th Regt.
The Grenadier Battalion.
Grenadier Companies of 1st Brigade
(1/9th, 1/27th and 2/27th BNI).
**Lieut. Colonel Hardyman**

0 yards  100  200  300  400

month. It now being the approach of the cold weather, I think this will prove a pleasant trip . . . I hope we may remain here till our departure towards Mr. Doondea. I fear P. I will not be able to go to you, but I yet will attempt. I was particularly glad to see Home in such spirit at his return from Muttra. I go in the Fort often and wish much you were with us, however you are well off for I hear two months longer.

Richard's absence was, in fact, more to his advantage than John du Feu might have supposed. Though disappointed that circumstances should have deprived him of participation in the Siege Force, he arranged with a friend, Monckter, to send him regular bulletins.

The village of Kamonah, outside the fort, had been taken on 12th October by Captain William Casement (George Casement's brother) with a party of Native Infantry and two guns. Since then, the Pioneers, under John Swinton, and the Engineers had been hard at work constructing trenches and parallels for the use of the assault party. It was dangerous work, under continual fire from the fort and on the night of 30th October two of the Pioneer officers were wounded — one, Lieutenant Ramsay, mortally. On 4th November Monckter sent his first bulletin to Richard:

Our mine will be completed tonight. Tomorrow will most certainly decide the fate of Doondeah Khan and whether Kamonah is to be in our or the enemy's hands.

On the night of 11th John Swinton, the last remaining Pioneer officer, was wounded in the head while placing the gabions which was reported to Richard by Monckter the next day:

Our approaches are almost completed, and nothing now can delay the storm, which will inevitably take place the day after tomorrow. Poor Ramsay is not expected to recover of his wounds. Swinton of the Pioneer Corps was last night wounded in the temple but is doing well. The roads are infested with horsemen, who of course declare themselves Doondeah Khan's people. He himself seems determined to fall with his Fort.

After much mining and counter-mining, preparations were at last ready for the assault. The main assault party, under Lieutenant-Colonel Hardyman, consisted of five companies of H.M. 17th Regiment, the Grenadier Battalion, including the two companies of the 2/21st, under Captain Drummond, and the Grenadier Companies of the 1st Brigade comprising the 1/9th, 1/27th and

2/27th Native Infantry. A second assault party of 800 rank and file from the 1st Brigade, under Brigadier William Duff, was to storm the fortified garden which adjoined the Fort. The Cavalry were ready to cut off the expected retreat of the enemy.

On 18th November the assault was launched but Dhundiya's men had prepared their defences well. Rows of holes had been dug all along the moat, filled with gunpowder and covered over with straw. Bamboo frameworks covered with thatched straw had been constructed and erected on the sloping faces of the parapet.

The garden storming party advanced first. When they reached the wall they found the scaling ladders were too short. Under heavy enemy fire they tried to extend the ladders on rifles with bayonets fixed. Brigadier Duff was killed and most of the officers killed or wounded. John du Feu was shot dead as he struggled most gallantly to lead his men up the ladders.

Half an hour later the main assault party attacked the Fort. As they reached the ditch the enemy threw down flaming torches which ignited the straw and exploded the gunpowder. The whole breach was engulfed in flames. Eventually part of the assault party managed to get to the walls and erect ladders but each wave was driven back by explosions of powder and the long spears of the defenders. John Robertson, at the head of one of the 2/21st's Grenadier Companies, was killed in the first assault. David Livingstone was seriously wounded. After nearly an hour of furious fighting on the walls, the attempt was abandoned and the battered remains of the assault force withdrew.

Monckter wrote to Richard the following day:

Bad tidings, my dear Purvis — We have failed, as you must have heard, in our attacks both on the Fort and Garden. Out of 300 of the 17th Regt. which headed the storm, 145 are either killed or wounded. Two of their Captains, Eadcliffe and Kirke killed — all the other officers excepting Col. Hardyman and a subaltern wounded. Poor Harrison dangerously so. Livingstone wounded. Poor du Feu killed while placing the ladders, after behaving most gallantly. Poor Fraser, the General's Aid de Camp, shot through the heart and killed in the Main Battery. Col. Duff wounded gallantly heading the Garden storming party and died last night. There are numberless others but I have not yet been able to ascertain their names. I saw the whole from the 12 Pounder Battery, a dreadful sight! No men could behave more nobly than both Europeans and Sepoys, but no courage, no bravery could surmount the obstacles thrown in their way. The ditch was filled with bags of powder covered over with straw. The enemy awaited until our men had advanced within shot point blank. They then opened a most tremendous fire. Our men coolly advanced to the breach. Immediately the enemy set fire to the straw which of course communicated to the powder and blew up several of those who were advanced. After the explosion the ladders were applied and found to be too short. This was remedied in [some measure] by fixing them on the musket and baonet — but as fast as our men mounted, they were either shot or scorched with powder bags thrown on them. You could see the poor fellows clinging to the bastion, striving to get up but unable to get a footing, and wholly exposed to the enemy's fire — without any cover or means of defence. Our loss I fear is great indeed.

David Livingstone and the other seriously wounded were carried into Aligarh and then, the following day, the British force discovered that Dhundiya Khan and his men had evacuated the Fort during the night and were headed for another fort at Ganaori which, it seemed likely, he was preparing to defend in the same way.

You must have heard ere this, My Dear Purvis, that Comona is evacuated. While Doondee Khann was in the Garden congratulating his son on the brave defence he had made, his people in the Fort (who had been paid up and who had to feed all their principal chiefs) took this opportunity of making off. When Doondee returned he found the Fort almost empty. He again returned to his son in the Garden, beat his breast, threw ashes over his head, and said he was ruined. His son proposed defending the Garden, but was over ruled by Doondee who said nothing was left now but to retreat to Gonouree. We had this intelligence about 10 o'clock. We instantly took possession of the Fort. The General Claud and all of us immediately rode into the Fort, Garden, etc. They had retired with such precipitation that they left all their guns, powder, grain, etc. Several of us went up and down the breach. I think I may say it was practicable tho' the defence was such that it would have been a miracle had we taken it. The General says he never in his life saw troops behave better. There were hundreds of natives looking on during the storm and they confessed they were perfectly astonished at the determined manner in which our troops advanced to the place. Part of the 17th are now on their way to Gonouree. We shall all follow tomorrow. I am sorry to learn poor Livingstone's wound is much more severe than was first supposed. I wish to God I could hear of ye re-establishment of your health.

Monckter was referring to a liver complaint from which Richard had been suffering for some time but from which he had now almost completely recovered thanks to the effective treatment administered by Dr. Ridges. However, in October the Regiment had received the news that a new Commanding Officer, Lieutenant-Colonel James Tetley, was taking over from William Nichol and, to compound this shattering blow, Josiah Ridges had been posted as Surgeon to another regiment. John Home summarised the feelings of them all:

Lord what an awful time for the Corps to lose our good <u>(the best we ever had)</u> Commander and our <u>better</u> Doctor – that fool Tetley (a greater never pissed) has struck Doctor off the strength of the Corps already and so we shall not have such another for many a day.

By 20th November, John Home had taken over the command at Bijaigarh and Richard had returned to base at Aligarh where he spent all the time he could at David's bedside; but his wounds were grievous and the doctors had little hope for his recovery. Another patient in the temporary hospital was Captain Dudingston whose brother was married to Richard's cousin Lucy. His right arm had been shattered during the assault and it was feared he would never carry a sword again. Richard wrote a letter for him to his brother adding a postscript of his own for Lucy. John Home was shocked to receive the news of their losses at Kamonah:

Many thanks for the news of our success, at least of our having got possession of the place — we had a report of it yesterday by a native but could not place much dependence on it. I hope we shall be more fortunate against the next fort. We cannot be so unfortunate, my dear Dick, we have no more Livingstones to lose — poor David, a more worthy, sincere friend does not breathe — as he yet came in to Ally Ghur, I have some hopes of his recovery . . . I hope I may be relieved before the muster that I may have the melancholy satisfaction of seeing him before his last, but still there's hopes of his recovery and in that hope will I remain. . . . Poor Jack du Feu too, . . . where was the Doctor and Ridge . . . I hope the former went out to Camp and will bring in Jack; but how I'm talking, how could he go to Camp and leave all the sick without assistance. Should poor David be with you, I beg you will remember me in the kindest manner to him. Perhaps I shall yet see him again.

But it was not to be: David Livingstone died of his wounds on the following day, 22nd November 1807, and the officers of the 2/21st spent a melancholy Christmas remembering their lost comrades and the happy days before the arrival of Lieutenant-Colonel James Tetley.

# 5. Bareilly

*Kotaura, India, 1808.*

James Tetley had been recommended for a Cadetship in the Bengal Army on 12th October 1778 by no lesser person than Warren Hastings himself. His origins were uncertain but his sister Elizabeth was known to be married to a younger brother of David Garrick, the actor. He obtained his Lieutenant's Commission in 1781 shortly after which he applied for transfer to the Bengal Civil Service as a Writer. His application was unsuccessful and he served with the 20th Battalion Sepoys for several years. In October 1798, as a Captain, he was appointed to command the newly-raised 2nd Bengal Volunteers which was taken into the Line in June 1800 as the 1/19th Native Infantry. The Regiment was known by his name as *'Titteelee-ki-Paltan'*.

On 27th September 1807, during the preparations for Kamonah, he was promoted Lieutenant-Colonel and was sent to replace William Nichol as Commanding Officer of the 2/21st. So, for Richard and his friends, began five years of petulant tyranny under a commander who would never gain either their liking or their confidence and whose:

. . . conduct could astonish those only who never heard how completely his conduct for some time past had been marked by a total want of principle.

In February 1808, the 2/21st were relieved at Aligarh and started their march to Bareilly — a much sought-after station:

Both the climate and country of and around Bareilly are said to be most delightful; so we are going to the very extremity of good — though we certainly deserve it, for we have long endured the extremity of bad. Aligarh is the worst station, I really believe, in the whole of the Company's possessions.

On arrival, however, though Bareilly itself lived up to its promise, the situation was much the same as at Aligarh with outposts to be manned at Kotaura and Bissalpur by detached companies of the Battalion.

Richard and John Home had bought a bungalow in Bareilly intending to share expenses and make themselves comfortable but, before he could get settled in, Richard was ordered to Kotaura, which was five days march from Bareilly, and which proved to be far less agreeable than the forts at Bijaigarh and Anupshahr which he had got to know so well:

This command is the most unpleasant I ever held, not only on account of its situation, being directly on the edge of the large forests, but we are placed here for the purpose of preventing the depredations of a Rebel, who occasionally makes a dash from the Nabob of Lucknow's country into ours, much to the prejudice of the inhabitants. Now I am obliged to keep my party in readiness to march at a moment's warning. Added to this I have no house, but am obliged to live entirely in my tent which is extremely unpleasant now that the hot winds are beginning to set in.

Moreover, Kotaura being some sixty-five miles from Bareilly, the periods of duty were extended to two months. Richard, though he had no recurrence of his liver ailment, was suffering from constipation and wrote to his old friend Josiah Ridges for his recommendations. These were quickly forthcoming though the doctor was anxious not to be seen to be in breach of professional etiquette:

I should recommend you to have always by you some opening medicine and a little Laudanum. I will enclose a paper which if you wish you can tell Lowe you have been long in the habit of taking and request him to send it you out by dawk but do not say I recommend it. One pill taken at bed time twice a month and a paper of opening powder the following morning will prevent an accumulation of bile and keep you in health. At night going to rest if you find [yourself] fatigued from the operation of the pill and powder, you may take 25 drops of Laudanum in a little brandy and water. Say you copied it off from a paper I gave you long ago — or otherwise it may give offence and appear something like interfering with another man's duty.

The old doctor was obviously not enjoying life in his new battalion and was homesick for the 2/21st:

I shall for ever regret leaving my old Battn. I do assure you the young men of this are, in my opinion, very far indeed from pleasant men. I know but little of them and from what I can judge shall never be very intimate with them. The young officers associate entirely by themselves. . . . Have you heard anything of poor

Home since he left you — I am extremely anxious to hear of him. He is in heart and disposition as worthy a young man as ever lived and possesses as high a sense of honor. He sometimes annoyed me by his rattling nonsense — something like a young puppy playing with a snarling old curr notwithstanding all which I have the highest regard for him. I shall write him soon directed to the care of his father. . . . I must not forget to enquire after the young butcha (Bowerbank) I hope he is well. A finer young man is not in the Service. He certainly possesses a sweet disposition and even temper which are valuable points in a young man.

Hardly had John Home and Richard settled into their bungalow at Bareilly but John decided to take leave to visit his father in Calcutta. With roads unsurfaced and the great railway system still some fifty years away, long journeys, where practicable, were made by river. Journeys on land were often made by *"Dak"* (or *"Dawk"* ). This was a network of covered litters, each carrying a single passenger, which operated between all garrison towns. The litters were carried by a team of natives who travelled at a fast pace for some six to eight miles where they were relieved by a fresh team — on the same principle as post-coaches in Europe. As the mail was always carried by *Dak,* the term eventually came to mean the mail itself in the same way as "Post" came to mean mail in Britain.

During his journey down the Ganges to Calcutta, John Home and his party offered hospitality on their boat to a Captain "Johnny" Cope Campbell whose craft had been swamped in a severe storm. Notorious for his argumentative nature, Campbell soon picked a quarrel with the others and became so bad-tempered that one of John's friends told him he was a bully and asked him to leave:

. . . at last he was told his company was very disagreeable, and requested to go out. He immediately began to equivocate and like Touchstone was bringing in his "ifs" and "ands" but he was told his conversation was not desired. He then walked out, some chits passed between D. and him . . . how such a man as Cope Campbell is supposed to be, to put up with the term of bully, which was twice given him, . . . wd. hardly be believed. I certainly expected a Duel at first but when D. had recd. the first answer, I saw very well that Capt. C. wd. not be the first to act contrary to the Articles of War. Would you believe that afterwards . . . he wished to meet D. on friendly terms without the intercession of any friend. He came to the house where D. lives, Encas MacIntosh's, and wished to make it appear as if nothing had happened, but D. went out of the room when he heard him coming. I know you never liked Cope so will not be sorry to hear what in his heart he really is — no man of true spirit wd. put up with the term of bully without a very ample apology.

Richard, missing John Home's company, volunteered to take
another officer's duty at Bissalpur which he found more agreeable
than Kotaura as he explained in a letter to his brother John:

My Father will have told you that I have again chosen for a short time, a solitary
retirement: but I have this time a house over my head, shelter for my cattle, and
every thing as comfortable as I could wish — widely different from my situation
at the place from whence I last wrote you. — Indeed I feel myself very nearly as
happy here as I could be at Bereilly; for I am grown familiar with solitude, and
the resources I at first made use of at common pastures to drive away tedious
hours, are now become habitual so that instead of dreading, and flying from
retirements as is the custom with some, I feel myself rather inclined to court it:
— not that I descend to the other extreme, and from a brutal kind of independence
endeavour to avoid the company of my fellow creatures; but after having been
two months thus detached from society, my return to it affords me the greater
enjoyment. However, my chief reason for taking the duty of another officer, by
which means I now hold the command of this post, was the absence of the friend
with whom I live — he is gone to the Presidency on a visit to his Father and I
don't expect his return till about the end of this month. His name is John Home,
you will see it next to mine in the Lieutenants of the Regiment if you have a list.
Our inclinations seem so well to agree, in every respect that I reckon it the
happiest friendship I ever formed. Whatever is pleasing to one, never fails of
being also agreeable to the other so we live together in perfect harmony. We are
both sportsmen and I believe that was the foundation of our intimacy: from being
companions in amusement we became perfect friends. By living together we
manage much more economically than we could do separately.

He also told his brother John that he was persisting with his
language studies in the hope that a proficiency in such might
eventually gain him preferment though he was becoming
increasingly aware that advancement in India could not be obtained
without toadying which he found obnoxious:

I find in this Country whatever claim merit may have to preferment it never
happens to be the means of procuring it — it is not sufficient for one to become
acquainted with a great man, and to recommend himself by a modest display of
his abilities, at the same time paying all the respect and attention properly due: —
No, he must degrade himself by following, bowing, cringing, allowing himself to
be treated contemptuously and so forth — then he'll get forward. I shall never
bring myself to submit to acting the sycophant. Consequently you will see me
return home (if it please God I will do), plain Captain or Major Purvis — or
whatever rank I may obtain at the end of my Service — upon two hundred, or two
hundred and fifty pounds a year. It is my constant pride to behave with all
possible respect to a man of Rank, till I see him inclined to behave haughtily, and
slacken in that respect (for I think there is some) due from a superior to an inferior
— I then lose all pleasure in paying attention to him.

Richard's brother, under their father's guiding eye, was doing well in the Navy. Not yet twenty-one, he had been given his first command in the rank of Commander — a fine Brig, the *Delight*, recently captured from the enemy, mounting eighteen 12-pounder long guns and with a complement of 110 men. On 23rd June he was on his way from Malta, where his ship had been fitting out, to join his father's command in the Blockade of Cadiz.

Admiral Purvis had now been on this station for nearly two years. Never even considering the possibility of evading himself the rigours of duty he had always imposed on others, the old seadog had kept *Atlas* at sea for nineteen months without once dropping anchor. During this time not one square-rigged vessel had entered or left Cadiz harbour without his authority. He was delighted with his son John's progress, he himself having had to wait until the age of thirty-four for his own command. During 1807 he had lobbied for his preferment and in February had written to Lord Collingwood:

. . . your Lordship will allow it to be very natural in a father to do all he can to forward the success of his son in whatever line of life he may be engaged. In addition to such common feelings I am more particularly anxious to get my son promoted as he has taken such pains in following the admonitions he received from me during the course of his time in the Service that I can safely say he never once occasioned in my mind an uneasy thought. All the testimony of the different captains he has sail'd under has convinced me of what my partiality to him might otherwise have betray'd me into. He has been two years a Lieutenant . . . I trust your Lordship will excuse me in asking what I have every reason to believe you would do without my solicitation were there more frequent opportunities of granting the favour I have to beg of your Lordship . . . to take my son under your patronage. He is now the only son I have in the Service and there is no other of my family now belonging to it except myself.†

In May, on Lord Collingwood's advice, he had followed this up with an approach to Lord Mulgrave, the newly-appointed First Lord of the Admiralty, and in November his perseverance had been rewarded by the First Lord's reply:

Lord Mulgrave presents his compliments to Vice-Admiral Purvis and has the pleasure to acquaint him that Lieutenant Purvis has been recommended to Lord Collingwood for promotion.‡

---

† N.M.M. Ref: PRV/39 *Loose Papers* 1807 MS.55/029 Part 1.    ‡ Ibid. Part 2.
(There was a clerical error here by the Admiralty: Rear-Admiral Purvis was not made Vice-Admiral until 15 October 1809.)

Richard's career, however, was another matter and the Admiral felt keenly his inability to do the same for his younger son:

If I had any interest with the Directors, my dear Richard, it should all be yours, and although I see no chance of my ever having such, yet if anything should arise whereby I could expect to gain any advantage for you, depend on it I shall not be unmindful of your inclination; but pray do not place any dependance on such an event.

If, however, the Company's armies should be taken into the King's service — a possibility he had heard discussed — he might have a better chance of assisting Richard with his career:

I have had many Officers of the Army staying on board and amongst others, Brigadier General Nightingale who has served long in your part of India. . . . I shall write home for a similar book to one shewn me by General Nightingale with lists of all the Officers and Civil Servants belonging to the Bengal Establishment and by which I can form a judgement of your progress. . . . General Nightingale thinks the Company's Army will be taken into the King's Service; if such should be the case I should like to know all the particulars respecting the plan, whether those so transferr'd are to remain in India under the same Regulation or whether they are to be in all respects like the rest of the King's Army. Should there ever be any changes of the sort, let me be acquainted as soon as possible.

John Home, having arrived in Calcutta, suspected Richard of having taken the command at Bissalpur in order to avoid having to supervise some building work they were having done on the bungalow:

I had no idea, Dick, you were so cursed lazy as to volunteer for a disagreeable command rather than [take the responsibility] of overseeing a few workmen.

He could not understand how Richard could have willingly accepted a posting to a place where there was a scarcity of game; nor did he fancy his chances of being able to bring the enemy to combat:

. . . as for your ever being able to catch Mr. Budja Singh with Infantry, you might as well be at Aligarh again for, with the restrictions [under which you operate], he will care very little about you. A troop of Cavalry might have had some chance by making a dash to cut off his retreat . . .

During his exile in Bissalpur, Richard heard the remarkable news that James Cock was giving up all shooting and hunting activities and was taking a long leave to visit a lady in Muttra. He wrote to Bareilly for confirmation which he, in due course, received from Edward Bowerbank:

I am sorry to inform you that Captn. Cock's resolution to give up the sports of the field seem irrevocably taken as he is selling off all his hunting apparatus as well as the remains of the Pack — even the elephant is for sale at the diminished price of 400Rs. After muster he sets off on a long leave of absence for Muttrah where report says is centred the point of attraction. He is sallying forth like another Don Quixote to prostrate himself at the feet of his Dulcinea, the fair Ellen Fagan, who is to have the honor of leading this hitherto untamed Knight of la Mancha victim to the Hymeneal altar. It is indeed a consummation devoutly to be wished.

Bowerbank himself was not to remain in Bareilly for much longer. In 1808 the Government, inspired by Sir John Moore's use of light troops in Spain, decreed that a Light Company should be formed in every battalion of Native Infantry. These Companies were then to be formed up into Battalions to be trained in the evolutions and practice of light infantry before rejoining their respective corps. Richard had set his heart upon being given command of this new Company and was greatly disappointed to learn that Colonel Tetley had appointed George Casement, his junior, to the post. His brother officers shared his outrage and believed that Tetley had only made the appointment to ingratiate himself with Casement's brothers. Edward Bowerbank, who had been sent to the Light Company as Casement's second-in-command, summarised the feelings of them all. He began his letter: "My dear old Blackbeard" (Richard had grown a beard during his exile at Bissalpur):

I assure you, my dear P—. I feel very sensibly what you say on the subject of the Light Company tho' of the two, I believe, I am the greater sufferer by your not having been appointed to the command of it which, as things have turned out, must certainly be a very pleasant and gratifying situation, nor would mine have been less so had you succeeded in your application. However, it is certainly not to the credit of any one to gain or accept an advantage by such means, and to be possessed of the highest place in Tetley's private good opinion is surely nothing very enviable. If we may credit the sincerity of T's confession to you, he did not give a preference to C. from any wish to act up to the meaning of the General Order on that subject, nor from a fair estimation of the professional merits and abilities of his officers, and in suffering himself to be influenced by any other motives, he was guilty of partiality and injustice. However, as this can only be known to the parties concerned, it must still in a public view appear a reflection (I need not say how unjust a one) on those more senior officers who wished for the command of the Company. The appointment which has been made does indeed great credit to the 2nd 21st in producing such a specimen in whom are supposed to be combined in an eminent degree all the good qualities requisite for a commander of light troops. Although I conceive Tetley's predilection for a person possessing disposition and manners so congenial to his own might in some measure influence his conduct on that occasion yet, I believe, the more inexcusable motive, of wishing to ingratiate himself with C.'s brothers, had more weight with him and indeed this alone, with such a weak sneaking old fellow, would be sufficient to cloak any wish he might have felt striving within to act in a just and impartial manner. As the case stands I fancy it will be productive of more harm than good to him. It has been a disappointment to you and is, and ever will be to me as long as I remain in the Company, especially when absent from the Battalion.

### Dr. Josiah Ridges was also sympathetic, writing to Richard from Kithor on 20th June 1808:

In regard to Tetley's conduct towards you in disposing of the command of the Light Coy. — it was indelicate in the extreme but I fear he has but little idea of delicacy — add to which a most thorough rooted degree of obstinacy will ever render him an object of disgust to his officers.†

### James Cock's wife-hunting expedition to Muttra had been to no avail and Dr. Ridges considered that marriage might even improve his life expectancy:

James Cock returned from his excursion and what is the result? I can only say I wish he could bring himself to do so wise an act as to marry; it would be the means of adding many years to his life in all probability. We have not a spinster of any description here; the one we had, Miss Grant, was shortly snapped up.†

### His posting to the Light Company was not a happy placement for Edward Bowerbank. The friction which had existed between him and Casement since he had first joined the Regiment had not improved and his opinion of Casement was low:

The more I observe of C. the more I find my dislike of him increase. The natural vulgarity and coarseness of his manners is rendered more glaring by his affectation. Instead of appearing conscious of the inferiority which certainly marks his conversation and appearance, he seems endeavouring to impress everyone with the idea that he is remarkable on the contrary account and makes himself perfectly ridiculous by seizing every opportunity of discharging all the quaint and figurative phrases and expressions he has been able to load his memory with either from novels, or the conversation of those like himself. I dare say he thinks that he has behaved very generously towards me in two or three

---

† N.M.M. Ref: PRV/101 MS.55/009

instances and believes that I think so too, but I conceive one may better judge of a man's real disposition and sentiments from little things wch. escape him unintentionally than from any thing which he says or does, purposely, to impress one with favorable ideas of him.

## Meanwhile in the Capital, John Home was getting bored:

Dick, I am tired of Calcutta, quite sick of it, and I shall not much regret leaving it if it were not for being in the middle of the family.

## He was also surprised to hear that Richard had taken on his old tailor, despite his reputation for dishonesty:

To tell you the truth I was very much surprised at the assurance of my old taylor entering your service. He was taken up at Futte Ghur selling some of my cloth etc. but that no other servant knew any thing about the cloth, so as to swear to it, he might have had a little employment on the roads, now I did not turn him off, even for that, and expected him to have accompanied me down here . . . I missed him very much on the River and gave him several hearty curses for his ingratitude, for thou knowest Dick I was ever a kind master unto him.

## John left Calcutta and started his return journey to Bareilly which was to take him the better part of two months, stopping off with friends and acquaintances on the way to raise sufficient money to enable him to commence the next leg of his journey. Richard sent him 200 rupees to meet him at Allahabad:

How much I am obliged to you for that mark of your attention and friendship, it was indeed a very seasonable supply, as it enabled me to repay the sum I had been obliged to borrow of Colvin, tho' I am sure he would have been happy to have supplied me with as much as I wanted, but you have kindly prevented me from increasing the number of my creditors tho' by that means you place me so deeply in your debt that it will be very long before I can even repay the money part.

## At Fatehgurh John had the despatch of some purchases for his friends to organise and had to see the Paymaster for some money. He had also run across George Casement at Nandangarh with his new Light Company:

I am at present cursedly confused and bothered about sending off the goods and chattels, all the things are across the river except your liquor which I got from Mr. Wattle and it goes this evening if possible along with the tent and camels to be pitched at Jalalabad, at which place I expect to be on the 25th if I can manage matters with the Buxy. I went there this morning but he had met with an accident a little before — a powder horn blew up in his hand and hurt him very much. I trust however he will be able to give me some cash and all will be well. I met Geo. Casement and party at Nunda Ghur and dined with them. He appears quite pleased with his appointment, I mean his being a Light Infantry Officer, but I think it has brought down his fat very much — I don't envy him in the least.

The return of Casement's Light Company to its mother corps was not to be as soon as had been expected. Early in 1809, up in the sensitive valley of the Sutlej, the great Sikh leader Ranjit Singh was rattling his sabre and Lord Minto had despatched the twenty-four year-old Charles Metcalfe as his envoy to the Sikh Court to attempt to negotiate a settlement. Meanwhile, a large force under General St. Leger, including the 2/21st's Light Company, had assembled at Sirhind from where Edward Bowerbank wrote to Richard on 8th February:

We are now at Sirhind and do not leave it till the day after tomorrow. From the orders that have been issued by Genl. St. Leger there can be no doubt but that hostilities will be the consequence of our crossing the Sutlej. Nothing has been lately heard from Mr. Metcalfe but the people here say that Ranjeet has carried him off to Lahore. Various are the accounts as to the no. of forces collected by Ranjeet for the purpose of opposing our entrance in to his territories wch. it seems he is determined upon doing. . . . A general engagement is expected on our arrival at the Sutlej, or rather on our attempt to cross it, as the Sutlej is not fordable at this season from its being swelled by the melting of the snow on the hills. Shd. Ranjeet make a proper use of the advantage this circumstance will give him against us, his artillery must occasion us considerable annoyance and severe loss — in the common course of events of this nature the two Lt. Inf. Bns. must suffer considerably in officers — Ho! Ho! Ho!, say I, and hope to write you in a whole skin when the game shall be finished — a few days more and I shall probably have it in my power to acquaint you how I like the music wch. gave so much pleasure to Charles XII.

In the event, Metcalfe had not been carried off by Ranjit Singh and a Treaty was negotiated and signed at Amritsar on 25th April 1809 which preserved peace with the Sikhs for the time being. A peace of sorts was also made between Edward Bowerbank and his Company Commander:

Should this business be speedily brought to a conclusion, I think there is a great probability of my shortly returning to you as, according to the general expectation, these Battns. are to be formed into Regts. and the noble Captn. is promised the retainment of his Compy. and probably the Adjutancy. As you might expect, his brother's situation and presence add not a little to his consequence [in the minds of some] tho' in mine it renders him more disgusting than ever. — I am however about to relate to you a circumstance wch. cd. alter my thoughts of him. — The other day under the supposition of my being in some urgent distress for money, he offered me an order on his Agents for 1000 dibs — I was even pretty pleased with the manner of his doing it than with the thing itself — for I never wish to receive favors from persons whom I do not esteem and rather consider it as an insult than an obligation to be offered them by anyone who does not esteem me. — I own however this handsome action has opened my heart towards Casement and makes me like him more than ever I had supposed I could but it is to be considered that many people make these offers from a wish to persuade themselves that they are not inferior in generosity of disposition but did they not witness it in others wd. not think themselves obliged to set the example. Still more make them from a desire to receive the praise which the world generally bestows upon such actions — but very few are prompted to them by any innate principle of generosity and benevolence. The manner of his doing it acquits C. from having acted from the first of these motives, from wch. of the other two I will not yet decide.

It is possible that Bowerbank eventually credited Casement with the third and most noble motive as there were no further acrimonious references to him in his correspondence with Richard.

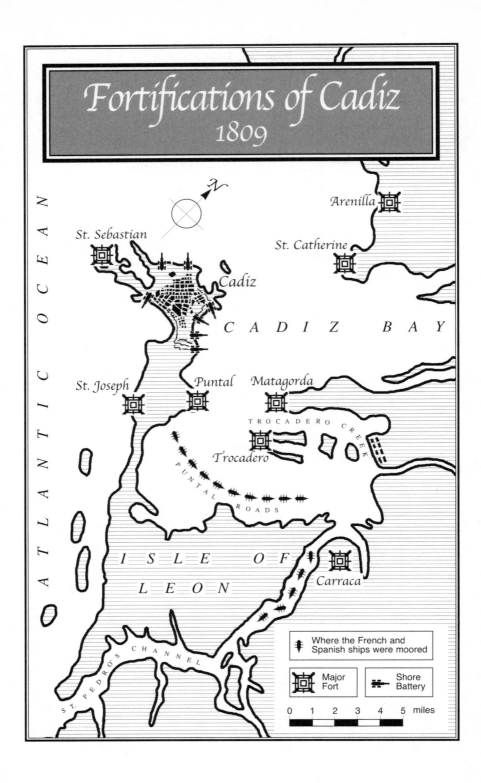

# Fortifications of Cadiz
## 1809

Arenilla

St. Sebastian

St. Catherine

Cadiz

C A D I Z    B A Y

St. Joseph

Puntal

Matagorda

TROCADERO CREEK

Trocadero

PUNTAL ROADS

ATLANTIC OCEAN

I S L E    O F    L E O N

Carraca

ST. PEDRO'S CHANNEL

Where the French and
Spanish ships were moored

Major
Fort

Shore
Battery

0    1    2    3    4    5    miles

# 6. Disenchantment

*H.M.S. Atlas, Cadiz Harbour.*
*20th April 1809.*

Admiral Purvis was now entering upon one of the most vitally important commissions of his career. In June the previous year, the Spanish people had risen in armed revolt against their French invaders and, heartened by the defeat of a French army at Baylen, the Spanish forces manning the shore batteries at Cadiz had opened fire on the French ships, under the command of Admiral Rosilly, which had been trapped in the harbour by the British blockade since Trafalgar. Rosilly could not escape as Admiral Purvis's Squadron was waiting for him off the harbour mouth and he had no alternative but to surrender to the Spanish.

As Bonaparte's forces threatened to invest the city, there was a grave risk, not only of their recapturing their own ships, but of taking the Spanish Fleet as well. The British had made several attempts to persuade the Spanish to move their ships from the creeks where they were moored, and were completely vulnerable to attack from the shore, into the harbour where they could be used for defence of the city when the French arrived. But the Spanish, who had only recently allied themselves with Britain against the French, viewed Britain's motives with deep distrust. To Admiral Purvis fell the task of persuading the Spanish authorities that our intentions were honourable and entirely in the interests of Spain. Lord Collingwood, at Minorca, had written to him on 26th March explaining the position:

You observe the anxiety which Ministers have that the Spanish ships should not, in any event, fall into the hands of the enemy; and to prevent this, in case of affairs going to extremity in Spain, will require much delicacy of conduct and skill: but it cannot be in better hands than yours.†

---

† *Correspondence and Memoir of Lord Collingwood,*
edited by G.L.N. Collingwood, 4th edition 1828

There were two possibilities if Cadiz fell to the French:

Do they mean to embark in their fleet, and go to America, taking all the loyal Spaniards and their property to a new establishment? Or do they mean, when resistance is no longer possible, to make the best terms they can? In the first case, the town of Cadiz would be the rendezvous of all who fled from the tyranny of the usurper. Cadiz should be made impregnable, and the ships placed so as to defend and be defended by it. Whatever will inspire them with perfect confidence in us should be done. It is their cause, in which we have no interest but their success. If, on the contrary, they have not determined to seek an asylum in America, but, in the case of Spain lost (which God forbid), prepare to make those evils as little ruinous to them as they can, and save from the wreck their unhappy lives, to swell the triumph of the tyrant, and be the reproach of the world, they will keep their fleet out of reach in the Caracas, in order to appease the violence to which they will have to submit.†

The Spanish navy was rife with French agents and sympathisers who were conducting a propaganda campaign to undermine faith in the intentions of their British allies and Lord Collingwood believed that the Spanish naval officers had the latter scheme in mind. Either way, Admiral Purvis had a highly delicate diplomatic mission on his hands in addition to a critical command at Cadiz.

In spite of the portentous tasks ahead of him, the Admiral was still very much concerned with Richard's prospects:

It has been sometimes thought by people acquainted with the Affairs of the Company, that it is probable Government will take the whole of the Company's Military into their service; should such be likely to happen I should wish to have the earliest intelligence that I may avail myself of any opening, whereby I might get you forward; and if you should at any time find out any means in which (by my interference) your prospects may brighten, you will not fail to make it known to me as soon as you can.

Richard, though pleased with the news from Europe, was disappointed that the French fleet had surrendered to the Spanish and not to his father. He wrote to his stepmother:

All the good news from the Continent have reached us within this fortnight, and most surprising they are. The happy turn that has taken place in the affairs of Britain surpass all that could have been expected or even hoped for. I only pray they may be followed up by the downfall of Bonaparte's influence and ultimately crowned with his total overthrow.

---

† *Correspondence and Memoir of Lord Collingwood,*
edited by G.L.N. Collingwood, 4th edition 1828

How much it must tend to the support of Loyalty and Patriotism, (which some croakers report to have been upon the decay), in England. And how much it must serve to attach every Briton to our Constitution to behold surrounding nations imploring her assistance. The newspapers in this Country said nothing of my Father's having received the French Fleet as Prizes; but that it had surrendered to the Spaniards – I wish the former had been the case as the Prize Money would no doubt have been acceptable to the Admiral.

The knowledge that his father had received some significant Prize Money would also have eased Richard's conscience in forwarding his next proposal: he had now been in India for nearly five years and had become increasingly disenchanted with the country and despondent about his prospects in the Bengal Army. Since the Regiment's move to Bareilly, a station with many more British civilians than the fort at Aligarh, he had made the acquaintance of several members of the Civil Service and felt greatly aggrieved at the far superior income they enjoyed. This grievance was heightened by the fact that he knew he had more brains and ability than many of them and could have qualified himself for their appointments in a far shorter time than it had taken them. For some time he had been considering how much better his prospects would be if he could transfer to the Civil Service as a Writer; but a Writership required a substantial cash premium.

He had asked for his father's assistance in clearing his debts which, when it had been offered, he had been able to decline as a result of his own resolve to clear his creditors by his own efforts. He had surely demonstrated that he was no longer a feckless boy and had developed a strength of character and sense of responsibility which would convince his father that his new proposal was not just another scatterbrained scheme. He had written to him on a previous occasion intimating that he might, at some time in the future, be approaching him about the possibility of a Writership and his father's response had not been wholly dismissive. On 25th June 1809 he wrote again describing in detail his present lack of prospects and asking for his father's assistance in a change of career:

At the time I mentioned to you what a profitable appointment a writership would be to me, I had not made myself acquainted with the advantages which would arise from my getting it so well as your last kind letter had led me to do and which I now find would be so great that I am prompted to enter again upon the subject, and to suggest to you a plan to procure that which I find would be so wonderful an advancement and tend so much to my future happiness in life. I much apologise for thus blatantly commencing with the subject without the least introduction or preface which must certainly be superfluous in an address that, as it will require to be so fully considered, ought to be written with the greatest possible clearness, however it may be wanting in common form. I must in the first place beg that you will not regard my suggestion as the sudden determination of a rash or unthinking boy, putting forth his hand to that which is beyond his reach; for be assured I would never think of opening this subject to you without having deliberately weighed in my own mind my circumstance relating to it. This I request because I confess my proposal may at first appear preposterous but I think I shall be able to convince you of the contrary. Judging by your letter you seem not to be aware that the appointment may, by some under hand means or other, be purchased. Neither had I myself any idea of it till upon enquiry I was given to understand, not only that it is purchasable, but that there are very few whose appointments are not purchased. I can not find out the sum which is generally paid but suppose it must be something considerable. However, if you could once manage to put me in possession of the Appointment, I know it to be such that I should very soon have it in my power to repay you with every farthing of interest so that you should neither suffer loss or inconvenience, if it should possibly be in your power to advance the money, or get it advanced for me.

I shall now proceed to point out the difference between the Civil and Military Service, that you may be convinced as I said before what an astonishing advancement in life it would be to me. I am now the thirteenth Lieutenant in my Regiment upon the allowance of £387 per year; we rise in regiments by seniority entirely; neither interest nor merit can possibly acquire advancement and that you may judge of the progress I am making towards promotion. I must here observe that I have got two steps since I have been in the country – a space of near five years! I joined the Regiment fifteenth Lieutenant; I am now thirteenth. My allowances until I rise to be 7th Lieut. will remain the same as at present. The emoluments of a Company, which I shall then have in my own right, will increase my income £72. Thus my allowances will remain till I attain the rank of Capt. Lieut., which cannot possibly be in less than 10 years – most probably a great deal more – my allowances will then be £614. A year or two more will make me a full Captain and increase them to £706. Now a higher rank than that of Captain I cannot reasonably expect to attain by the expiration of my period of service: that is to say that, provided the Army remains of its present strength, and I am sorry to add that we now have no hopes whatever of an augmentation. My twenty five years thus ended, I shall retire upon a pension of about £180 a year, and whatever I may hereafter save out of my allowances, which must indeed be but a trifle. Or if an unexpected increase to the Army should fortunately give me the rank of Major by that time, my pension will be £270. You must observe that I have here throughout mentioned my income under the head of allowances – for this reason, that the whole is classed under the following heads; for instance, a full Captain's Pay is 120 Rupees a month; then comes Batta 180 Rs., Gratuity 36 Rs., Lieut. Allowance 75 Rs. and his Company 45 Rs. making altogether 456 Rs. a month, what I call his allowances and of which what is actually collect pay is not the principal. Here also I shall remark that it is certainly true we may retire upon the full pay of our rank but it is only that which is literally called pay, and not the full of our allowances as people, particularly those in Europe, might be led to imagine. This is a quibble which required to be explained, for I have frequently mentioned to you the amount of my income, which probably you had considered as my pay and expected to see me in the enjoyment of it hereafter as a pension.

Now, my dear Sir, I have finished as precisely as possible the prospect I have before me as a soldier. I neither hope nor even think of its being better except it happen by miracle. In my last I believe I told you what might be expected from recommendatory letters; but I also told you of what kind they must be, but the difficulty of procuring such, and the possibility of their not succeeding even after they were procured, prevented and still prevents my placing any confidence in what I wrote expecting a staff appointment which, however, if it could be got, would better my situation in a great degree; but since we are to have no new Regiments, I see no possibility of my ever holding one, tho' the best of letters were provided for me.

I shall now endeavour to shew you how widely different would be my situation and prospects were I transferred to the Civil line by giving you as exact an idea of that service as I have myself been able to form from the enquiries as well as observations I have made. Even in the event of my now being transferred to the Civil Establishment, I should immediately enter upon a salary of £578 a year, which is almost £200 a year more than I receive now after five years hard service. A civil servant of five years standing is generally in the receipts of £1,100 or £1,200 a year – this I can instance in one who is on the Register of the Court of Appeal at this Station whose salary is £1,115 a year besides his being allowed a house to live in. This, I shall add too, is a gentleman of even far below common abilities, from whence we may infer that he was much longer than necessary at the College and there being nothing particular to recommend him to such an appointment we may reasonably suppose that every one has a right to expect the same after the same length of service and this gentleman arrived in India the same season with myself. I can also flatter myself, of the knowledge I already have of the Persian and Hindostanee languages that I should finish my studies at the College in less than half the time that is generally taken. You may remember when I was first nominated Cadet, you were told (by whom I cannot recollect) that the appointment was equally good with a writership. Pray observe the difference between my situation and that of the gentleman above mentioned. His salary £1,115 per annum and a house provided for him, mine £387 and obliged, not only to provide my own house when in cantonments but to keep up a perfect camp equipage viz. tents, camels, servants of all descriptions etc. etc. at all seasons. With respect to the payment of the money you may lay out in pursuit of this my present plan, you must be aware that I have now arrived at that age when I can aspire with punctuality to such resolutions as I make; or at least that I would not make them without first ascertaining in my own mind my perfect power of adhering to them, and after once giving my word that you shall be paid, rely upon my not departing from it tho to that end I were to confine myself to the most rigid parsimony – but you may easily see, by the description I have given, that I should never be driven to that necessity. I must again assure you that I have not suddenly fixed upon the plan of making you this address but that I am led to it by deliberating coolly upon the information I gathered. Neither do I address you as positively expecting your compliance with my wish; but from being prepossessed with the full persuasion that you ever seek opportunities to serve me, it would be a kind of neglect on my part to refrain from doing it. I know should it be in your power you will not let pass an opportunity of procuring me such an advancement; and altho' it should not be in your powers I should suffer no disappointment from your not doing it for rely upon it I have not presumed to entertain much hope; notwithstanding I have written with so much [correctness] upon the subject. I must lastly beg you that if my suggestion meet not your approbation you will destroy my letter and think no more of the affair. I would wish that no third person be made acquainted with it unless it be questioning him as to the truth of what I have written upon which point you can satisfy yourself by applying to any old Indian – for all must be well informed of the advantages of the civil line. People are very apt upon these occasions to set one down as an idle profligate who cannot make himself contented with the situation allotted to him in life. The very contrary, however, is the case with me, I have no fault to find with the life of a soldier; but I have that most natural of all wishes – namely to better my prospects in life. . . . The length of this letter will most probably prove tedious to you. I shall therefore conclude – but first, regarding the principal subject of my epistle, I shall add that, if there be a possibility of a son's entertaining more grateful sentiments of his parent's kindness than I have ever done of yours, such will be mine should you make it convenient to comply with the wish I have here expressed.

There were ample precedents for a change from the Military to the Civil that Richard knew of: Robert Grant, for example, the Collector at Cawnpore, had actually transferred as a Captain in H.M. Army, first to the Bengal Infantry and then to the Bengal Civil. He had then worked his way up from a Writer, the most junior rank, through various intermediate appointments to that of Collector, the Chief Administrator of a District, carrying a very substantial salary and ancillary benefits. This progression had taken him twenty-four years — after which period of service Richard considered that he would be lucky to reach the rank of Captain.

By 1809 the 2/21st's Officers Mess had been augmented by four Ensigns — Jolliffe, Ferrell, Clarkson and Smith; three Lieutenants junior to Richard — Watson, Ross and Dwyer, and one Lieutenant senior to him —Wrottesley, who had transferred from the 1st Battalion. Hugh Wrottesley was a younger son of Major-General Sir John Wrottesley Bart. and Hon. Frances Courtenay, a daughter of Lord Courtenay of Powderham Castle, Devon. Any officer who was patently well-connected found immediate favour with Colonel Tetley and his consequent favouritism of Wrottesley was much resented by the other Lieutenants in the Battalion.

John Home also believed that Tetley would try to insinuate his own son into the company of the 2/21st's Mess. He wrote to Richard:

. . . young Tetley has just come out to join his Papa; the one that was a Writer in the Auditor General's Office. I don't imagine the Officers will admit him into their society, it will breed a quarrel I think, for Tet. will certainly introduce him at the Mess. The fellow had the impudence to write to me to lend him a horse to carry him out to Camp and I was fool enough to lend him my pony.

Rattray had planned a three-day hunting trip and had asked Johnson and Watson, who were not required for duty at the time, to join him. They had requested, and been granted, the necessary leave from the Colonel and Rattray had organised elephants and all the necessary accoutrements and servants:

. . . but the night before they were to start, he [Tetley] wrote each a letter on service recalling the indulgence and ordering them to join if they had left cantonments. I believe this was done as much to annoy Rattray as anyone else for he was obliged to go then, even by himself, having written to Government that he intended going out in the district — all hands are as mad as hell with Tetley.

Nor was the Colonel popular with his Indian officers and NCOs. While stationed at one of the outposts, Richard heard that there had been some sort of altercation between Tetley and Jemadar Rambuccus, a highly-respected Indian officer in the Regiment. He wrote to John Home for details but John had only a muddled knowledge of the affair:

. . . I fear I must be still silent regarding the crime sent in against poor Rambuccus for to give you a clear account of it is more than I can. All I can say is that when the Volunteers were ordered to turn out he came forward amongst the rest and when the Colonel told the Jemadars to fall back as their services were not required, Rambuccus staid behind to tell Tetley that he wished to go on as Jemadar . . . Jupen also staid behind contrary to orders . . . Tetley was terribly annoyed at Rambuccus and went up to abusing him and giving him a violent push (a gentle one, he says) ordered him to fall in with the Battn. immediately, which he did, tho' looking at the same time very much displeased, or as the crime says insolent and disrespectful looking. This is I believe all that occasioned his being put under close arrest. When the parade was over the Jemadar came forward, gave up his sword and demanded a Court Martial. Tetley was well pleased at first but afterwards wanted him to take his sword again; but the man refused it. So much for the Jemadar tho' I doubt that you will be much the wiser for all I have written for the truth is I know very little about the matter.

Although there was a preponderance of Scottish officers in the 2/21st, as indeed in the Bengal Army as a whole, they were, in the main, educated people of gentle birth with the same comportment and ethos as their English and Irish colleagues (strangely, there were very few Welshmen in the Bengal Army at this time). There were, however, a very few of the abrasive, finger-wagging type of central-belt Scot who ruffle the harmony of society wherever they go. One such was William Menzies of the 1st Battalion. Son of a clerk in the Edinburgh Customs House, Menzies had arrived in India in 1800 and was now a senior Lieutenant. His coarse manners and loud, hectoring voice had made him deeply unpopular with his brother officers who were duly incensed when he won a lakh [100,000 rupees] in the Lottery — a circumstance which was the constantly dreamed-of ambition of them all. Then to their amazement and disgust, he won it again. George Casement wrote to Richard:

Think of that animal Menzies getting another Lakh in the Lottery. How blind the Goddess must be, Dick, to shower down her favors on such a "Ya, Nay" devil.

And then, on the assumption that his newly-acquired wealth would enable Menzies to retire immediately and return to Scotland:

There is, however, one good resulting from it — namely a step to the 21st Regiment which I trust I will not be removed from.

But Menzies did not retire and, in the event, was to plague them for a further three years, his wealth, as is often the case with such people, making him even more offensive than before. There was general rejoicing, however, when John Home's brother won a lesser prize in the Lottery. John wrote to Richard:

. . . he had half the ticket that came up 10,000. He has offered me, after paying his own debts etc. what may be over, at least 2,000. I must confess I intend to accept of the loan of it, and by that means consolidate my debts, and when the little that I shall owe besides is paid, I can then pay him by instalments; you know it is a great comfort being in only one person's debt and as at present the money will be of service to you, receiving it at once, so I hope you will have no objection to receiving it, for as I may be in somebody's debt it is better to be in my brother's who at present is not having any call for cash, than to stay in yours, when you are using every effort to answer the demands against you and as you must be paid it is better to have it once than in little drafts that you can feel no benefit from. The pecuniary transactions between us will I hope soon be settled tho' I must ever be your debtor for the many obligations I have received from you.

Though he would never have considered pressing his friend for repayment of the various sums he had lent him over the years, it must have been a great relief to Richard's own fragile economy to have his loans repaid under such satisfactory circumstances.

Richard also learned from his father that his aunt, Lady Bellenden (his mother's sister), had died recently leaving him about £800 in stock which would be transferred into his name when he came of age in January 1810. Moreover, his father had insisted upon adding to this legacy the £100 which he had offered Richard during his difficulties, but which Richard had refused.

The Admiral's finances, also, were looking up. Not only had he earned significant Prize Money during his command at Cadiz, but had inherited the property of his cousin, Thomas English, who had died in 1808, which included lands in Essex and in Wiltshire. Richard wrote to his brother on 12th August 1809:

I heard a long time ago of Mr. English's death and of the Admiral's good fortune in succeeding to the possession of all his property. What an excellent income he must now enjoy. I suppose this addition to what you mention in your letter regarding the Atlas, together with the prize money he is daily sharing will make him on his return to England the greatest man in the Wickham county: God bless him and give him many years to enjoy it! I am sure I have no wish for him to remain toiling in a foreign climate to make me (as you say) an "Honorable".

Two months after Richard's request to his father to assist him with the purchase of a Writership, he realised he had done the wrong thing. Back in England, Parliament, spurred on by the reforming journalism of William Cobbett, was looking closely at the corruption which was rife in the East India Company. Richard realised that he had asked his straight-laced father to be party to an arrangement which would shortly be publicly exposed as corrupt and knew he must retract his request without delay:

Altho' the suggestion contained in my last letter dated the 25th of June, was to procure me an appointment through corrupt means, I hope you will not think me at all the more corrupt for having written it; since I so well knew that Writerships were put up to sale and sold just as freely, as your neighbour Mr. Cobbett says as "Packwoods Razor Strops"; and in fact that money was the only means by which they were possibly to be procured. The proceedings in the House of Commons

respecting the Duke of York will of course awaken the East India Company to
some examination into the conduct of the Directors in this particular, especially
as Mr. Cobbett has spoken so openly of it in his gazettes the sale of Writerships
and Cadetships will therefore of course be put a stop to, and render needless all I
have written on the subject of the former appointment. If the contents of my last
letter have been at all offensive to your feelings by my having supposed that you
would have recourse to a corrupt method of serving me, it is my duty to apologize
for it in the most earnest manner; but so common was the practice and from its
having, as I hear, been resorted to by some of the most respectable people in
England, that it might be said almost to have lost the appearance of corruption;
also from it being as well – so publicly known there are so few Writerships that
are not paid for. I know of one or two instances of even relatives of Directors
coming out Cadets, by reason of being unable to pay for the other situation. It
gives me the greatest possible uneasiness when I reflect upon the feelings which
will probably have taken possession of your heart on reading my last letter, and,
I must confess, that after reading so much of bribery and corruption in the late
English papers, I even seem little in my own imagination. But pray, my dear Sir,
consider attentively what I have said above, and I trust you will be convinced that
I never had any idea of proposing a scheme that could in the least degree prove
prejudicial to, or inconsistent with, either your honor or my own: I merely
intimated to you what I thought – and what really was then – the only means
whereby to procure a situation which would be so advantageous to me.

With a transfer to the Civil Service out of the question, Richard now
saw his only hope of improving his prospects in what he was
increasingly referring to as "this detested country" in some sort of
recommendation to a staff appointment. But such a letter, to have
any chance of success, had to come from someone of importance
who had social access to the high command in India.

Also in 1809, a growing disaffection among officers of the Madras
Army regarding the withdrawal of certain allowances came to a
head. Many officers refused to report for duty in what amounted to
a minor mutiny and the situation was made worse by the insensitive
handling of the Governor, Sir George Barlow. The mutineers
received little sympathy from Richard and his friends in the Bengal
Army as he related in a letter to his father dated 27th August:

I have now very good reason to be rejoiced that my friends recommended my
being appointed, and indeed in getting it – to the Establishment of Bengal for
there are disturbances between the officers of the Madras Army and the
Government, almost amounting to a Mutiny. The European Regiment of Madras,
officers and all, refused to embark on board Sir Edward Pellew's ship – on what
pretence I know not; but really they could have no just one as they had been
ordered by the Commander in Chief. This was the first act of positive

disobedience they have been guilty of, but there had been a continual kind of opposition to those measures of Government manifested for four months before in consequence of Sir George Barlow, the Governor General, having assumed some authority which the Army thought proper to dispute his title to. In short they have behaved in a manner more resembling a party of transported Convicts than the sons of Gentlemen who have the ties of relationship and other connexions with their own Country. It is impossible for me to give the full account having no correspondents in that Country and we are only made acquainted with the circumstances by private letters; because nothing dare be published in Calcutta without the sanction of Governments who of course suppress every thing that might tend to weaken the confidence of the natives in their measures, which any thing of the nature of a dissention between the Powers Civil and Military would certainly do. Lord Minto has judged it expedient to visit these refractory Gentlemen and has accordingly sailed in the Dover Frigate for the Coast with the idea of reconciling them to their wonted performance of their duty; but I fear they have gone too far to be reclaimed until some of them are deprived of their Commissions. And what is more to be regretted, if true, is that the Army of Bombay has offered to support that of Madras in their mutinous cause; one would think them all deranged and I trust there will be no such proceeding on this Establishment; indeed there is no danger for the conduct of the others is regarded with abhorrence.

By the time Lord Minto arrived in Madras, the matter had blown over and most of the officers had returned to their duties.

# 7. Paths of Venus

*Mirzapur, India. 1810.*

Sita Ram, the only Indian sepoy of the period to have written his memoirs,† claims that most British officers of the Bengal Army kept Indian mistresses. This was certainly not the case with Richard and his friends. Though some more senior officers, such as Josiah Ridges, did keep what was called a "sable venus", the junior officers, if for no other reason, simply could not afford such a luxury. However, it would be unrealistic to suppose that young men, deprived of normal contact with women of their own background, would not resort to periodic relationships with native women. This was often followed by deep remorse as was the case with Edward Bowerbank who wrote to Richard:

I do not attempt to deny the truth of the reports which have reached you of my late misdeeds though I assure you I am not bent on a repetition of them, on the contrary, the remembrance of such filthy embraces serves but to heighten my disgust against the ugly inanimate partakers of them. There are times when firmness of constitution and extremity of lustful desire are too strong to be allayed by the dictates of reason or to be opposed with success by mere human arguments, but that any one should in cool blood speak of these devils incarnate with seeming pleasure is my utter astonishment and I can still less comprehend how they can gain such a pernicious influence over mind and indeed with common sense of which we have here too many instances to doubt its reality.

Richard himself had acquired a reputation for frigidity and lack of interest in the opposite sex which was strengthened by his eagerness to accept long periods of command at isolated outposts where no women were present. It let him in for much good-natured teasing:

I am at a loss whether to congratulate you on your emancipation from the dreary wilds and forests of Bisalpur or to condole with you on your return among the fashionable beings at Berailley where you are obliged to shave at least once a

---

† *From Sepoy to Subedar* by Sita Ram. First English edition 1873. Reprinted by the Military Book Society 1970 by arrangement with Routledge & Kegan Paul.

week and run the risk of being disgusted by a tender glance from the bright eyes of Clara or by the inviting smiles of the pretty Sylph. Pray, during this last seclusion, as on your former one, did you meet with any sympathising beauty of the monkey tribe, who enjoyed your attentions and won your affections by her playful leaps and fascinating grimaces?

Pray, how happens it that the beautiful, the all accomplished Europasia, the desire of many hearts, is now known by the vulgar and familiar appellation of "the Doctor's Daughter", or is it only you who, relying on your frigid philosophy and the natural, or rather unnatural, strength of your heart, continue to shew your contemptuous disobedience to the will of Cupid by dubbing her with such indifference.

John Home, also, took little interest in women or anything else which interfered with his sport or his food. He had one brief flirtation which ended when his ladylove turned her attentions to another:

My old flame is making love to a Mr. Fraser, a boy younger than herself a good deal, and after all no great beauty, in my opinion very ugly, at least his mouth is enormously so — but no accounting for taste.

Richard, despite his reputation for indifference, did not remain celibate all the time and confided to his brother:

In answer to your enquiry regarding the other sex, if you mean those of the Cyprian class; I can tell you as Sam Luke has probably done before, that they are in no scarcity throughout all parts of India. I sigh while I write upon the subject for what innumerable curses do they bring upon the sons of Adam. I am extremely sorry to read that you have been so unfortunate as to suffer from the enjoyment of the embraces of these kind of beings. Such may be unavoidable in England; but luckily in this Country, where the heat of the climate must be allowed to kindle certain flames in the Constitution, we have such an extensive variety that a little extra caution and a little extra cash will always prove security against scrapes of that fatal nature; at least it is chance if otherwise. For my part, since I trod the paths of Venus I have made but one unpure connexion and then my sufferance was of the slighter kind – you comprenez, j'espere. My dread of furnishing you with whitey-brown nephews, as you call them, is a sufficient argument to deter me from keeping a Sable Venus to tuck my clothes in at night etc.

Gonorrhoea, which one must assume John had at some time contracted, was widespread among servicemen in India and in the Navy. Naval surgeons received a fee of fifteen shillings, deducted from the patient's pay, for each case which they treated. The extremely unpleasant treatment consisted of a six-day course of injections of mercury up the penis which, in itself, must have acted as a deterrent to liaisons with "those of the Cyprian class" and led to the old admonition: "One night with Venus — six days with Mercury".

Richard had noticed that, in his letters, John was continually making mention of their cousin Renira and what an accomplished and pretty girl she was growing into. His interest, Richard thought, was clearly more than casual. Marriage between first cousins was quite common in those days and Richard had a feeling that ultimately, this might be in his brother's mind:

Your taking to yourself a wife would undoubtedly be the best plan to preserve a whole constitution; for what between the disease and the remedy (both are equally bad) a wound in the War of Venus proves a dreadful canker – and if you await my opinion in the choice of this essential I will not direct you farther than Blackbrook, but then remains the question whether you would be considered an eligible candidate for the hand of the all-charming princess – you are very warm in her praise.

Richard also told John how much he himself looked forward to marriage with a good English girl but, with his present poor prospects, he had doubts as to whether he would ever be able to afford it. Every penny counted; he even begrudged the money it cost him to receive the newspapers which the well-intentioned Mr. Grant sent him out from England and wrote to his stepmother asking her if she could, very tactfully, put a stop to it:

I wish you would do me the favour to give Mr. Grant a hint – but let it be a particularly delicate one, not to send me any more news papers; because there are plenty published in this Country giving us all that is important of the Europe news; and the one which Mr. G. sent me cost in postage – it having been forwarded over land from the coast, which all are equally liable to be – 16 Rupees and 10 Annas – which turned into English coin, makes exactly £1. 16s. 8d. which is an expense I cannot afford to have often repeated. You must be aware that I have every proper sense of the kind intentions which prompted Mr. Grant's sending the paper which were to give me the earliest information of our success in Portugal; but they were, as they always would be, defeated by the delay at the general post office occasioned by the multiplicity of letters which they have to sort and despatch on the arrival of a packet, during which delay the public news are always received and published by the Calcutta editors. If this were not the case – that is to say if I could have the satisfaction of getting good news before my neighbours, and the pleasure of imparting it to them, I would certainly not begrudge that – or even a greater account. I leave it to your judgement how to open this to Mr. G. and communicate to him my sentiments in the manner least likely to give offence; because, to tell the real truth, notwithstanding the expense it put me to, I feel extremely grateful to Mr. G. for his having had in view my gratification by giving the speediest account of the success of my Countrymen.

The 2/21st was ordered to move from Bareilly in November 1809 to relieve the station at Mirzapur, some 350 miles south-east of Bareilly on the south bank of the Ganges. Two months prior to the move, Richard was sent to survey the route. The Battalion commenced its march on 25th November arriving on the north bank of the Ganges opposite Mirzapur on Christmas Day. From here Richard was despatched with one Company to the outpost of Azamgarh, some seventy miles, or eight marches, to the north-east. It was manned by two Companies, the other from another Battalion, under the command of a Captain.

On 15th January 1810 Richard, now reconciled to the fact that the only chance of bettering his position would be by a suitable recommendation to a staff appointment, wrote to his father:

Your goodness in offering to get me forward whenever your interference may prove advantageous I am likewise thankful for and depend upon my not failing to inform you whenever the opening occurs; at present the only service I am aware of your being able to do me, is procuring such introductions as I mentioned in one of my letters from Bareilly, to some of the persons high in office then, should there be any increase to the Army, or should any vacancy in Staff situations occur, they might be instrumental to my preferment. As to our Army being made over to the British Government, it is never even thought of in this Country; and I should suppose (if it ever took place) you would get the information much earlier than myself. However, I shall write to you if it does.

His Manton gun had arrived in November and appeared to be exactly what he wanted but:

. . . this season must pass over without its having a fair trial for I have been out shooting very little for want of time to indulge in recreation of that nature.

His cousin Barrington Purvis had also arrived in Calcutta:

Poor fellow, I am sorry to say his prospect is a very dreary one as he will most probably be a year in India before he gets even an Ensign's Commission and altho' I have not the pleasure of his acquaintance, I thought it a kind of duty to point out and exhort him to avoid those snares which generally lead young men into the most unpleasant circumstances on their first arrival in India.

It also seemed probable that Richard would, at last, be able to meet up with his cousin, George Purvis, Barrington's brother, whom he had not seen since his arrival in India, as his Battalion was now stationed at Benares, within a day's journey of Mirzapur. This, he realised, would please his father who was a great believer in family unity and never failed to enquire after his nephews.

Though the news had not yet reached Richard, his brother John, aged twenty-two, had been promoted Post Captain on 16th September when he had left the *Delight* and had joined his father in the *Atlas* at Cadiz. Admiral Purvis had been heavily involved in refitting the Spanish fleet, which he had found in an appalling and unseaworthy condition, and in preparing the town for the arrival of Bonaparte's army. He had apparently had some success in meeting Lord Collingwood's instructions to overcome the distrust of the Spanish people and to gain their goodwill. James Hall, Surgeon of the *Repulse,* 74, recorded in his diary:

September 20th. Admirals Collingwood and Purvis breakfasted on board here; they then went and dined with the Governor of Cadiz. In the evening they went to the theatre, which was numerously attended. On their entrance they were loudly "huzza'd" and "Viva l'Inglese" resounded from every corner. The two Admirals returned here to sleep and early in the morning went to their ships.†

On 23rd January 1810, Vice-Admiral Purvis (he had been promoted on 25th October) had learned that the French army had forced the passes and were advancing in considerable strength on Cadiz. At last, he obtained the Governor's consent for the plan he had long advocated — to blow up the forts and batteries on the east side of the harbour. There was much loss of life as the French overran the city and gained possession of the shore defences. Fort Matagorda was gallantly defended by the British soldiers, seamen and marines who were manning it until the French batteries at Trocadero reduced it to rubble and the defenders were evacuated by the boats of the British warships.

In March, the Spanish Admiral Valdez had proposed, through the British Minister, that the British Fleet should attack the French

---

† *Sea Saga* edited by L. King-Hall, Victor Gollancz, London, 1935. P.30

stronghold at Trocadero. Admiral Purvis, having witnessed the devastation caused by the French hot shot from this fort, and realising that his ships would stand no chance in such an engagement, refused. However, he proposed a compromise: if Valdez would provide the ships, the British would man them and undertake the attack he proposed.

On 7th March, Lord Collingwood, whose health had been failing for some time, had died aboard his Flagship. Admiral Cotton had been despatched from England to replace him as Commander-in-Chief. On his arrival, Admiral Valdez had again forwarded his reckless proposal. Admiral Purvis referred it to his new Commander-in-Chief who, realising that the British Fleet would face almost certain destruction, endorsed Admiral Purvis's decision.

In April, the Admiral had sent his son John back to England with despatches and, shortly thereafter, had received orders to return to Spithead himself. This was to be the old Admiral's last voyage after nearly fifty years of distinguished service in the Royal Navy — the last four spent in one of the most difficult and important naval commands of the Peninsular War.

Now a rich man, he sold his house in Wickham and bought the mansion house and estate of Vicar's Hill, near Lymington, from where he wrote to Richard on 19th November 1810:

I have sold my house at Wickham and bought one as above which is pleasantly situated, and only twenty nine miles from Wickham. I should have been pleased to have got one nearer to our old neighbours but there was none to be had; John you will have heard got Post and is in expectation of getting a Frigate very soon, he is here and amuses himself with his gun; . . . Indeed, my dear Richard, I have every reason to be pleased and made happy by your conduct, I have heard of you from various quarters and very gratifying they have been, I wish with all my heart I could render you any assistance in your professional career, but I know not how it can be done, if you can point out the way I shall be very glad to follow it up. . . . I have had a long and fatiguing station off and in Cadiz Harbour and had calculated to come home with my late friend Lord Collingwood and for which purpose I applied for leave but before Lord Collingwood could be relieved, he sunk under the illness which induced him to wish to retire.

Now content that Richard had overcome his earlier difficulties and was leading a blameless life, he hinted to him, for the first time, his long-resolved intention of dividing his property equally between his two sons:

It has ever been my intention, my dear Richard, to divide my attentions equally
between you and your Brother and whilst your conduct continues fair and
honourable I shall not in any way change my plan.

During the year 1810, Richard entered into correspondence with his
cousin Renira who was just eighteen. She told him that her father,
George Purvis, was carrying out major improvements to his
Blackbrook Estate at Fareham and reminded Richard of the time he
had come to visit them at Blackbrook and had failed to tip the post-
chaise boy. Richard replied:

The circumstance respecting my generosity to the Post boy I had perfectly
forgotten, and was at a loss for some time to discover your allusion. We have
none of that class in this Country on whom I could exercise such sentiments of
liberality; I was taught by yourself and your Father on that occasion; but if you
please you may publish for the information of the Gosport Postillions, that the
next time I hire a chaise to travel from thence to Blackbrook they shall most
assuredly be rewarded with a present something exceeding <u>one whole Shilling</u>: I
could only wish Fate would so direct it that the same poor unfortunate fellow who
suffered before by my Ignorance – not my parsimony, may be the happy man to
drive me and thereby receive reparation for the loss he formerly suffered.

Renira also asked him to look out for her "very particular" friend
Miss Becker who had recently gone out to Calcutta:

I should like much to see your <u>very particular</u> friend Miss Becker but I fear it will
be some years before I am gratified: I imagine it must be one of the two young
ladies I occasionally saw at Fareham on Sundays in short blue Spencers who
lived somewhere near where your poor Grandmother did. However, whether or
not, and notwithstanding the <u>very particular</u> friendship which may have subsisted
between you and her, I doubt (even should I be fortunate enough to meet her)
whether I could a bit the more dare to expect a smile: indeed I will almost engage
for it her nature has by this time under gone much surprising alteration that even
yourself could scarcely make certain of it. . . . Your friend will have rather a
mortifying trial to go through at first: The Rules of Precedence amongst the
Ladies in the Calcutta society are as rigidly laid down and as strictly adhered to
as they are with respect to the several ranks of the Army. . . . However, if your
friend is, as you say, a pretty girl, she will not long have to endure these
humiliations: – but by attracting the notice of some person of distinguished rank
will shortly become a leading character in Society.

Richard told her that he had heard from John Scott, his old shipmate
from the *London* who had distinguished himself with such bravery
at Ferrol and in whom his father had always seemed to take a
particular interest:

I received a letter from Scott at the same time with yours: Barrington met him at Madeira where his ship was last May. It gave me pleasure to hear from so old a friend; but his letter does not appear to be written in such good spirits as I could wish: – not in such good spirits as yours was – notwithstanding it was a rainy day's performance.

James Ridge, Adjutant of the 2/21st, was on his way back to England on furlough. His mother lived in Fareham and Richard asked Renira to look out for him:

You will shortly see an acquaintance of mine in your neighbourhood Capt. Ridge of this Service, whose Mother has, I believe, lately removed from Winchester and settled at Fareham: you will find him a very pleasant and genteel young man should you meet him, which I trust you will in the midst of all the Gaiety which you mention is now carried on at Fareham.

Richard was charmed by Renira's letters with their news of home and their lighthearted, inconsequential chatter about balls and parties. She had added a postscript demanding an early reply with which he was only too happy to comply.

One of the civilian friends that Richard had made at his previous station was Thomas Thornhill who had been the Judge and Magistrate at Bareilly since 1804. Thornhill had prospered in his profession and indulged his passion for racing with the ownership of several thoroughbred horses which he ran in the Bareilly race meetings which attracted a large attendance from many miles around. Now, Thornhill wanted some leave before his return to England but every application he made seemed to be thwarted by the Government for whom he had a low regard:

Government have with their usual good nature refused to grant me leave of absence notwithstanding I told them I was going home next year and wished to take leave of my friends in this part of India, but being given to lying themselves, I suppose they suspected me of the same vice, however I don't much mind as I am determined to travel up by Dack to the Races and shall have my sport and save my Batta.

Young Edward Bowerbank was still serving under Casement with the Light Company which had not yet rejoined its parent battalion. Richard had for some time been concerned about him; he had seemed to have become increasingly listless and lacking in his previous high spirits:

Believe me, I rejoice in the hope of soon seeing you. This weather disagrees with me — I can neither read, write or employ myself in any other way with ease or pleasure.

This had been confirmed by James Ridge:

The Butcha I'm sorry to say looks exceedingly ill. This weather is certainly sufficient to take the Europe bloom out of any body's cheeks.†

Richard had last heard from Bowerbank just before Christmas when the Light Company was in the middle of a march from Cawnpore to join a force which was assembling at Aligarh — for what purpose nobody yet knew. Certainly Edward's description of his entrée into fashionable Cawnpore society had shown a flash of his previous puckish humour:

I made an unfortunate tho' remarkable entree among the Cawnpore fashionables, for I did not arrive till dinner was nearly over and being something staggered by the stare which was bestowed on me in endeavouring to make my best bow to Mrs. S. and just as my eyes in this act of obeisance were turned up under the lids, a black rascal carrying an immense goose stepped before me, and the whole of my face coming in contact with the upper crust of it, my nose dived to the bottom and on pulling it out I was immediately known for a Yorkshire yokel.

But it was the final paragraph of his letter which heightened Richard's anxiety for his young friend whose behaviour had never previously been marked by diffidence or contrition:

Make my best remembrances to Hunter, Matthew and all friends. I shall be an old soldier by the time I come back and have learnt subordination which in this country is the most difficult part of one's duty. I often look back with the sincerest regret at the pert and insolent conduct which I have been guilty of on many occasions since I joined my Corps and which might have missed me for life had I met with men of less sincerity and consideration than those whom I had the folly to offend.

It was the last that Richard ever heard from Edward Bowerbank who returned home on Sick Certificate on 17th July 1810 and died shortly after his arrival in England. His death is recorded thus: "Died at Chiswick 31 May 1811 at the house of his brother, Revd.

---

† N.M.M. Ref: PRV/101 *Loose Papers* MS.55/029

Thomas Bowerbank, Vicar of Chiswick, after excrutiating suffering of more than two years, brought on by fatigue and the effects of the climate". He had not yet reached the age of twenty-three.

# 8. Recommendation

*Mirzapur, India. 1811.*

In March 1811, during operations in the Rajah of Rewah's territory, the 2/21st, led by their Commanding Officer Lieutenant-Colonel Tetley, mounted an unsuccessful attack on a fort known as the Bapawy Ghurry. The *"East India Military Calendar"* reported that Colonel Tetley had been slightly wounded but tells nothing of the action other than to record that:

Having destroyed all the forts of the Sirdars, of the banditti, who had plundered and murdered the riotts of Mirzapore, and fulfilled the orders of Government, by receiving compensation for losses, and surety for future conduct; he [Colonel Tetley] received the thanks of Major-General Wood, commanding the Benares Division of the army.

He did not, however, receive the thanks of his own officers who had a different tale to tell. Both Richard's and John Home's Companies were on outpost duties at the time. George Casement received a full account of the action from one of the officers who was present. John Home wanted to send it on to Richard but Casement would not part with it.

I should enclose it could I but persuade George Casement to permit me, tho' why he keeps it I don't know but he is so annoyed about the d----d Light Company that he does not know what he is about; the truth is, the Colonel has not behaved very well . . .

On the approach to the fort, the guns, which were necessary for the success of the action, had been left behind with Johnson and Watson. The attack had therefore failed but Tetley was accused of having detained the Battalion under heavy fire from the fort without exposing himself to danger. There had also been some sort of serious altercation between the Colonel and James Cock, the latter, it was said, having refused to obey an order.

On 7th May, Richard's friend Thomas Thornhill, the Judge at Bareilly, wrote to him with another facet of the sad affair:

The other day I received a letter from James giving an account of the masterly generalship of your Commandant, but James's powers of description fall very short of those of his master who has written a detail of his warlike deeds to Mrs. Gillman. I have not seen the letter but am told by those who have that it surpasses all belief — "To Mrs. Gillman, Bareilly, Ceded and Conquered" — and in the corner — "Lt. Col. J. Tetley, Commandant" — the cypher of vast dimensions and inscribed "[Toolpacan Jung] Colonel. Colonel Jas. Tetley Bahaudar" — two flaming swords crossed, drawn on the envelope and the words ["fall two hours"] written underneath. He gives an account of the country, its produce and inhabitants and the cause of the war but no mention of a retreat. He weeps for the loss of his beloved sepoys and glories in the wounds recd. by his gallant son and gives an account of Cock's mutinatious behaviour . . . and of his having in consequence degraded him from the Right Grenadiers to a Battn. Compy., desires that Mister Brooker may be informed that he is not yet too old or infirm for active actual service and concludes with a fervent hope that his late conduct has entitled him to the applause of his fair correspondent's good man John Gillman.

Even Dr. Ridges had heard about it:

I am sorry to hear the loss your Battn. has sustained in the late attack. Poor T. is, I fear, no general and like many others too obstinate to listen to advice.†

He also used the opportunity to lobby for the return of his old cook for whom, it seems, John Swinton did not share his regard:

Casement told me when last here that Lieut. Swinton did not like Ram Sing my old cook. If so, I wish he would resign him, I should feel myself much obliged to him. The man suits me better than any other person I could get. Indeed I never had any other cook since my arrival in India [who suited me better].†

About the same time, Ensigns Ferrell and Jolliffe left the Battalion to join the force which was to invade the French-held Island of Java in August. The French-occupied islands in the Indian Ocean had for long provided sanctuary to a fleet of privateers which preyed on the Company's shipping. In 1809, no less than six Indiamen had been captured by French privateers which partly accounted for the fact that so much mail went missing between Europe and Bengal in this year. In 1809 the British had taken Rodriguez and in 1810 Réunion and the Isle of France (Mauritius). Bonaparte attached great importance to retaining Java, his last stronghold in the Indian Ocean, and the capital, Batavia, had therefore been heavily fortified by the French who believed the town to be impregnable.

On 26th August 1811, Batavia was stormed and the French routed with considerable loss of life on both sides. The invading force included 7,000 volunteer sepoys of the Bengal Army for whom it was a signal victory against European troops on foreign soil. Ferrell and Jolliffe remained in Java as part of the occupying force.

Also in 1811, Lieutenant-General Sir George Nugent replaced General Hewett as Commander-in-Chief in India and an opportunity at last presented itself for a recommendation for Richard. His stepmother had apparently met Lady Nugent, or had mutual friends, and wrote to her, before her departure for India, recommending Richard to her husband's attention. The Admiral wrote to Richard on 24th November:

In consequence of the hint you gave us expecting a recommendation for the attainment of a Staff appointment, your good Mother applied to some of her Friends to solicit that favor of Sir George Nugent who writes he has taken down your name with others on a list from which he means to make memorandum on the voyage out, but that independent of kindness and civilities, essential services cannot properly be promised as that must depend on individual merit and a variety of circumstances that can only be judged of and acted upon on the spot; so that you will perceive how uncertain the chance is of your succeeding, unless your good Character has or may be made known at Head Quarters, from some Officer of Rank and consequence; you may be well assured my dear Richard I feel every possible anxiety to render you all the services I can and if these applications made by your Mother should prove fortunate, it will make us both extremely happy;

Life at Vicar's Hill apparently suited the Admiral and his wife. Before their move from Wickham, Elizabeth's health had not been good, necessitating regular trips to Bath, but by 17th March 1812:

. . . your good Mother has indeed wonderfully recovered her health since she came here, the sea air agrees well with her, and we have plenty of it being only a mile from salt water, and can see the ships pass to the Needles from the windows of the house. You will by this time have received an Account of your being recommended to the attention of Sir George Nugent, through the influence of your Mother and though I wish you not to place too great dependence on its success, for fear of disappointment, yet we have great hopes from the reply made to the application and the lively interest shewn by Lady Nugent in your favour. I am well pleased with the contents of your letter and I have no doubt of your endeavours to establish as good a character as I can possibly wish you to possess by which means you will not fail to share with your Brother such advantages as I may have the means ultimately of giving you.

John, commanding the *Gannymede,* a small frigate, was presently on passage from Cadiz to England transporting the newly-appointed Spanish Ambassador to the Court of Saint James.

Richard was due for home leave in 1814 to which he greatly looked forward. However, should he, in the meantime, obtain a staff appointment through Sir George Nugent's interest, he would have to consider whether to defer his leave which, if he took it, might have a detrimental effect upon whatever improvement to his prospects he had gained. This point had not escaped his father:

In respect to your coming home in 1814 you may be assured it will not fail to afford us great satisfaction and this will of course be your Head Quarters. You must be the judge however as to the propriety of leaving any Staff Appointments which may fall to your lot, and at any rate take the advice of Sir George Nugent before you finally determine, he having expressed himself in such a way as to give us cause to think he will endeavour to serve you if he should find your character and abilities such as to warrant the measure.

Admiral Purvis, though enjoying the peace of his retirement after a very busy life, missed the company of the young men who had always surrounded him and no doubt benefited from his good advice, and told Richard that any of his friends returning to England on furlough would always be welcome house guests at Vicar's Hill. When John Johnson left India on furlough in 1811, Richard therefore entrusted him with some letters and legal papers to be delivered into the hands of his father and knew that he would be well received. Johnson arrived in Lymington in May 1812:

Mr. Johnson landed at Lymington and sent the Letters up to me here, I immediately went and brought him up, but could not prevail on him to stay more than two days he being so anxious to meet his Friends from whom he has so long been separated, but he has promised me he will pay me a visit when he is more at liberty. In the short time he favor'd us with his company, we were too much pleased with him to let him depart without this promise of coming again, he is indeed a very nice well inform'd young man.

During his stay at Vicar's Hill, John Johnson no doubt gave the Admiral a full account of his son's activities and achievements which clearly pleased him:

I certainly do amuse myself about my little domain but never at a time when I can communicate to you the pleasure I always have in hearing such good accounts of you; I have already in former letters told you what I now repeat, that whilst your conduct continues such as it has been you will always share my esteem, love and future favor.

Richard had consulted his Agents in Calcutta regarding the inheritance he had received from his aunt, Lady Bellenden, and had been advised that it would be in his interests to have dividends credited to his account in India rather than in London. He therefore executed a new Power of Attorney and, anxious that his father should not misinterpret his motives, wrote to explain:

You may possibly be led to suspect I have it in view to get my cash remitted to this country for the purpose of supporting some extravagance for which my pay has proved insufficient, but allow me to assure you the fact is so far contrary that I have a balance in my favor already in my agent's hands even after paying the sum mentioned in my last letter for my house.

\* \* \*

One profound benefit which the British brought to India, and to which even the most extreme critics of the Raj must concede, was the destruction of the Pindaris. These were massive bands of mounted outlaws who left a trail of devastation through Central India and the Deccan in the early 19th century. They were a product of the anarchy which raged unchecked as the Moghul Empire disintegrated. The bands comprised both Hindus and Muslims, many being ex-soldiers of the partially-suppressed Marathas.

Having targeted an area, the Pindari bands of up to 3,000 mounted men and women, unencumbered by tents and baggage, would sweep down on their victims at a speed which made their interception almost impossible. They swept the area clean of cattle and property, destroying what they could not carry away, murdering and raping the inhabitants of whole villages and inflicting the most barbaric tortures on those who would not divulge the whereabouts of their valuables. Their cruelty was quite unprecedented, even in the lawless conditions of the time. Every village lived in dread of their arrival and many women committed suicide on news of their approach.

Early in 1812, Pindari bands raided Mirzapur, where Richard's Regiment was stationed, and other targets in the Company's territories in South Bihar. It would be several years before the British mounted their major, and successful, offensive to destroy the Pindaris but, during the first half of 1812, the 2/21st was engaged in checking their incursions around Mirzapur.

In May 1812, the 2/21st moved to Barrackpore, just north of Calcutta, but William Price of the 2/5th was still in action against the Pindaris in the Mirzapur area:

We are all in motion in this district. Our detachment at present consists of Colonel Martindell and a squadron of cavalry of the 3rd and a galloper, C Company of our battalion and half a company of pioneers. We marched from Kita on the 21st ulto. We have not yet exceeded 50 miles from Kita as yet, and I suppose it is the Colonel's object to remain in this vicinity as it is a favorable position for pursuing the Pindaris should they be so lucky as to elude the detachment above us. I think these preparations will end in something, for Government will hardly be at the expense of making these arrangements every year solely for the protection of our territory — it is supposed that Taindeah is encouraging these marauders to visit our provinces; should it be the case it is to be hoped that Government will hold him responsible for all depredations they may commit. Three more troops are coming in to Bundelkund and great preparations have been made at Mirzapore, Benares and Sassevar for the reception of the Pindaris.

Richard's new posting at Barrackpore entailed periodic garrison duties at Fort William and he soon learned that an officer with access to the shops and bazaars of the capital was expected to shop for his friends up-country for items which they could not obtain. William Price, not unsurprisingly, wanted a gun:

Will you do me the favor of enquiring at the various shops in Calcutta whether there are any Jack Mantons of the old construction similar to the one that Home got for me — if you should by chance fall in with one that you think what answers me (and you know that your taste and mine agree) with open locks, purchase it immediately and write me a line, and I will send you an order on my Agents for the amount and will give directions how it is to be forwarded . . . buy also a good stock of powder and shot for me.

The shopping lists of his friend Wilkinson at Gorakhpur were of a more domestic nature:

. . . a set of tumblers, Claret and Madeira glasses to match, say 3 doz. of each and 3 sets of Smyths tooth brushes — a boat which Joseph Taylor is about to send up to Forde could be a grand opportunity of forwarding these. I am not anxious for a border to the glasses provided they have cut stems and the tumblers are fluted, but I am sure I shall approve anything you select. 12 yards of each of the accompanying breadths of ribbon and a couple of nail brushes may be added to the assortment if the funds are adequate and will claim Mrs. W.'s best thanks.

Richard had met "Griff" Wilkinson when he was stationed at Mirzapur. ("Griff", short for "Griffin", was a sobriquet applied to all newcomers to India who were green in the ways of the country and which Wilkinson, for some reason, was to retain.) He was a businessman with interests in saltpetre, indigo and timber and lived at Gorakhpur with his wife and mother. Being "in trade" carried a certain stigma in British India and there was consequently little social contact between the business and military communities. Wilkinson, however, was an exception. His background was similar to that of the 2/21st's officers and he became a great favourite with them all.

In 1812 his future prospects seemed to depend upon whether or not he could obtain a contract from the Government for the supply of saltpetre. If this could not be secured, it would entail his moving his operation to Java which he was disinclined to do:

[My time] has of late been engrossed by a correspondence with Government on the subject of a contract for saltpetre which, if accepted on the terms I have proposed, will prevent the necessity of my going to Java . . . I am just now in a most unpleasant state of suspense and Govt. are in general so dilatory in their discussions on all matters of this nature that I cannot hope to know my fate in less than another month. The circumstances of Gladwin's death, as preventing the possibility of reference to an experienced Resident, will retard the discussions, but may ultimately prove beneficial by removing those obstacles which I know he was prepared to throw in the way of a measure which, if acceded to, may have tended to diminish the amount of his commission. To you who know how many inducements I have to remain stationary, it is needless to enlarge on the anxiety with which I await a determination that probably involves all my future prospects and must lengthen or curtail the period of our beloved mother's residence with us, since her encountering the climate of Java is totally out of the question . . . I have the promise of ample support whenever a considerable capital can be invested to advantage and the situation is favorable for the purchase both of cloths and sugar. In the interim I can jog on quickly [if need be] by the sale of my Indigo Factories from all apprehensions of incurring heavy loss.

Nearly two years had now expired since his stepmother, so Richard had been led to understand, had written to Lady Nugent regarding his recommendation to the Commander-in-Chief. A vacancy would occur within the next couple of years for the quartermaster's appointment in the Regiment which would be of great benefit to Richard. Although not directly in the C-in-C's gift, with his recommendation Richard would be sure to be appointed. He had never met his stepmother, though their correspondence had always been most cordial, and had no particular reason to trust her. There had been no response whatever from the C-in-C's Headquarters and doubts began to form in Richard's mind: what if his stepmother had not written to Lady Nugent at all, or perhaps did not even have her acquaintance, but had told his father otherwise to calm his anxiety to do something positive for his son? He expressed these fears to Wilkinson who suggested a simple solution:

The [terms] of your recommendation to the Commander in Chief warrants I think more sanguine expectations from his patronage than you have ventured to indulge nor should you be backward in soliciting his attention to your interests whenever a favorable opportunity occurs for so doing . . . petticoat influence may now safely be relied on [to be] as effective [as] any other and . . . if the Quartermaster-ship is your object, I would on no account delay a communication on the subject since this may obviate the plea not infrequently made use of by men in power when an application is deferred till the vacancy takes place of its being too late and I believe you are aware that others in the Regiment have an eye to Swinton's promotion. A letter to Lady Nugent might have a good effect now. Can there be any impropriety in your thanking her for the interest which you are given to understand from home she was kind enough to evince in your favor — [it would be well] on this occasion to refresh her Ladyship's memory by mentioning the name of the parties with whom she communicated and <u>her answer will confirm or remove your suspicions of the deception practised on your father.</u> My anxiety for your success has suggested this hint, my dear Purvis, and your better judgement will adopt or reject it as circumstances may render advisable.

When Richard arrived in Calcutta it had been his intention to attend one of the Public Breakfasts which were held twice a week to enable new arrivals to to be presented to the Commander-in-Chief. But on making application he learned that they had just been discontinued as the C-in-C was about to leave for a tour of the Stations up-country. Instead, he wrote to Lieutenant-Colonel Murray, the C-in-C's Military Secretary:

Sir,  In consequence of my misfortune in losing the opportunity of doing myself the honor to wait upon His Excellency the Commander in Chief in Calcutta, by means of the Battalion to which I am attached arriving at the Presidency only a few days previous to His Excellency's departure for the Upper Provinces and further owing to letters I have recently received from England urging me not to be backward (although it is with reluctance I am obliged to resort to this means) in making myself known to His Excellency, in consequence of my having been recommended to His Excellency's notice by my friends in England. I am induced to take the liberty of soliciting you would do me the favor to address His Excellency in my behalf, mentioning that as I am informed His Excellency had the kindness to answer my friends, his providing for me rested upon the character I supported in the Army as an Officer, (on which point I venture to trust His Excellency has been satisfied,) and on my capacity to hold any situation which might better my prospects in the Service, I should esteem myself ever obliged and indebted to His Excellency would he have the goodness (provided it does not interfere with any previous arrangements) to have me in remembrance at the time the appointment of Quarter Master of the Regiment to which I belong becomes vacant. I rely upon His Excellency's pardon for the liberty I have taken in thus daring to address him, in consideration of its being the only means by which I could hope for the honor of any notice from His Excellency.

If Sir George Nugent had not yet favoured Richard with his interest, he certainly received the credit for the next momentous incident in the history of the 2/21st — the hated Lieutenant-Colonel Tetley was removed and sent in command to the 2/24th. Wilkinson wrote to Richard:

I must sincerely congratulate you on the removal of your late commanding officer and rejoice that it took place in a manner so well calculated towards the feelings of one who for years past appears to have thought any regard to the feelings of others unnecessary and has done every thing in his power to irritate the minds of those who were in any degree under his control. The examples that have lately been made of some obnoxious characters by supercession and removal will have a good effect throughout the army and I suppose your present Commander-in-Chief bids fair to be more popular than most of his predecessors.

Richard, speaking of Mirzapur in a letter to his father added:

It was in that direction, from Mirzapur, where our late obnoxious Commanding Officer, without exposing his own person, detained part of the Battalion under the fire of a fort in the manner I described in a former letter – Johnson may have enlarged upon this subject and divers others relative to that Commanding Officer: but I am now happy to say the penetration and justice of Sir George Nugent has at length released us from the tyranny we had for years been obliged patiently to suffer. To my shame I have neglected writing to Johnson since the fortunate event occurred, and it is a subject on which, as brother sufferers, we could have exchanged long discourses. We have an excellent Commander now, Gentlemanly and Friendly in his private character but justly strict in exacting the full performance of our duty.

Great had been the jubilation in the 2/21st Officers' Mess and in the barrack rooms of the NCOs and Sepoys when the Regiment had learned who was to join them as their new Commander — recently promoted to Lieutenant-Colonel — none other than their old and trusted friend William Nichol.

# 9. Progress

*Vicar's Hill, near Lymington, Hampshire.*
*19th October 1812.*

Admiral Purvis now had much more time to write to his sons, though he had never been negligent in so doing, even during the most demanding period of his professional career. But now he could write in the comfort of his own study with its windows overlooking the rolling, green, English lawns of Vicar's Hill. He could wish that he had a view of the sea from the ground floor; but he had a vantage point at a first floor window from which he could see the ships beating up the Solent from the Needles. His telescope, which had accompanied him for so many years, in so many of His Majesty's Ships, lay on a table beside the window and, from time to time in the course of the day, he would find himself drawn to his observation point to scan the distant water for sail.

His son John had commanded his frigate the *Gannymede* for a year now. He was in the Mediterranean under the command of the Admiral's old friend, Sir Edward Pellew, who had promised him to attend to his son's interests. Would that he would give him a really good cruise so he could get some Prize Money.

He had so much enjoyed having Richard's friend Johnson to stay with him at Vicar's Hill and had been much gratified by the good account he had given him of Richard's character. Johnson had promised to pay them another visit, and not such a fleeting one, before he returned to India but he had heard nothing from him since. Richard had given him some cause for anxiety in the past; but that was all over with now. He had not seen him since he was a boy of fourteen and had no doubt that he had now grown into a fine young man. Having written down the family news he felt he should remind Richard of his expectations:

I have in a previous letter told you that the greater part of my Property will hereafter be divided between your Brother and you, provided I see no cause for altering my plan, which has always been to place both my Sons on an equal footing.

Then, the old Admiral, who had been a major protagonist in the war against Bonaparte, who had corresponded and discussed command decisions with such men as Lord Collingwood, the Duke of Wellington, Sir Colin Campbell and Sir John Moore, set out for Richard his personal view of the political situation in Europe:

The fate of all Europe is now depending on the result of two vast Armies in the heart of Russia: Bonaparte has headed one to overthrow the Government of Russia and they have had some desperate battles already and, each being determined to persevere, there is every reason to expect there will be very hard fighting. The French have possessed themselves of Moscow but not before the greater part of that fine City was reduced to ashes; it is said Bonaparte has made offers of peace to the Russians but their Emperor has declared he never will directly or indirectly enter into any negotiation until the Enemy shall have quitted [Russian soil]; the season of the year, the difficulty of obtaining Provisions and Ammunition and the very great distance Bonaparte has to look for his supplies of men and necessities of all kinds, gives us hopes that his Army will, by desertion and sickness, crumble away and be no more formidable either to Russia or any other country; the French are said to have lost in one Battle 40,000 men and the Russians not a great deal less. Lord Wellington has done wonders in Spain: the Armies of France in that country have been very roughly treated by that great General and please God to spare his life and bless him with health, he will be the happy means of relieving the Peninsula from the oppressions of a faithless Enemy. Cadiz is relieved from the Siege, and many of the great Towns are evacuated by the hated French; Lord Wellington has shewn Bonaparte his soldiers are not Invincible and what they are to expect if ever they should visit this Country; the deep rooted [hatred] of Bonaparte against this Nation is beyond any calculation and, should he succeed in his views against Russia, nothing can satisfy him short of the [total] destruction of our Navy, and our complete humiliation, but I trust we shall continue to frustrate all his wicked views and not only save our own Country but spur up others to a sense of their degraded situation and induce them to shake off the tyrannic yoke they have so long submitted to. America you will find has [recognised] also the danger of Bonaparte and has been induced through him to make war against us; but as the great Body of the people in that Country are completely against the measure I think peace with them will soon be established.

The circumstances which eventually vindicated Richard's step-mother from the deceit of which he had suspected her, were the result of a curious, and ultimately unprofitable, sequence of events. On 19th February 1812, James Ridge had married Harriet Essex Nichol, daughter of William Nichol, at Calcutta. Wishing, the

following year, to take his bride on a belated honeymoon, he put in
for six months local leave which meant that the Adjutancy would be
vacant for this period. Colonel Nichol had Richard in mind for the
temporary appointment but deferred to his new son-in-law's
recommendation that George Casement should be given the job. No
sooner had the decision been made than an order was received from
Sir George Nugent, who was 800 miles up-country at the time,
nominating Lieutenant Purvis for the appointment. By this time,
James Ridge had decided he would not take his leave after all so, in
the event, the Adjutancy never became vacant.

Nevertheless, the C-in-C's intervention proved to Richard that he
did enjoy his interest, despite his previous doubts. He wrote to his
father telling him how he had followed this up with a letter to Lady
Nugent:

In this I was guided by the supposition that it was to her Ladyship in particular I
had been recommended. I took occasion to hint that there would be a vacancy in
the Regimental Staff ere long, when I should hope to be honored with similar
remembrances from her Ladyship and his Excellency which I have no doubt will
be the case should the opportunity of Quarter Master fall vacant while in his gift.

By now, Richard saw the hopelessness of the quixotic sentiments he
had expressed to his brother five years earlier: to stand any chance
of accelerating the turgid progress of his career he must be prepared
to prostrate himself before anyone who could conceivably assist
him. Moreover, the value of Sir George Nugent's patronage would
shortly be usurped with the arrival of the new Governor-General,
Lord Moira, who, it was said, was to take upon himself the
appointment of Commander-in-Chief. In England, his father was
doing what he could:

I have been trying to obtain letters to his Lordship on your account but have not
yet succeeded.

Clearly, Richard must make efforts of his own and not rely upon
those of his family at home:

. . . for I trust it will afford you almost equal pleasure to hear of my advancement
by interest of my own making as it would were it to happen through the means
provided by yourself.

Richard made himself known to Mr. R.P. Ricketts at Benares, a very senior civil servant who was a friend, or relative, of the Garretts. He was friendly and sympathetic to Richard's appeal but his mind was occupied at the time by the illness of his little daughter, Louisa, whom he was having to send back to England with his wife. Nevertheless, he promised to keep Richard in mind:

It has afforded us much real satisfaction to find that the little attention we had it in our power to evince towards you during your sojourn in this District was as gratifying to your feelings and have to regret that circumstances should have occurred to prevent my fulfilling my wish of furthering your prospects but you may rest assured whenever I have it in my powers so to do you will not be forgotten.

James Ridge did not approve of Ricketts's sporting standards:

Mr. Ricketts has killed a tiger from a machan [shooting platform] — this is murder without sport and would not give us Bareilly logue [people] the smallest pleasure . . . †

He had, however, before his marriage to Harriet Nichol, thought highly of Rickets's wife, Sophia:

I could not say enough in her favour. She is exactly the woman I think I should out of a great number choose for a wife. †

Richard was delighted to hear again from his cousin Renira at Blackbrook. She gave him a full description of Vicar's Hill and included a sketch she had done of the mansion house. But the main topic in her letter was the recommendation of a bride for Richard when he returned to England.

A first cousin of the Admiral, William Purvis, had married Susannah Eyre, daughter and heiress of Samuel Eyre, M.P. for Sarum and proprietor of the Newhouse estate near Salisbury. William Purvis had changed his name to Eyre on his wife's inheritance of Newhouse. He had died in 1810 (the Admiral and his brother George were chief mourners at his funeral) leaving four daughters the eldest of whom, Harriet, was the heiress to the Newhouse estate and the object of Renira's astute recommendation.

---

† N.M.M. PRV/101 *Loose Papers* MS.55/009

I have to thank you . . . for the recommendation of a wife in Miss Eyre, should I
be inclined for one on my return to Europe: but let me tell you, your interest with
the Heiress of Newhouse must be exceeding great to induce her to favor any offer
from one so devoid of personal recommendations as your Cousin Richard who,
to the pretty figure you may remember him, can boast no additional attraction
except the Mahogany tint resulting from constant exposure to the effects of an
Indian climate.

He had not, he told her, yet had a chance to present himself to
Renira's friend, Mrs. Thackery, who had recently arrived in India:

I have not yet been in company with your friend Mrs. Thackery, except in
Ballrooms and the like, where she is amongst the most admired of the females,
and really is in my opinion the finest looking woman I have seen at the Calcutta
Assemblies: but this you must understand is no great compliment for generally
speaking we can boast no display of Beauty, the female society chiefly consists
of such ladies as have despaired of attracting admirers at home, and resolve to try
their fortunes in a land where the trifling charms (a white face, for instance)
which they do possess are higher valued.

He hastened to reassure her that this did not apply to young ladies
whose families already resided in India, such as her friend Louisa
Ridge, James Ridge's sister, who was shortly to come out to join
him and:

. . . who it is most likely will become a member of our Regiment, as the Brother,
our Adjutant, is a married man, therefore it may be expected she will chiefly
reside with him, and may probably engage the attention of some of the gallant
young men so as to be permanently attached to our society.

In his letters to Renira, Richard was more forthright in expressing
his homesickness and his ever-growing dislike of the Indian life. He
explained to her that he was compelled for financial reasons to seek
preferment even though its attainment would delay his return:

So long and so anxiously as I have looked forward to the blessing of returning
amongst you all, this place, I confess, is greatly at variance with the genuine
wishes of my heart; inasmuch as I could be content it were ordained that no
situation should be offered me, the emoluments of which would oblige me (such
is the duty we owe ourselves) to remain in this detested Country – and the anxiety
expressed in your letter, in the name of all your family, tends not a little to
enhance, in my estimation, the sacrifice I shall make in the pursuit of my present
plan.

He returned Georgina's love and begged Renira to get her to write

to him; he described the wonderful tropical fruit which they daily
enjoyed in India — pineapples, bananas, pomelos, mangos and
lychees — but admitted that:

I should exchange them all for a simple Nectarine out of your Blackbrook garden.
You will have a comfortable fire-side at the time this reaches you: and it seems
to me at this moment I could resign all my prospects for the same enjoyment with
your happy family: – such as we were wont to have, and with poor John Leman
too.

Richard's correspondence with Renira had been warm, affectionate
and completely correct as Richard knew by now that his brother
John was in love with her. He wondered if the playful matchmaking
in her letter might be a gentle way of telling him that she entertained
the same feelings for John and that Richard should never venture to
hope that the relationship between her and him could ever be
anything other than that of affectionate cousins and friends. Every
letter he had received from John contained some tender reference to
Renira and, to rationalise the matter in his own mind, Richard went
through all John's letters and copied out the relevant passages:

10 Feb 1808 – You cannot conceive what a nice girl our Cousin Renira is – very
accomplished and is now at Bath with her Father and Mother, just about to be
introduced into company. She will not be long single when once her value is
known.

25 May 1808 — Our Cousin Renira will be a very accomplished pretty girl and
I hope will meet with a good husband.

21 Apr 1809 — Do not marry or get in love abroad: I have been so once: it is all
over now and I will never again entangle myself.

5 May 1810 — At Fareham Assembly, I thought Renira the prettiest girl in the
room: more this deponent sayeth not.

1 Nov 1810 — The Blackbrookites and I are, entre nous, a la distance: – now for
the story: I, sailor like, kept backing and filling in the wake of our Cousin Renira
who, by the bye, to a seaman's eye, is a Light Frigate, straight stemmed, fine head
sails, figure head lean, and in every respect true built; in fact I thought her just
suited for a young Post Captain like myself; but as the devil would have it, just
as I was about to ask the First Lord for her, he took notice of my attentions and
thus addressed me: – "I do not like you paying so much attention to your cousin
– I shall not allow it." Upon which, with good steerage way, I threw all aback and,
paying off on the other tack, have not been near any of the family since.

27 Mar 1811 — Twelve months on shore which is a good spell, and what is extraordinary – not married: however, it shall not be long first if I can accomplish it. – Renira is a fine bouncing country wench and just opening upon the world, and in appearance calculated to attract any man: she is a good tempered girl, but in my opinion was taken away from school a little too young: you may possibly discover my remark as I understand she is in the habit of corresponding with you; I have not seen her lately.

20 Aug 1813 — The Blackbrook people I never hear from – such a history I will give you when we meet as will certainly astonish you. Poor Renira cannot help herself and between ourselves, the more I see of her the deeper in love I get: the time will come (if a certain person does not make a previous disposal of her hand) when I shall be happy. From her letters to me I am sure he cannot dispose of her heart: she is an affectionate good girl, and in a cottage, with a little attention, will make a good wife. I try to forget her – still if an eligible good offer is made her I should be the first to advise her to accept it.

Richard could not understand what his uncle had against John: he had made Post Captain at the unusually early age of twenty-two and had prospects of an excellent career in the Navy and good expectations on his father's death. Indeed, Renira had told Richard in one of her letters that her father had it in mind to entrust his only son, George, to John's patronage at sea in due course. It could surely not be because John and Renira were first cousins — marriage between such was quite common. Yet his uncle clearly did not wish them to marry and Richard could only assume that his uncle had ambitions for an even better match.

Unless, of course, that paragraph in John's letter of April 1809 held the clue. George Purvis knew many senior officers in the Navy and, if this affair, whatever it may have been, had left any taint on John's good character, news of it might well have got back to his uncle. There again, Richard knew that his brother had "suffered from the embraces of those of the Cyprian class" which knowledge, if transmitted to his uncle by the same means, might very well account for his hostility.

In 1813 two newly-commissioned Ensigns joined the 2/21st. The first, Wemyss Macleod, was another Highlander, the fifth and youngest son of Revd. Angus MacLeod, Minister of Rogart in Sutherland. The second, John Neufville, had been educated at Eton and was the son of Jacob Neufville, a French emigré who lived at

Grove House, Lymington. Admiral Purvis had been approached by his mother to request the favour that Richard might be asked to "notice" him but, by the time Richard had received his father's letter two years later, Neufville had decided he had had enough of India and was on his way home on furlough.

Meanwhile in Java, Ferrel, Jolliffe and James Bates, a friend of Richard's from another regiment, were finding the climate almost intolerable though life was not entirely devoid of amusement. Ferrel, in a letter to Richard, described a reception which Government had held for the Malay Chiefs:

There was a Grand Feast given to day at 12 o'clock to all the Malay Chiefs who have a Guard of Honor of 50 Sepoys, loaded mussquits, invitations to all the settlements to partake of the same. You will see them with beef, custard, port jelly, etc. all heaped together on the same plate, completely wild some of them. We go bitted and sashed — all the half cast ladies, of which there are a great number, are to be seen in the galleries — what a scene, they drink Cherry Brandy like Wine till they begin to get unruly and then they [are given] no more.

The climate was having such an effect on their health that Ferrel thought he might have to leave the island on Sick Certificate. Poor Jolliffe was even worse and was hardly recognisable from his former self:

I fancy with due deference to Mr. Jolliffe be it said that if the Isle of Wight ladies were to see him now they would not fall desperately in love with him.

To John Home, who was something of a hypochondriac, Ferrel wrote:

If you were to be here for one or two months it would cure you of all your imaginary complaints for life as you would be convinced what the real ones are.

He also asked John to remind James Cock that he had promised to write to Swinton on his behalf, to try and get him into the Pioneers.

At Gorakhpur, Griff Wilkinson had at last heard from Ricketts on the subject of his saltpetre contract:

. . . which had at least the good effect of annihilating suspense, by the assurance that I had nothing to hope or expect from the present Government.

His timber was doing well though and he hoped soon to be sending down some fir spars large enough for the main masts of 74-gun battleships. Richard had been toying with the idea of taking his furlough in 1814 and applying for a Writership when he was in England so he could start a career in the Civil Service on his return. Wilkinson advised him against it:

I . . . can imagine your impatience for the expiration of that period which is to afford a release from this vile country but if this is to be merely temporary you would surely have cause hereafter to repent the sacrifices of such an appointment as a Writership for the transient gratification to be derived from a residence in England for a couple of years the certain effect of which will be to increase your aversion to everything in India [whereas] by the exercise of a little self denial at present you had a fair prospect of quitting it for ever at the age of two and thirty.

George Casement was similarly surprised:

You are surely jesting when you talk of going home as I should think your friend Ricketts could have no difficulty in getting you some staff situation worth your acceptance as he is Principal Private Secretary to Lord Moira.

In December 1813 John Home and Richard were again in isolation at an outpost at Nudiah. They had hoped to be relieved before Christmas so they could enjoy the festivities in Barrackpore but Christmas Day arrived with no sign of a relief. A few days later Richard received a letter from Casement written on Christmas Eve:

There are not any men at Barrackpore now that can be sent to relieve you but the 25th Regt., and General Blair told Swinton two days ago that he would not send them but talked of sending two Companies from the 18th Regt. when relieved from Garrison duty so that your relief cannot march from hence before the 5th proximo and I think there is every reason to think you will not be relieved till February but of this you will form your own conclusions from what is stated above. . . . James Ridge and family came up last night and we are all to eat our Xmas dinner with Lt. Colonel William Nicholl. . . . We have no news here of any kind except that the Masonick Body are to give Lord M. a dinner on St John's Day at which Cock and I will have the honor of being present having become Masons. — We all go to Fort William on duty next month so in the event of yr. being kept at Nudiah another month I will be able to execute what commissions you or Jack may have for me in the China Bazaar after Muster.

His Masonic involvement had apparently done nothing to quench James Cock's ardour and reports of his amorous pursuits were as numerous as ever:

Our friend Cock will surely not continue for ever unsuccessful in his chase after a wife and if the Buddhpur Spinster answers his description I hope he will find her less coy than the fair Mary-Anne upon whom, if a report current after his departure is true, he tried to rain his utmost powers of persuasion.

Wilkinson, talking of the arrival in Mirzapur of a new family with two charming daughters and the departure of one similar from Gorakhpur commented:

Cock's trip to Mirzapur at this particular period looks a little suspicious but if he makes any play at Chuprahs I think he will find attractions in the Muston family sufficient to prevent his further progress. We have little chance of seeing him here as the magnet will be gone ere he arrives in the neighbourhood.

On 1st July 1814, Richard's long quest for interest and longer study of the Persian language were rewarded with his appointment as Interpreter and Quartermaster of the 2/21st. Previously, his pay had been 62 rupees per month plus *Batta* and other allowances amounting to 239 rupees making a total monthly income of 301 rupees His new appointments brought him a massive increase of 225 rupees per month which was more than enough to persuade him to defer his furlough for the time being.

Then, later in the year, in expectation of a renewed conflict with the Nepalese, the Government raised a further three regiments of Native Infantry — the 28th, 29th and 30th. This was the opportunity for advancement for which many officers had been waiting. Richard, John Johnson and John Home immediately applied for transfer to one of the new regiments and in January 1815, the year of Waterloo, were appointed to the 1/30th — Johnson in the rank of Captain and Richard and John Home as the 2nd and 3rd most senior Lieutenants respectively. In May, Richard was confirmed as Interpreter and Quartermaster of the new regiment. Things were, at last, looking up for him.

Richard's brother John was also doing well: he was still commanding the *Gannymede* in the Mediterranean and now two further ships had been placed under his orders. He realised, however, that he was lucky to have a seagoing appointment at all in view of the present situation in the Navy where a great influx of sons of the nobility over the past decade was blocking promotion channels and keeping many good officers ashore on half pay. The problem had been recognised six years earlier by Lord St. Vincent who had told the King during a private audience on his retirement:

. . . at present the Navy is so overrun by the younger branches of nobility and the sons of Members of Parliament, and they so swallow up all the patronage and so choke the channel to promotion that the son of an old officer, however meritorious both their services may have been, has little or no chance of getting on.†

Admiral Purvis also was aware that if John lost his present employment he might never go to sea again and reiterated Lord St. Vincent's fears in a letter to Richard:

It is very uncertain where John may be when you come home, for as he is employ'd his business will be to keep so, for there never was so much interest required to get off the Half Pay List as now. There are Captains of ten years standing who never commanded a Post Ship and all their applications are and have been without effect. Promotion from [due to] the multitude of Noblemen's sons introduced into the Service is totally out of the question, unless the person soliciting it has greatly distinguished himself by his bravery, in which case he is never forgot.

He also advised Richard of the death of his "Aunt Mop" (Mary Oadham Purvis) during a visit to Blackbrook the previous December.  Just before she died, she had written a little note to her brother, the Admiral, desiring her blessing and good wishes to her nephews, John and Richard.

---

† *Old Oak, The Life of John Jervis Earl of St. Vincent* by Admiral Sir William James, Longmans, Green & Co. Ltd., London, 1950. P. 209-10

# 10. Preparations for War

*Dinapur, India. December 1815.*

In the 14th century, Hindu Rajputs from India moved north to escape persecution by the then dominant Muslim Turks. They established themselves in the town of Gurkha from where, over the next 500 years, they were to conquer most of the land which today constitutes Nepal. By the early 19th century their conquered territories marched with those of the Company and conflict was inevitable. After several years of periodic armed incursions by the Gurkhas, the British eventually went to war with them in May 1814. This conflict lasted one year and saw the death in action of the great General Sir Rollo Gillespie, the conqueror of Java, and the triumph of the equally great General Sir David Ochterlony which caused the Nepalese to sue for peace. During the lengthy negotiations leading up to the consequent Treaty of Sagauli, the Gurkhas used the time to strengthen the fortifications around their capital, Kathmandu, and then refused to ratify the Treaty.

This was the situation in December 1815 when John Home and Richard arrived in Dinapur with the 1/30th to join the force which was assembling to resume war with the Nepalese. They had recently received the news of Wellington's victory at Waterloo and, with the threat of Bonaparte now finally lifted from Europe, a new spirit of optimism prevailed.

John Johnson had returned from furlough just in time to join the Regiment. He arrived driving a very smart new buggy which seemed to his friends a curious purchase in view of the fact that the Regiment was about to go to war. George Casement wrote to Richard:

He must have bought the new buggy to sport at Birhampur as John's prudence would not have thought of such a thing had there (in his opinion) been a prospect of your going into the Field.

From John Johnson, Richard received news of his family and a full description of Vicar's Hill. He had already seen Renira's sketch of the house, so he knew what it looked like, and Johnson filled in the details: it was a three-storey, white stucco mansion, built about 1767 by a Mr. Luther, with a pillared portico at the front door and a pentagonal wing protruding from each end of the main frontage. There was extensive stabling and coach houses adjacent to the house which enjoyed privacy, without isolation, on high ground above the Lymington River. The vicarage for Boldre Church was close by from which the hill had acquired its name.

The Admiral and Mrs. Purvis, Johnson told Richard, had been extremely hospitable, had gone to great lengths to ensure his comfort and had pressed him to stay longer. They kept a staff of eight — a butler, Richard Smith; a footman, George; a coachman, also George; a groom, John Gold; a housekeeper, cook and two housemaids. Of these, the only one known to Richard was Dinah Smith, the housekeeper, who had been in his father's service since he was a boy at Wickham. At that time, she had been betrothed to his father's excellent manservant, Martin, who, to the distress of the whole family, not least poor Dinah, had died in 1805. When Johnson had gone to England on his furlough, Richard had given him a sum of money with which to buy a present from him for Dinah. His father wrote:

In consequence of Mr. Johnson having mentioned your wish that he should make Dinah a present in your name, your Mother bought a handsome shawl and gave it her as from you, and I suppose the enclosed is an acknowledgement for your kindness towards her.

His stepmother added:

Dinah has desired to thank you herself for her shawl, which she is highly delighted with as well as indeed struck by your remembrance of her. She is going tomorrow for a few days to Wickham to see her old Friends there and it will be shewn in great triumph. She is a faithful good creature . . .

Also living at Vicar's Hill was Richard's old nurse, Ann Porter, who had looked after him after the death of his first stepmother, Mary Garrett, when his father was at sea. She was now eighty and in poor health:

Poor Mrs. Porter is very unwell, her power of speech has entirely left her and, although her intellects remain unimpaired, yet she is very much alter'd. She desires her best regards to you.

John Johnson told Richard that his father seemed happy and well though ever concerned for his sons' advancement and success. Like his old and revered commander, Lord St. Vincent, he took great pleasure in the running of his farm and in well-meaning, but no doubt none-the-less irritating, interference with its day-to-day routine (though not to the extent of Lord St. Vincent who, in the summer months, would greet his farm workers in the fields at 2.30 a.m. to discuss the day's work!). His father, Johnson told Richard, seemed to miss the company and conversation of men and he had felt badly about having to cancel his final visit to Vicar's Hill due to a change in his sailing orders. The Admiral had been disappointed and had written to Richard in April:

I this day receiv'd a letter from Mr. Johnson, in which he tells me he shall not be able, (as we had previously settled) to spend the latter part of his time here before he left this Country, for that he had received notice from the East India House that the ship he was to proceed in was to be dispatched from the Downs next Wednesday and sail for India without coming to Portsmouth; we saw him about three weeks ago, but his stay was then only two days, as your Uncle and his family were with us which fill'd all our beds, he had however an opportunity of becoming acquainted with them . . . Indeed, my dear Richard, we are all well pleased with Mr. Johnson and had it been convenient to him to have given us more of his company we should have been very happy.

He was also disappointed that Richard was having to delay his furlough though naturally pleased with the circumstances that had made this necessary:

I was very much pleased to find you had obtained the appointment of Linguist in so handsome a way, and altho' it will occasion a delay as to the time of our meeting, yet considering all circumstances we may hereafter be satisfied it was all for the best; for after having spent a year or two in this Country, you would probably feel a degree of reluctance at being obliged to return again to India, there to remain a longer time than if you had not avail'd yourself of your furlough.

John was still commanding the *Gannymede* but was now on the American Station, having sailed from Gibraltar with sealed orders the previous September. On 18th August 1813, he had captured the

French privateer *Vauteur,* of 7 guns, but the Prize Money had not
been significant. The Admiral finished his letter by, once again,
reassuring Richard of his expectations — as always, dependent
upon his continued good character:

You may rest assured my dear Richard that although the time for our meeting is
placed at a distance, you will find my promises respecting the division of my
Property is already secured, and that a proportion equal to that of your Brother
will ultimately become yours, unless great changes should occur on your part,
which I have no reason to think can ever happen, for indeed I am much gratified
with all I have heard of you.

Richard had, on a prior occasion, expressed his gratitude for this
comforting, if recurrent, pledge with due diplomacy:

The prospect which you mention in writing of the division of your property is, I
hope, a very very distant one but that gratitude dictates an acknowledgement of
some kind . . . to force a few cheerful words from a troubled heart – such is mine
at present, thinking on the subject – I shall barely say I thank you for the promise
of a favor which I could hope by the Blessing of God were never to be conferred!
but to conclude this, to me, gloomy subject I shall add my promise of constant
endeavours to support such a character in the world as will give you pleasure: not
for the property's sake; but to insure to you that happiness which from our earliest
years you have expressed to John and myself [to be dependant] upon the course
of our behaviour.

He had also submitted a similarly dutiful response on the subject of
his father's gout and the restoration of his good mother's health:

. . . what happiness it afforded me to see confirmed your perfect recovery from
the Gout and also that you can express yourself on that subject with such apparent
indifference, which gives me good reason to hope you are under no apprehension
of a second attack: to the Grace and Blessing of God, which by your excellent
instructions and example I have been taught daily to supplicate for those who are
dear to me. Of course I fail not of adding the Thanks and Praise which are due in
particular for His goodness herein, as well as the reestablishment of my Mother's
health

The year 1815 had seen some changes in the 2/21st. In February,
Daniel Smith had died in Chittagong, aged twenty-three, less than
six weeks after his promotion to Lieutenant. He had been present at
Tetley's attack on the Bapawy Ghurry and was a very popular
young officer. Casement wrote to Richard:

I was truly sorry to hear of Smith's death as he was as honorable a little fellow as ever lived. I trust the 2nd Bn. will not be deprived of any more of its members, a few of the 1st Bn. I think could be better spared.

In June, John Jolliffe had died in Malacca, aged twenty-eight, a victim to the crippling Java climate and in July Hugh Wrottesley had been transferred to the 1/28th. He had been trying to get out of the 2/21st for years as he had never lived down the stigma of being Tetley's favourite and had become the butt of much sarcasm. John Home had predicted his move some years ago:

I should not be surprised if . . . the continual witticisms that are put on Wrottesley would induce him to get out of this Battn. Since he came down, there has not been a day that wit has not been flying about at his expense.

George Casement, still with the 2/21st, had been engaged in the pre-Treaty phase of the Nepal War in 1815 and had reported to Richard in March that their particular section of the front seemed to be well under control. They had been expecting a hard fight at the Hurchund Ghurry and had advanced in strength only to find, to their surprise, that the enemy had evacuated the fort:

Had the enemy defended Hurchund Gurry a number of us must have got our heads broken as the place was very strong being a small mud fort surrounded by a considerable ditch outside of which there was a formidable stockade also surrounded by a ditch. In the course of the 4th and 5th we completely destroyed the stockade and blew up the fort, so that in the extent of frontier we are ordered to protect by that Great General Barrie Latter there is not a place of strength remaining in the enemy's possession. You will learn by my letter to the Colonel that on the evening of the 28th Ult. we got possession of their stockade at Ceiliah and took their best gun a brass 3-pounder without much annoyance from the [enemy].

Casement enclosed a letter he had received from Monke who had been in action against the Gurkhas on 19th February. Casement's half-brother William had taken a prominent part in the action:

As the enclosed is full of a brother's praise who I sincerely love I cannot deprive myself of the pleasure of making his actions known to you, being aware that no man admires a brave soldier more than Dick Purvis.

Monke wrote:

When we came into Camp, the Irregular Horse were preparing to go after a party of Goorkahs supposed to have taken Lieut. Pickersgill the Surveyor. Altho' I had just come off a march of 7 hours I could not resist the temptation, but set off on a small black pony. The Pickets were ordered out some time after the Cavalry. Col. Dick was mounted on an elephant. About 20 officers volunteered and were before the Infantry two miles. The Cavalry in the mean time got between the Forces and the Goorkhas. The Goorkahs charged, the Cavalry pretended to give way that the Infantry might come up. But the enemy at this time seeing the Infantry coming, retreated towards the jungle in good order. Your brother at this time said to us that as the enemy would escape unless we charged (the Infantry being two miles behind), we all set off full speed. Your brother is blood to the bone, he led the charge himself exclaiming "Now is the time for a charge" and I saw him surrounded on all sides and when the [Subedar] was fighting like a lion he said "that's a brave fellow". Wilson of the 25th cut down two men and then his sword broke. Paton of the same Corps fought most furiously as he charged . . . God knows how he escaped. However he has about a dozen slight wounds and his horse seven. I escaped but my pony was wounded by an arrow. At this time the Cavalry came amongst them and they instantly ran. And then the slaughter began, in 20 minutes not a Goorkha was to be seen, they left 90 killed, 19 wounded and 60 prisoners. The Infantry were too late for the fun. They lost two Chiefs, one named Burwannee Dutt Pappa, the name of the other I have forgot. I have got the accoutrements of the second in command and have got a lot of their poison. Muskets and matchlocks are as cheap as dirt in Camp.

The "Great General Barrie Latter" to whom Casement referred was, in fact, Captain Barré Latter who had commanded the Rangpur Local Battalion since 1813 and, during the Nepal War, was commanding a mixed force of over 2,000 Native Levies tasked with guarding the northern marches east of the Kosi River. Educated at Rugby, Latter was originally intended for the Bar and had been admitted to Lincoln's Inn in 1791 before deciding to join the Bengal Army. Throughout his career in India he collected Tibetan manuscripts with the intention of compiling a dictionary. Major R.J. Latter (who was not related) was commanding the 1/30th when Richard joined the Regiment in the absence of Lieutenant-Colonel Charles Crawford on furlough.

When the new regiments had been raised and Richard had applied for transfer, George Gordon of the 1/21st, a Highlander from Spinningdale in Sutherland, hoped he might succeed to the appointment of Quartermaster of the 2nd Battalion should Richard vacate it. He had written to him expressing this hope but, having received no reply, feared that Richard might have taken offence:

. . . as I have never heard from you since, it strikes me now that you may have conceived from my letter that I wished for nothing more than your removal at all events in order that I might grasp at your appointment; but if ever you entertained any idea of this kind you certainly were never more mistaken for at the time I wrote I had not the most distant notion of so indelicate a sentiment; . . . It did not strike me at the time that it might be possible to attach any idea of indelicacy to the communication and if you have conceived it in a selfish and rapacious light, I am sorry you know so little of me as to induce you to believe it possible I could mean it so. No Purvis, this would be beneath me, almost to any man; and to you utterly impossible; for perhaps there is no man more sensible of the excellent and amiable qualities of your character and disposition than I am, and perhaps few that have a more sincere esteem and regard for you.

Gordon had also written to the Earl of Moira but perhaps not in quite the terms likely to secure his interest:

I wrote a letter since to Lord Moira which I fancy was too plain for his delicate mind and irritable temper for his Secretary used his discretion in not producing it unless I should particularly desire him. I felt obliged to Major Doyle [for this] act and I told him not to produce the letter at all, for the Lord is a hot, passionate and pettish Irishman and he might come to harm in his paroxysms.

Gordon, in common with many officers in India at the time, had perhaps underestimated the Earl of Moira (later to become Marquess of Hastings). His military career to date had not been particularly distinguished and his reckless spending of a family fortune by extravagant living, coupled with his close friendship with the Prince Regent by whose interest he had obtained his appointment, made questionable his suitability for a job requiring serious commitment and hard work. In the event, the job was the making of him and he was to become one of the greatest and most dedicated Governor-Generals of India, never retiring to the hills in the hot weather and never failing to be at his desk at 4 a.m. each morning.

Richard assured Gordon that there was no question of his having taken offence and Gordon replied:

. . . I am extremely glad that my conjecture respecting the cause of your not having wrote to me from Chittagong was erroneous — but you know "Burnt Children dread Fire" (this is an adage with us in Scotland, I don't know whether you have it in England).

Gordon had for some time suffered from the behaviour of several of the worst sort of his own countrymen in the 1st Battalion, including Menzies, and one Williamson to whom he had a particular aversion:

The fact is I seldom saw a man more easily thrown out of the cool and prudent possession of himself by any sudden event or change of fortune than he is — except where the opinion of those whose good opinion it is the interest of his vanity and worldly advantage to preserve is concerned when he is a true MacSycophant. He has made himself rather ridiculous in this Battn. by his haughty, pompous and consequential manner and conduct and though he were Adjutant General or any thing else you please he could hardly be more puffed up than he is. He has even forgot his former gait and as he is not yet habituated to a new one I fear he may not escape breaking his neck!

### Richard had spoken highly to him of a Scottish Minister's daughter at Dinapur:

I am very glad also to hear such good accounts of my countrywoman Miss McQueen as you give and I dare say she would make a good wife if taken before she is corrupted with the manners and sentiments of the generality of Ladies in this Country — especially about Calcutta . . . For my part, as I have no thoughts of going home soon, I shall marry as soon as I can consistent with the ideas I entertain of the mind and accomplishments of a woman whom I would make my wife. But these ideas, perhaps together with objections on the other side, will ever stand in my way as insurmountable obstacles and very likely I shall live and die a bachelor though no one could detest the life of a bachelor more than I do or more earnestly wish for matrimony.

Richard's brother John, on the other hand, was not prepared to live and die a bachelor. Early in 1815 he had returned from America in the *Gannymede* and, during Bonaparte's "Hundred Days" he had commanded the *Amphion,* 32, in home waters. In October he was transferred to command the *Magicienne,* 36, with orders to proceed to the East Indies early in the New Year. In both *Amphion* and *Magicienne,* he had his thirteen year-old nephew, George Thomas Maitland Purvis, under his care as a Volunteer First Class.

Then, despite the strong opposition of his uncle, and the advice of his father to wait until his return from the East Indies, he announced his intention of marrying Renira and taking her to sea with him. They were married on Christmas Eve 1815 and sailed for India the following month. Young George Purvis left the ship before they sailed and was placed by his father in the Royal Naval College. Admiral Purvis wrote to Richard on 4th October 1815:

John is to have the Magicienne — a fine frigate of 36 guns and nearly a new ship. . . . I think you will have heard before this reaches you, that your brother has made known his desire of marrying his cousin Renira and, from what I understand, the intention is that the ceremony is very shortly to take place. I have expressed my wishes that they should not marry until his return to England, but their plan having been settled before I was made acquainted that there existed any sort of attachment, I have little expectation that any change will be made; but on the contrary that Renira is to proceed with him to sea, a measure which I think very imprudent and such as I fear he will himself be convinced of when it is too late.

The Admiral also gave news of his special protégé, John Scott, who had distinguished himself with great gallantry in the storming of a strongly-defended American fort on the Mississippi — an action which had earned him the commendation of both Sir Edward Codrington and Sir Edward Thomas Troubridge:

I believe I told you — Scott was made a Commander for his bravery on the American Expedition and since that has married his old flame Miss Cole, a very nice young woman.

Despite his great gallantry and an outstanding service record, John Scott was relegated to the half-pay list in 1815 where he was destined to remain for the rest of his life.

The force assembled at Dinapur was under the command of Major-General Sir David Ochterlony, one of the most colourful characters in the history of British India. To his sepoys who, though revering him, had difficulty with his name, he was known as "Loneyackty" and in the Irish regiments under his command he was "General Malone". Later in his career he adopted the lifestyle of a Moghul prince and paraded through Delhi each evening with his thirteen Indian wives each following on her own elephant.

Whether through the influence of Mr. Ricketts or by some surviving ember of Sir George Nugent's interest, Richard, to his surprise and delight, was brought to the attention of General Ochterlony who appointed him as Quartermaster of the 4th Brigade.

It was only temporary, of course, for as long as the campaign against the Gurkhas would last, but it was a staff appointment of some significance, especially in a war situation, and Richard had reason to hope that General Ochterlony's interest might lead to better things when the campaign was over.

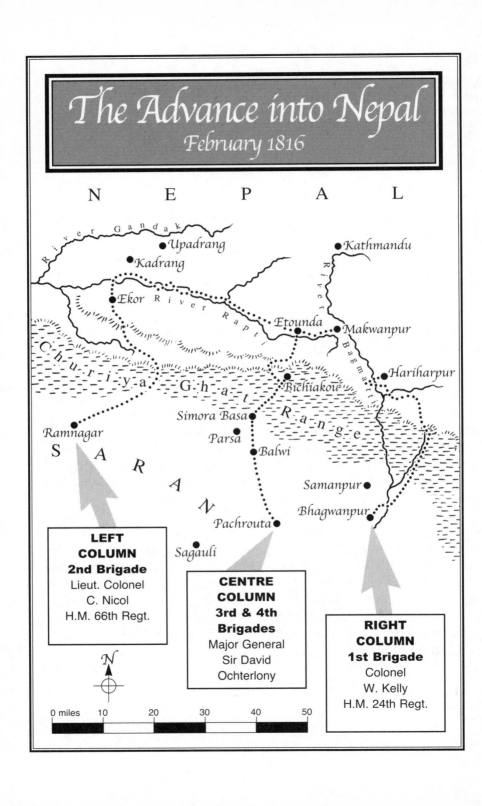

# 11. Makwanpur

*Nepal. February 1816.*

Though he had no way of knowing it at the time, the war with the Gurkhas in which Richard was about to be engaged was to forge one of the most enduring and worthwhile international alliances that Britain has ever had the privilege to enjoy. And that this great friendship should have been preceded by bloody conflict is entirely appropriate as it was to be an alliance of two warrior castes who had tested each other on the field of battle before deciding that their ethos was so similar that they would sooner be friends than enemies. Forty years later when the sub-continent erupted in violent revolt, every Gurkha unit in the British Indian Army remained true to its vow of allegiance and Government troops from Nepal marched into India to assist their British friends. The story of the valour and loyalty of the Gurkha Regiments through nearly two centuries of warfare, right up to the present day, is one of the most heart-warming in British history. This is where it all began:

General Ochterlony's force was divided into three columns *(see map opposite):* the 1st Brigade formed the Right Column, the 2nd Brigade the Left Column and the 3rd Brigade and 4th Brigade, of which Richard was Quartermaster, the Centre Column. The General's plan was that the Centre Column should advance into Nepal towards Kathmandu with the Right and Left Columns crossing the border some thirty miles on either side. Between the advancing forces and Kathmandu lay the Churiya Ghat — a rugged mountain range cut by deep and rocky ravines in which the enemy had constructed massive defensive stockades. Once the Ghat had been crossed, the outer columns were to turn inwards and join up with the Centre Column south of Kathmandu.

The Centre Column, under the personal command of General Ochterlony, moved forward from its camp at Balwi on 3rd February. It halted for five days at Simora Basa where the heavy guns were left and a depot established. On 9th February the Column entered the dense forest in the foothills of the Churiya Ghat and on the 10th took up a position at Bichiakoh. The direct road from here into the hills was heavily defended by enemy stockades and the next four days were spent in reconnoitring an alternative, but very difficult, route by which the pass might be turned.

On the evening of the 14th the 3rd Brigade set out. To conceal this movement from the enemy, they left their tents standing which were immediately occupied by the 4th, Richard's, Brigade. The ascent of the Churiya Ghat was an amazing feat of strength and ingenuity. Picking its way through rocky ravines and deep watercourses, the Brigade eventually came upon a steep upward slope, some 300 feet high, up which the pioneers constructed a staircase of tree-trunks to enable the elephants to proceed. The guns had to be dragged up by hand using luff tackles secured to posts wedged into gaps in the rock. One attempt to send a gun up the "staircase" on the back of its elephant ended in disaster with the poor beast stumbling under the weight and falling to its death on the rocks below. The 4th Brigade followed one day behind the 3rd and by 27th February the whole Column had crossed the Ghat and had reached open ground below the heavily-fortified heights of Makwanpur.

Up until now the Gurkha army had sat cross-legged in vast crowds watching with obvious interest as the British moved into position. The following day they attacked in strength. At one point three companies of Native Infantry and eighty men of H.M. 87th Regiment held a hilltop against an estimated force of 2,000. Reinforcements reached them before they were completely annihilated. Two British 6-pounders were brought into action spraying grapeshot into the advancing hordes but still they kept coming. The battle raged for several hours on the hills and in the gullies in front of Makwanpur and there were dreadful casualties on both sides. More artillery was brought into action and, eventually, the Gurkhas retired with honour. The British had been deeply impressed by their bravery. Ensign John Shipp of the 87th Regiment recorded:

A Sergeant and a Grenadier Sepoy of the Bengal Native Infantry c.1812. The Sepoys recruited for Richard's Regiment, the 2/21st, were mainly high-caste Brahmins or Rajputs from the province of Oudh and enjoyed a high reputation for bravery and loyalty to the Company.

**Left:** A Grenadier Sepoy of the 30th Bengal Native Infantry *(from a black and white pen drawing by R.C. Lovett).*

**Below:** Darsham House, Suffolk, bought by Richard's great-great-grandfather, Captain George Purves in 1712. Richard's grandfather was born here and the house remained in the family for 173 years. In 1877 it was inherited by Captain Purves's great-great-great-great grandson, Arthur Kennedy Purvis, one time Captain in the 87th and 107th Regiments of Foot, who sold it eight years later for £19,000 in order to pay his gambling debts.

**Above:** The children of Edward Holden Cruttenden, a Director of the Honourable East India Company, with their ayah, Juba, who saved them from incarceration in the Black Hole of Calcutta. The child on the right is Elizabeth who married Charles Purvis of Darsham (1743-1808) whose influence was sought to get Richard appointed to the Bengal Establishment. The original painting by Sir Joshua Reynolds remained in the family until 8th June 1928 when it was sold at Christie's to Leggatt Bros. of St. James's Street for 7,200 guineas. It is today in the Mueum of Art, São Paulo, Brazil.

**Left:** Lieutenant-Colonel Charles Purvis of Darsham (1777-1859) who served as a Major in the 1st Royal Dragoons with Wellington's army in the Peninsula. He was present at the Battles of Vittoria and Fuentes d'Onor and later transferred to the Canadian Fencibles to obtain his Lieutenant-Colonel's commission.

*© Reproduced by courtesy of the National Maritime Museum, Greenwich.*

**Above:** H.M.S. *Magicienne*, commanded by Captain John Brett Purvis R.N., leaving Trincomalee, Ceylon.

**Left:** Vice-Admiral of the Red John Brett Purvis in old age.

**Below:** Bury Hall, his elegant home in Gosport. The house was sold by his grandson in 1905 and was demolished in the 1950s to make way for the Northcott House Old People's Home which now stands on its site.

*© By permission of the British Library Ref: Maps 136a10[8-9]*

I hate a runaway foe, for there is no credit in beating him, but these were no flinchers. I never saw a steadier bravery than they showed in all my life. Run they would not, death held no terrors for them, though we were so near that every shot told. †

The following day the British buried over 1,000 Gurkha dead in a mass grave and moved the wounded into hospital tents where they were tended with the same care as our own casualties. General Ochterlony had ordered that Gurkha casualties should be attended by men of their own caste and there was no shortage of volunteers. John Shipp wrote:

It gladdened my heart when I went into the tents where the enemy wounded were housed, to see some of our native soldiers waiting on the poor wretches in the most devoted manner; speaking to them in their own language, comforting them, and calming their fears, which was the more necessary as some of them thought that their lives were only being prolongued for a more cruel and lingering death . . . It was delightful to see men who, the day before, had been bitter enemies, showing the deepest kindness to each other. †

The Right Column, which included Richard's old Regiment the 2/21st, was commanded by Colonel W. Kelly of H.M. 24th Regiment. Their advance had gone according to the General's plan and, once through the Churiya Ghat they had turned inwards and commenced their march to join up with the Centre Column. About halfway to Makwanpur they came upon a detachment of the enemy holding a hilltop position at Hariharpur. The hill was attacked and the enemy dislodged at 6 p.m. on 1st March; but the Gurkhas were not prepared to give up their position that easily and, in Colonel Kelly's words:

. . . in very considerable force made a most desperate attack to recover this point. I was therefore obliged to send a few companies to support the rear of the position which was threatened. It was impossible, from the nature of the ground, to close or use the bayonet, and the musketry continued without interruption till half-past eleven o'clock, when the arrival of two 6-pounders on elephants in a few minutes decided the affair. ‡

---

† *Memoirs of the Extraordinary Military Career of John Shipp, Late a Lieutenant in His Majesty's 87th Regiment.* London, T. Fisher Unwin, 1890.

‡ *History of the Organisation, Equipment and War Services of the Regiment of Bengal Artillery* by Major F.W. Stubbs, London, King, 1877.

Meanwhile, the Left Column, under Lieutenant-Colonel C. Nicol of H.M. 66th Regiment, had met no opposition to their advance and joined up with the Centre Column at Makwanpur on 1st March, the day after the action there.

Seeing the British force consolidated and encamped only twenty miles from Kathmandu, the Gurkhas realised they had no chance of successfully defending their capital and sent an envoy to General Ochterlony to confirm that they would now ratify the Treaty of Sagauli. In due course, the Regent of Nepal arrived at the British camp in a magnificent palanquin attended by twenty armed men. John Shipp described him:

He was a most noble and venerable looking personage, superbly dressed, with numberless daggers stuck in his cummerbund, his sword studded with diamonds and all sorts of precious stones, his neck, turban and hands one mass of jewels.†

It was an extraordinary situation — here, on a battlefield soaked only a few days previously with the blood of both sides, there was an aura not merely of mutual respect but of positive regard. It was almost as if both sides realised that this was the start of an historic friendship which had required each to demonstrate its valour to the other in order to ensure its permanence.

A British staff officer led the Regent to the General's tent. His way was lined by British and Native Infantry who presented arms as he passed — a compliment which he perfectly understood and to which he responded with a majestic bow. The General met him in the doorway of his tent where the usual oriental compliments were exchanged and, after two hours of amicable conversation, the Treaty was signed and a unique alliance had been forged. Waves of smiling Gurkha soldiers poured into the British camp, anxious to trade goods and reminiscences of the battle with their erstwhile enemies. Parties of British went to look around the great fort of Makwanpur where they were welcomed with the strains of *"The British Grenadiers"* and were conducted round the fort by the *Keeledar* [Governor] who even drew up his own regiment for their inspection.

---

† *Memoirs of the Extraordinary Military Career of John Shipp, Late a Lieutenant in His Majesty's 87th Regiment.* London, T. Fisher Unwin, 1890.

When General Ochterlony's army marched from Makwanpur, the Gurkha soldiers flocked around them in great numbers, shaking hands and wishing them well. Richard's involvement in this short campaign occupied a mere two months of the twelve years he had already spent in India yet, in historical terms, it was perhaps the most significant event in his Indian service.

\* \* \*

The Admiral's fears that Renira would not take to life aboard a warship had apparently been groundless. In April 1816 *Magicienne* had reached Madeira from where John wrote to his father with:

. . . very good accounts of Renira's supporting so well a sea life, which she certainly did not calculate on.

Also in John's care aboard *Magicienne* were two young members of the Garrett family — Henry, a Midshipman, and William, a newly appointed Writer in the Company's service. He also carried an important passenger — Rear-Admiral Sir Richard King, Bart., who was travelling out to take over as the naval Commander-in-Chief, East Indies and China. It was not yet known to what part of the East Indies John would be sent. Richard hoped it might be Bengal but, no matter where it should be, he was determined, if practicable, to take local leave to travel and meet up with John and Renira.

While still in Nepal, Richard had written to his father with news of a Lieutenant Walcott who had been wounded at Makwanpur and whose parents he knew were known to his own. The Admiral was duly appreciative of the gesture:

Your good Mother transcrib'd that part of your letter which related to Lieut. Walcott for the purpose of its being forwarded to his family, with whom we are well acquainted. They had not heard of his being wounded and consequently would have been infinitely more distress'd had they heard it from any other quarter. Mrs. Walcott wrote your Mother a very handsome letter on the occasion and beg'd she would convey to you her's and Mr. Walcott's grateful thanks for your kind and benevolent attention.

They had learned from the newspapers that peace with the Gurkhas had now been established and the Admiral assumed that Richard's regiment would now return to its previous station:

Wherever that may be, you may be always assured of the true regard and affection we feel for you and which, if possible, has been heighten'd by the repeated handsome manner in which your friends have spoke of you and I have no doubt you will continue to merit the favor of those who may have the power of rendering you essential and lasting service; but even without such inducements there is a self satisfaction in knowing you have always deserved that which may not ultimately fall to your lot. Indeed, my dear Richard, I bear in my mind very great pleasure and satisfaction the various accounts I have heard of you, and I rejoice that I have made those promises which will, on a future day, place you and your Brother on as equal terms as possible.

Young Neufville was still hanging around Lymington and clearly did not enjoy the same esteem which the Admiral had for those other brother officers of Richard's whom he had met:

Your friend Neufville dined here yesterday. I am inclined to think he likes England better than being with his Regiment.

He had, however, been impressed by William Nichol, who had visited them together with his niece, and had been delighted to receive a letter from Lady Nugent in which she spoke highly of Richard and promised that she and Sir George would visit them at Vicar's Hill when they were next in the area.

John and Renira arrived at Trincomalee, Ceylon, around the middle of the year 1816 and, in September, Richard took leave and passage to Ceylon to visit them. The meeting appears to have been cordial and plans were discussed for Richard to return to England on furlough with them, in the *Magicienne,* in 1818. However, there was an incident, the exact circumstances of which we shall never know, which was to cause an estrangement of several years duration between the two brothers. It appears that Richard agreed to make certain purchases, on behalf of Sir Richard King, for which John had instructed him to draw up to £100 on his own account. Then, it seems, John had heard something, or learned something; or Richard had said something, or done something, which caused John, without notice to his brother, to cancel his sanction for this sum. Richard returned to Bengal in the *Orlando,* frigate, and John had no further communication with him for several years.

John's service in the *Magicienne* on the East Indies Station over the next two years was eventful. For some time he was employed as

Senior Officer off the Mauritius where he was actively engaged in the suppression of the slave trade — an activity which Admiral Sir Richard King considered unlikely to yield any financial reward as he told Richard in a letter written from Admiralty House, Trincomalee, dated 22nd November 1817:

> . . . your brother, Mrs. P. and Inf. are again gone on active service to the Isle of France where I think she may pass the time more pleasurably than on this island, which station is now within the limits of my command; the service required there is against the slave trade therefore a little slave money may be picked up; your brother and officers were sanguine but I am not as there is but very little chance.†

John, in *Magicienne,* was also involved in two daring rescue operations of wrecked ships: in the first he rescued the passengers and crew of the Free Trader *Albion* which was wrecked on Foul Point, near Trimcomalee, and for which he was presented with a piece of plate valued at 100 guineas by the officers of the Madras Establishment. In the second, he rescued the crew of the Indiaman *Cabalva* which was wrecked on the Cargados Garragos Reef and for the "zeal and promptitude" he displayed upon this occasion, he received the thanks of the Court of Directors accompanied by the sum of 200 guineas for the purchase of a piece of plate. For part of his time in the East Indies he was acting Commodore, Ceylon — a senior position for someone aged twenty-nine.

Richard was later to learn that John had asked for his ship to be withdrawn from the Indian States without giving him even "the most distant hint of his intentions".

On his return from Ceylon in February 1817, Richard rejoined his regiment, now stationed at Barrackpore, at the time when the Government was preparing to launch its major initiative to destroy the Pindaris. A great army of 120,000 men and 300 guns had been mobilised. This was divided into the Army of Hindustan, under the personal command of Lord Hastings, in the north and the Army of the Deccan, commanded by Sir Thomas Hislop, in the south. It was the biggest operation which had ever been mounted in India and the plan was to surround the Pindaris in a vast circle and to then gradually tighten the drawstring.

---

† N.M.M. PRV/101 *Loose Papers* MS.55/009

Richard, with the experience of a staff appointment in the Nepal War to his credit, was now determined to mount his own massive operation to obtain a better job. On 18th February he wrote to Colonel Nichol, the Adjutant-General, asking for a staff appointment in the forthcoming campaign and offering to pay his own expenses in travelling to join the army in the field:

Sir, — By the increasing rumour of expected war with the Native Powers I am induced most respectfully to renew an application with which I before took the liberty of troubling His Excellency the Commander-in-Chief for any Employment in whatever Brigade or Army may be destined for actual service in the Frontier. In submitting for the consideration of the Most Noble the Marquis of Hastings this entreaty, addressed from a situation so remote from the probable seat of war (a circumstance which I particularly lament,) it might be favorable to my [views] would you be so obliging as to state that I am myself prepared to defray the expenses necessarily attendant on adopting the most expeditious mode of proceeding to the Upper Provinces. — Also . . . I respectfully beg to submit for His lordship's consideration the fact of my whole service in India having passed in the unremitting performance of Battalion Duties — excepting only my having held the situation of Quartermaster to Colonel Burnet's Brigade in the 2nd Nepaul Campaign — a distinction with which I was honored by the selection of Major General Sir David Ochterlony.

Then, on 10th March he wrote to Colonel Doyle, Military Secretary to the Commander-in-Chief, to try and establish just how he stood in his Lordship's interest:

Sir, — The little ceremony I use in addressing you without any previous introduction requires, I am fully sensible, infinite apologies on my part; but such introduction is an honor I have promised myself for the past two weeks at this station, constant duty having prevented, and still continuing to do so, my visiting Calcutta since my return from Ceylon.

I beg you to be assured, that in troubling you as I am now about to do, it is by no means my wish, or my intention to intrude myself upon your notice, or that of the Earl of Moira, as a tiresome suitor for an appointment such as you may have known and found difficulty in satisfying. — On the contrary, I am only solicitous of being candidly informed whether I may consider myself on that footing, or whether I can, with any probability of ultimate success, further encourage those hopes of being better provided for which have been inspired by divers of my friends.

Mr. Ricketts on my sailing for Ceylon in September last not only repeatedly expressed himself so interested in my favor as induced me at the time to suppose he would mention my name to yourself; but I also know he did on that occasion make some reference or other to satisfy himself that I had been, through his recommendation, near four years on his Lordship's list: under this persuasion I doubt not of your agreeing that I should be wanting in proper respect to my own

Interest, did I not make some effort to introduce my name or my person to those by whom alone my views might be forwarded.

Would you therefore be so obliging as to inform me, (in case of my having so fair a chance as I have flattered myself with) what would be the most delicate method, and such as would be most likely to meet the Earl of Moira's feelings on these subjects, of applying to be better provided for . . .

## Colonel Doyle replied on 31st March:

No: 2470. Lieutenant Colonel Doyle presents his Compliments to Lieutenant Purvis, and in reply to his letter under date the 10th Inst. begs to acquaint him that his name is noted in this office for consideration by His Excellency the Commander-in-Chief as favorable opportunities for serving him may present themselves.

In April, Richard obtained an interview with Colonel Doyle at which he pressed his case then, on 11th May, he tried again; this time with a public letter requesting a staff appointment on active service and a private letter proposing various specific staff appointments for which he hoped to be considered should Colonel Doyle not think it appropriate to place the first letter before the Commander-in-Chief:

Public Letter. — Sir, — Having certain grounds for supposition that a considerable force is likely to take the field for service on the N.W. Frontier during or at the conclusion of the approaching rainy season, would you have the kindness to lay before The Right Honble. the Earl of Moira my earnest and respectful entreaty, in the event of there being foundation for the above conjecture, for Employment in the capacity of Brigade Major, or otherwise on the temporary Public Staff of any Army or Brigade that may so assemble. In thus communicating a request for active and responsible employment I have conceived it may form some apology for my apparent confidence would you be so obliging as to mention to His Lordship at the same time, that I had the honor of being selected by Major General Sir David Ochterlony as Quartermaster to the Brigade which penetrated the Chooreea Ghattee Pass in the Nepaul Campaign concluded by Treaty before the Fortress of Mackwanpoor. This circumstance, added to the length of time my name has been on His Lordship's list, your assurance contained in Letter No. 2470 of its being noted in your Office for consideration by His Excellency the Commander-in-Chief as opportunities for serving me may present themselves, and there being no immediate prospect of opportunities by other means, encourage me to hope that this application may be honored with a favorable reception.

Private Letter. — Sir, — With reference to my late conversation with you upon the subject of an appointment, and report tending still to confirm me in the supposition on which it was founded, I have framed the accompanying application with the view of assuring the Right Honble. the Earl of Moira that, in reaping the benefits which I have been promised by the interest of my friends, I am as well prepared to encounter the active and toilsome duties of the Profession as to enjoy those advantages under any other circumstances. — Indeed, as connected with my private views, and the satisfaction such distinction would afford my friends in Europe, an Employment of the nature expressed in my application would be the most congenial to my wishes. In the event, however, of your not conceiving it expedient, (trusting to the kind exertion of your judgement in my favor,) to lay my application before His Excellency the Commander-in-Chief, I avail myself of the permission you obliged me with to offer the following memoranda for further consideration. — Captain Hampton, Extra Assistant Commissary at Prince of Wales's Island is about to apply for leave of absence to return to Bengal when, in consequence of receiving an equal salary in the temporary command of the 2nd Battn. 20th he will most probably remain until his promotion to a Major. Would his Lordship have the goodness to appoint me to act for Captain Hampton on his applying for leave, with a prospect of succeeding him. — I have also learnt that there is an additional assistant about to be granted in the Auditor General's Office. These vacancies in addition to a probability of the same in the Adjutant General's Office are the only emunerations with which I shall for the present venture to trouble you.

On 12th June Richard decided to try civil channels and wrote to Mr. Adam who was acting as Personal Private Secretary to Lord Hastings in the absence of Mr. Ricketts:

I had trusted that an earlier return of my Friend Mr. Ricketts would obviate the necessity of troubling you for the exertion of that Interest in my behalf which I believe he requested you would use upon the offering of any favorable opportunity for procuring me a staff appointment more lucrative or more pleasant than the one I at present hold. Such opportunity having now arrived, I hope I may not be so intrusive as to over-rate your desire of meeting Ricketts's wishes when I request the favor of your soliciting from the Governor General the situation of Junior Assistant in the Adjutant General's Office which has become vacant by the promotion consequent on the demise of Major Gordon, late Deputy A.G.

And finally, on Sunday 6th July, again to Mr. Adam:

Having received positive information of the unexpected death of Captain Ashurst, Deputy Paymaster with the Nagpur Subsidiary Force, I avail myself of the injunction you kindly laid on me, to repeat my application for your Interest with the Marquis of Hastings, in requesting you would endeavour to procure for me the above appointment which has probably become vacant in too sudden a manner to admit of the obstacles which before interfered.

I did myself the pleasure of calling at your house this morning, judging it the only day you might be disengaged from Public Business, but was unfortunate in finding you absent — when it was my design as well to communicate the foregoing, as to express how thankful I feel for your attention on the former occasion and obliging promise of its continuance.

This was to be Richard's last, grovelling attempt to better himself in the Bengal Army by his own efforts. The promise of five years ago seemed to have dissipated as had Sir George Nugent's influence in India. He had suppressed all vestiges of pride as he tried to cultivate both military and civil inlets to Lord Hastings's interest, prostrating himself in the manner required, all with a complete lack of success. His Staff Appointment in General Ochterlony's army, which he had believed might invoke a turn in his fortune, seemed now to count for nothing.

In deep despair, Richard went into Calcutta and arranged for his passage back to England in the Indiaman *Thomas Grenville* which was expected to sail early in the new year 1818.

# 12. Soldier's Return

*Barrackpore, India.*
*December 1817.*

L ord Hastings's campaign against the Pindaris, which would later be known as the Third Maratha War, was being conducted with considerable success. Like a reaper working in decreasing circles in a cornfield and driving the rats into the centre, the British drawstring was tightening month by month and vast numbers of the ruthless marauders were being cornered and destroyed. Richard's disappointment at being stuck at Barrackpore on battalion duties instead of earning glory in the field was perhaps mollified by the news in November that Lord Hastings's camp had been hit by cholera which was to kill one tenth of the great Army of Hindustan.

On 23rd June, Wemyss MacLeod died at Barrackpore. He was aged twenty-four and had fought with the 2/21st on the hill at Hariharpur. The day before, Richard's cousin Lucy had died in Edinburgh and, when he received the news later in the year, Richard grieved for his aunt who had now lost four of her six children. The remaining two, George and Barrington, were both in the Bengal Army and unable to be at their mother's side. George, however, had just been appointed Adjutant of his regiment, the 1/4th, which was at least a shred of good news for his poor family.

The Admiral, unaware of the rift between his two sons, was delighted that they were, comparatively, so near to each other and hoped that Richard would have the opportunity to show John and Renira some of the sights in Bengal should John have occasion to bring the *Magicienne* to Calcutta. He also had news of John Scott:

Scott has a Son and at present he lives at Bishops Waltham. He is very anxious to get a Ship that he might place a hope by some of getting made a Post Captain.

Richard also learned that he had missed his chance with the bride that Renira had proposed for him: his cousin Harriet Eyre, the heiress of Newhouse, had been married to George Matcham, a nephew of Lord Nelson. Neufville, his father told him, had been in London for some time and had now condescended to return to his regiment in India.

On 1st December 1816, whilst still in Ceylon, Richard had written to his father begging him to pay no heed to any reports detrimental to his character which might come to his ears. This was obviously connected with whatever disclosure, whether with or without foundation, had caused the estrangement with his brother. The Admiral had, apparently, heard nothing of it and, in any case, was not disposed to think ill of Richard, having heard so many good reports of his character and behaviour in recent years. He replied on 2nd June 1817 which reached Richard in December:

Your letter to me of 1st December last, and that to your Mother of the 10th are only now receiv'd, and before I proceed to any other points, I must set your mind at ease with respect to reports which you fancy I have heard not favorable to your character; but indeed, my dear Richard, so different have been all the accounts I have receiv'd respecting you, that I have been very much gratified and pleased with what I have heard, and I trust that I shall never have cause to be otherwise: I am quite at a loss to account for what you imagine has been told me, and more particularly so, that John and Renira should appear to be acquainted with such stories.

Richard, it seems, also believed certain of the Garrett family to be aware of this imputation.

I have no idea of any of the Garretts being displeased with you, they have always been particular in their enquiries after you and I have as often delivered your messages to them.

The Admiral concluded:

When you receive this letter take the earliest opportunity to tell me you are made happy by my assuring you I never had a thought of your having acted in an unbecoming manner; and that if you had at any time suspected any one of fabricating any reports unfavorable to your character, you had completely replaced them in your esteem or friendship as the case may seem necessary. Your Mother joins me in every kind wish that every possible good may constantly attend you and be assured I am, My dear Richard, Your truly affectionate Father, Jhn. Chd. Purvis.

On 1st January 1818, Richard was made Brevet-Captain, which

meant that he had the authority of the rank of Captain but without the pay. At the same time, he handed over his appointment as Interpreter and Quartermaster of the 1/30th Native Infantry to his old friend John Home, bade farewell to his friends in the Regiment and set out for Calcutta to join the ship which would take him home.

The Indiaman *Thomas Grenville,* commanded by Captain Robert Alsager, sailed from Diamond Harbour New Anchorage on 7th January 1818. Richard's fellow passengers included two officers of the Bengal Native Infantry — Captain Nicholson of the 11th, whose wife was also aboard, and Lieutenant Snodgrass of the 4th. Also aboard were Captain John MacRa of the 1st Royal Scots, ADC to the Governor-General, and Lieutenant David Warburton of H.M. 24th Regiment, in command of invalids. There were several civilians and a few servants.

As soon as he had settled into the routine of shipboard life, Richard got down to the difficult task of writing to his brother. He had been deeply hurt by his behaviour towards him — not simply by the implied slur on his integrity of John having cancelled his credit, but by his lack of consideration in not having advised him in advance; by his complete silence ever since; and by his having arbitrarily rejected their provisional arrangement for Richard to have returned to England with him in the *Magicienne.* If, in his own mind, Richard knew of any truth in the allegations against him, he certainly did not consider them of sufficient weight to justify this ongoing censure; and if he genuinely knew of nothing which could have caused John's withdrawal from him, he doubtless felt very aggrieved that he had chosen to take someone else's word against that of his own brother; or, if John had been presented with seemingly incontravertible evidence, that he should not have challenged Richard with it before making his own judgment.

Whatever was the case, he would no doubt meet John in England within the next year, before which matters between them must be brought out into the open:

My dear John, — It will doubtless astonish you to receive this letter from on board the Company's Ship Grenville in which I have taken my passage for Europe; and the candour which I have practised all my life now prompts me to tell you that your long, and as I thought little affectionate, silence has chiefly urged this measure. You can have no hesitation in acknowledging that in the course of return I should expect answers to those letters which awaited you at [.....] – as to this they intimated the result of a reference which I had at some pains caused, to the south in this country upon a pecuniary subject that in good breeding you should have answered; and I was galled by the little tenderness shewn to my character for integrity, when, after desiring me to draw on you for about £100 on account of Sir Richard King, you should have written an unconditional order to Mr. Palmer to stop payment of the sum, verbally to me in Mr. P's. office at the very moment I was about to avail myself of what yourself had directed. Suppose I had in the interim given an order to Mr. Custer the merchant at [Ducen], 400 miles away, for Sir Richard's [muslin], you cannot dispute the injurious effect of not having had [such a transaction] fully protected. You may probably despise the punctuality which I would here inculcate as being beneath gentlemen, if so, how much more gentlemanly it would have been to have said to me "don't draw" and then to Palmer "don't pay", and such is generally practised in India. Probably you doubted my compliance – such have been causes [distressing] to me for months past; – while in declining health and drooping spirits I had no letter to renew the hope with which I parted from you on Orlando's gangway — that of a happy return to England in the Magicienne. I was left to doubt whether such an arrangement would be desirable, or even acceptable, to you: a suspicion which in some measure meets confirmation in the circumstances, recently made known to me, of your having actually applied to [Mr.] Hay to have your ship withdrawn from the Indian States without giving me the most distant hint of your intentions. These are [grievous] causes of complaint against you which I should have considered as much hypocrisy to have concealed from you as it might be injurious to make known to others;

On 13th February, Lieutenant Warburton died and was buried at sea and on 11th March the ship anchored at Green Point, Capetown to provision and load rice for shipment to St. Helena. Richard wrote to his father:

Our voyage thus far has been by no means expeditious being prolonged to nearly a fortnight beyond the expectation of the Captain and Officers of the ship, but it has, thank God, been agreeable in point of weather with the exception of one gale of wind. It will of course be my peculiar endeavour on reaching the British Channel, to take passage in a fishing or other boat to Lymington, or failing in that, Portsmouth. I hope the former may be possible in order that I may be sooner gratified by the meeting with yourself and my good Mother, and that by the blessing of God [finding you] in perfect good health and corresponding with the joyful [date] on which this, my greatest happiness, is promised me – namely the 1st of June. I reflect with the greatest satisfaction on the step I have taken in resolving to quit India at the time I did – the [difference] that I feel enjoying this taste of a cold latitude, seems to persuade me I should not have survived another hot season in India. The [renewed] strength I have acquired in but a few weeks points out the low extreme to which I must have been before reduced . . .

The *Thomas Grenville* sailed from Capetown on 14th March

arriving at St. Helena on the 27th. Here Richard and George
Snodgrass hired horses on which to explore the island at a cost of
£2. 5s. per horse for three days. They no doubt went to have a look
at Longwood, the wind-swept farmhouse where the great Napoleon
Bonaparte was living in exile since his defeat at Waterloo three
years earlier. Before going into the interior of the island, however,
it was necessary to obtain a pass about which Richard had a curious
story to tell his father.

On their arrival at St. Helena, Richard was told by Captain
Alsager that the Deputy Adjutant-General on the island, Lieutenant-
Colonel Sir Thomas Reade, had expressed interest in seeing
Richard's name on the passenger list and had wondered if he was
related to his old friend Admiral John Child Purvis. Captain Alsager
told him that he was, in fact, his younger son and Richard waited in
confident expectation for some invitation or offer of attention from
Sir Thomas. However, nothing was forthcoming:

The following day I landed in the Captain's boat with him but parted from him
immediately on my own pursuits, after the accomplishment of which I waited on
Sir T. to request a passport (which is necessary to every stranger) to the interior,
not doubting that the name would lead to the acquaintance which I flattered
myself he desired, but no: the following is verbatim what passed. – "I wait upon
you, Sir, according to the bidden custom, to obtain a pass to the interior of the
island" – "You shall have it, Sir." said he taking the pen and paper; "Your name
Sir?" I answered "Captain Purvis." which he wrote down without the slightest
emotion, or even checking the pen in its course. I have been more particular in
this detail than probably the subject deserved, but it is possible you might desire
the means of answering any reported backwardness on my part. Although as
careless of Sir Thomas Reade's acquaintance as of Sir Thomas Reade's
footman's, I could not help asking myself if J.B.P. would have so treated a
brother of Sir Thomas Reade's that is to say provided he is at all warranted in
[taking] to himself the title of your old friend.

Having unloaded her cargo of 200 tons of rice, the *Thomas
Grenville* sailed from St. Helena and on 8th April spoke the
American ship *Columbus,* bound from Calcutta to Massachusetts.
She had run short of provisions and Captain Alsager ordered a
cutter to be lowered and for twelve casks of salt meat and one of
"split pease" to be taken to the American ship.

The *Thomas Grenville* entered the English Channel on 2nd June
and the ship's officers started looking out for a fishing boat
operating from the Solent area, to which Richard and George

Snodgrass might transfer. Eventually they raised one which was returning to Lyme Regis which, to Richard, seemed better than having to sail all the way to Gravesend with the ship. It seems that they transferred in rather a hurry as Richard did not even have time to settle his Mess Bill before leaving the ship. However, he and the Purser, George Homer, had become good friends during the voyage and Homer promised to send the bill on to him in due course.

Immediately upon landing in Lyme Regis, Richard sent a note ahead to his father with the intention that he and George Snodgrass would spend a night in Lyme Regis, travel up to Lymington the following day, spend the next night at an inn near Lymington, then present themselves at Vicar's Hill the following morning:

This is my Forerunner to inform you of my forthcoming arrival in your neighbourhood, but as I am unacquainted with the hours kept at Vicar's Hill, I have persuaded myself a view to prevent your being disturbed too early, to breakfast with my fellow passenger, Snodgrass at the [Port] and intend to present you with my unworthy self as early afterwards as possible. If you could make it convenient to send for my conveyance a horse, and for my guidance a servant, it will save me a long walk which after the fatigue of travelling from the [east] of [Devonshire] will be grateful.

The reunion between Richard and his father can only be imagined. Last time they met Richard had been fourteen; he was now twenty-nine. Their knowledge of each other was founded on an extraordinary consecution of letters, over a period of fifteen years, which had itself been continually dislocated by the length of time each took in transit and further so by the fact that many never arrived at all. Pleas for assistance had been received long after their need had been satisfied; expressions of remorse, censure, concern and approbation had lost much of their relevance so far were they removed from the event which had invoked them.

In the course of this strange dialogue, Richard had passed from boyhood to manhood and his father from the height of his manhood to the frailty of old age. In earlier years, the Admiral had not hesitated to castigate his son for anything he perceived as weakness, inconstancy or caprice; but now, with the mellowness of old age, he was increasingly unwilling to harbour any sort of misgivings concerning Richard's character or behaviour.

There can be little doubt that the fatted calf was killed.

Richard spent the first six months of his furlough in getting to know his father and stepmother, settling into the pleasant and relaxed routine at Vicar's Hill and renewing his acquaintance with relatives and friends. George Snodgrass was delighted with Vicar's Hill and seemed in no hurry to continue his journey to rejoin his own relatives in Edinburgh.

Within the first few days after their arrival, Snodgrass accompanied Richard to Blackbrook Cottage where they received a warm welcome from Richard's uncle and aunt. Snodgrass was enchanted with the great thatched house, set in its beautiful gardens, proclaiming that he had never seen anything remotely like it in his native Scotland, nor anywhere else.

Richard, for his part, was enchanted with his cousin Georgina who was home on holiday from her boarding school in London. She was now seventeen and a half and promised to be as great a beauty as her mother. She was bursting with vitality and youthful humour and delighted the company with her fashionable mannerisms and *mots justes.* Richard found it difficult to keep his eyes off her for long enough to converse with his aunt and uncle as courtesy required.

His young cousin George, just sixteen, was also at home on holiday from the Naval College, Portsmouth Dockyard — the same establishment, though then called "Academy", at which Richard had suffered nearly two claustrophobic years before going out to India. George had been to sea under John's care in the *Amphion* and the *Magicienne* but little mention was made of John or Renira in the presence of his uncle and aunt from which, Richard concluded, their disapproval of the marriage had not abated. George was to return to the College in September and Richard promised he would write to him there with some "Good Advice" from a former inmate.

On the way back to Lymington, Richard talked incessantly about Georgina and told George Snodgrass that he intended to pay court to her and that he should watch the newspapers for an engagement announcement. At the end of June, Snodgrass reluctantly packed his bags and left Vicar's Hill for the Port of London where he intended seeking passage on a coastal smack for Leith.

John Johnson had returned to England on furlough three months ahead of Richard and, together, they took a trip to Cheltenham and Bath in August calling on friends and acquaintances. They had hoped to call on Mrs. Ricketts, for whom James Ridge had expressed such admiration some years previously. She was in Bath at the time with her little daughter, Louisa, who had been sent home from India, but the child's health had deteriorated and she was not expected to live:

My dear Captain Purvis, — I am indeed grieved to say that my reports of my dearest Louisa are by no means so favorable as I could wish or indeed as I had flattered myself by this time they would be when I last wrote to you. Her head ache and pain in her right side continue unabated and are now [accompanied by] such violent spasms and other unfavorable symptoms that her recovery in my own opinion will be almost next to a miracle – she is perfectly resigned herself and has certainly poor dear child suffered such a martyrdom that I know not if it is not selfish in me to wish for a prolongation of her suffering. . . .I feel most grateful to you and Captain Johnson for your friendly enquiries and anxious good wishes about my dear Louisa and most truly rejoiced to hear such favorable accounts of your friend. – My present state of mind is better imagined than described and will I am sure plead my apology for not entering upon other subjects at such a painful and distressing period as the present.

In August, John Ramsay, the Shetlander, died in Calcutta and the following month James Ridge himself died in Southampton shortly after his arrival in England. His wife, Harriet, Colonel William Nichol's daughter, was thus widowed at the start of her long awaited honeymoon, the postponement of which five years earlier had deprived Richard of the temporary appointment of Adjutant of the 2/21st. The chances of an officer in the Company's service living to enjoy his pension were slight: between the years 1796 and 1820, only 201 officers retired on pension while 1,243 were killed or died in service.

Richard had long since decided, probably before he sailed for England, that nothing on earth was going to persuade him to return to India. He had not, however, mentioned this decision to his friends, who assumed he would go back after the normal two and a half-year furlough, and certainly not to his father who was treating him with the greatest kindness and affection and whose displeasure he was loth to invoke. The Admiral had even insisted on pressing £50 on him as a contribution towards the expenses of his trip with Johnson to Cheltenham.

Happy as his life presently was at Vicar's Hill, three months of his leave had already expired and with it more of his precious savings than he had reckoned on. The longer he let things continue, the less he would have and the more difficult it would be for him to launch himself in a new career. He hoped for his father's indulgence though he knew it would not be given without recrimination and a loss of the happy position in his father's esteem which he presently enjoyed. On the other hand, his father might positively refuse to help him, in which case he would have to support himself on whatever was left of his capital until he could find some sort of employment or, worse still, if his money was all gone, he might be left with no alternative but to return to India — a prospect which did not bear thinking of.

Then there was Georgina whose behaviour towards him gave him some reason to hope that the growing feelings of affection he had for her were, at least in small measure, reciprocated. He certainly could not support a wife on the wages of a lowly clerk or petty official, which were the only sort of positions he felt he might be able to obtain without his father's assistance; whereas, if his father would help him, one more time, to get his foot on the ladder of some worthy and reasonably remunerative profession — farming perhaps, or better still, as it would make use of the brain he knew he had, the Church — he would feel able to make an honourable proposal to his pretty cousin, even though they would have to exercise some financial restraint in the early days of their marriage.

The more he thought of it the clearer it became that he could not delay any longer. He must broach the subject with the Admiral and the sooner the better.

PART 3

# Holy Orders

# 1. Confrontation

*Vicar's Hill House, near Lymington, Hampshire.*
*Christmas Day 1818.*

Richard had been good to the promise he made to his young cousin George at Blackbrook Cottage back in June. In September, he had written to him at the Royal Naval College enclosing a handsome pair of razors, a stout leather strop, a badger brush and a china shaving mug with a saucy nautical motif, containing soap with a pleasant, but masculine, scent of cologne.

Having himself experienced in the same establishment, albeit fifteen years previously, incitement from fellow students to err from the path of academic commitment, he felt himself ideally qualified to treat young Cousin George to his first letter of "Good Advice". His, however, would be in lighter vein than those he was wont to receive from his father, and good Mr. Garrett, consistent with the lesser age differential between him and his cousin:

My dear George, — After some hesitation in determining upon a suitable remembrance to you in the way of a small present, the stubble upon your chin in June last has occurred to my recollection, and I have therefore put you up a pair of Razors etc. which will, as yet I conclude, serve to remind you of me once in a month — hereafter weekly — and ultimately (Purvises being notable for strong beards) daily. I might have chosen articles of a nature more acceptable to yourself, as firearms or the like, were it not that such an offering would draw upon me my aunt's displeasure as endangering your personal safety. The instruments now provided I shall only sanction your applying to any destructive purpose in case of your failing to support that credit which must distinguish the name of Purvis in the records of your College upon its original and still more intricate plan. But without any joke, I am now led into this subject — to you the most important temporal one which your youth has yet to reflect upon — you will I hope conceive me justified in prolonging it a few words more.

Your excellent Father has no doubt urged this point with you frequently and set forth the advantages promised by earnest application to your studies, in illustrations far beyond my capacity; but I have still your advancement, not unmixed with a little family pride for my own sake, very much at heart, and therefore cannot (however little may remain to be said) withhold my suite of entreaty — not to give it the formal term of admonition. I could furnish you with an hundred quaint rules by which I (profession interpreter) have forwarded young men in the study of languages during my residence abroad but I shall with you confine myself to these two precepts: —Never imagine your time of leisure too short to sit down to your studies, but fill up every moment — if it be but for five minutes. Your rising from work reluctantly will ensure your resuming it cheerfully — nay, with avidity. My second injunction is, that being so engaged, you resist both the force of example in your fellow students, and all their persuasions to discontinue for the pursuit of pleasure. Such are simply my recommendations: but I cannot flatter myself with possessing the shadow of that influence over your conduct which should induce you to act up to them merely because I have judged them advisable. I entreat you bring the conviction home to yourself by calculating the benefits they will tend to secure you. The first to be considered, and most important is, I need not say, an early and rapid promotion in the most honorable profession in the world! Does your fondness for that profession render you impatient to enter on its more active duties? — Serious application (in my day termed fagging) is the only means of gratification. Are you impatient of restraint in the Dock Yard being under the bolts and locks of your College? — Fagging is your only Master-Key. Do you begrudge the trifling recreations between the hours of study? — You have them in store an hundred fold by a present temporary sacrifice. Do you look forward with the same pleasure as I do to our being associates in the pursuit of amusement during next Winter? — That pleasure will be prolonged, as well as unalloyed, by the Plan being safe out of your hands, and off your mind, which I know your Parents expect at Christmas. Lastly, but by no means least deserving of your serious reflection: Do you seek to relieve an anxiety (founded on the excess of her love to you) of the tenderest and kindest Mother that ever owned a son? Would you gratify an honest and natural pride in a Father, an Uncle, a Brother-in-Law, and a renegade first Cousin, who all possess, or have claims to an interest in the Naval Profession? — If you have (which I doubt not) a heart susceptible of happiness from the attainment of all these objects, you have only to let application keep pace with those distinguished abilities which, as I am informed on every hand, you have been blessed with from Nature.

Think silently on these sentiments, and what others connected therewith your own good sense may suggest, whenever you take the Father in hand upon a secret resolution — act upon them according to what they will infallibly dictate, and my offering will [become] to be a gift but you will have amply repaid, my dear George.

As Christmas approached, Richard knew he could delay no longer and must speak to his father about his proposed change of career. The Admiral's first reaction was surprise: How could this be? he had asked Richard, it had been his own choice to go to India against all advice of his family and friends. Richard accepted this but tried to explain that, at the age of fourteen, he had not really been qualified to make such an important decision. But he had been quite adamant, his father pointed out, he had countless letters to prove it.

On Christmas Eve, Richard Smith, the butler, delivered to Richard's room a bundle of letters with a request from the Admiral that he should read through them. They were old letters dating back to 1803, mainly from Richard and Mr. Garrett. The Admiral had been through them and underlined in pencil every paragraph which related to his son's determination to leave the Navy and go to India.

Richard had made little headway during his two recent interviews with his father — the subject was of such fundamental importance to him that he had found it difficult to marshal his thoughts logically and to present his case in a way which stood any chance of eliciting his father's sympathy and understanding. Moreover, his father could not possibly absorb and remember every point he made verbally whereas, if he were to present his case in writing, he had every confidence that his father would read it carefully and give fair consideration to every part of his argument. This was the sensible course of action, he decided, and, as he was due to leave Vicar's Hill in a few days to visit the Garretts in Bath, his father would have a couple of weeks to study and consider his plea. For the same reasons, he would also request a written answer from him.

So, at 11 p.m. on Christmas Day 1818, when the household had retired, Richard, though suffering from a severe headache, sat down in his bedroom at Vicar's Hill to compose what would probably be the most important letter he would ever write to his father:

My dear Sir, — I have directed Richard to return herewith the letters you desired me to peruse: I have done so, and so far as they respect my entering into the Company's Service, are unanswerable. That you had documents of this nature in your possession I believe I professed myself well aware at our last conference on the painful subject; but I cannot confess that a boy between 14 and 15 years of age was by any means competent to making a prudent decision between a protracted confinement within the Dockyard walls of Portsmouth, and the fancied parade of an Indian life (which were then submitted to my choice) to be concluded, as I falsely judged, by all the ease and affluence enjoyed by your then neighbours, Majors Goodlad, Ives, Anderson, etc. under my own immediate observation. Previous to your taking command of the Dreadnought (I think it was) we had conversations on the subject of my appointment, of which however, as I cannot adduce similar proof to that contained in Mr. Garrett's letters against me, I shall conclude the subject with fully admitting that I acted unwisely; but in being left to act at all, more was expected of me than my years were adequate to. I hope and trust that affair may now be allowed to rest; nor did I (I confess) expect it to be agitated at this remote period – I mean from the time of its conclusion at Blackbrook. The present however, I imagine a fair opening to enlarge on a subject which I have much at heart, and which would torment me with increasing anxiety and suspense until I should disburthen myself to you. Six months of my allotted time in England have elapsed without my ever imagining that I possessed the opportunity (however diligently I have sought it) of disclosing to you the state of my finances, my wishes and prospects in future life: and judging from your kindness to me in most other respects that such information, although interesting, and even desirable to you has remained unsolicited by means of the very same mistaken delicacy which has hitherto opposed my offering it, I embrace this opportunity of communicating the subject, as well to avoid any embarrassment of personal conference as to be fully explicit myself and afford you ample leisure for replying to certain points with that deliberation I conceive required by an affair of (to me) so great importance. First, with respect to the provision of my purse, it is, proportionate to its scantiness, to be exposed in very few words. I left India proprietor of £2,500 which is necessarily reduced during the voyage and by my expenses since landing in England. But on another matter I have more to say, in spite of the late hour and a bad head ache – more on which to entreat your serious consideration. The unfortunate difference which caused your offering these letters for my perusal has laid me open, I am well aware, to a certain retort from which I must in the first instance ask your forbearance and that you would in no wise revert to the circumstance or manner of my exchanging into my present profession, but give me the benefit of your judgement and experience in advising how I may extricate myself from it; for no less than that is now the object of my wishes – my present profession, however, I have perhaps erroneously expressed, because there is every thing to be said in its favour. The Service of the East India Company is respectable, honorable, the friendships I have formed in it would be ever valuable, and certain opulence, under a prolongation of life, its final result. But these are advantages alluring us to a destructive and justly dreaded climate, where all the respectability and all the honor in the world sit but as mockery on an emaciated frame; when the hopes which in our more sanguine moments we do venture to build on highly estimated friendships it is so common to see in an instant fatally disappointed; and where even the opulence I speak of, even supposing it to be attained, is valueless in the hands of one returning to his native Country scarcely of an age, seldom with even the inclination, and never with a constitution to expect the commonest enjoyment. The certainty of wealth here alluded to is founded by our rise in the Service by gradation obtainable only by resigning the prospect of settling, at all events till the last stage of life, – in my native Country, and presupposing my arrival at the head of a Regiment by surviving all those who are my seniors. This is not a prospect to my liking; the alternative is accepting the Company's pension; namely full pay after 22 years service in India. My past progress from fifteenth to third Lieutenant during the number of years I have already served demonstrates that I can expect no higher rank than that of Captain at the expiration of the above period: my pension will then be £180 a year. Now I foresee no difficulty in deciding upon a new profession calculated to yield me that income at the end of (reckoning it will be two years before I should reland in India) the ten years yet remaining. As to the intervening span, I candidly own, its passing in the drudgery of any profession in England would be preferred before all the idle splendour of the East. You will, I hope, acquit me of any desire to impose myself upon you as an useless and expensive dependant at home: the circumstances of my requiring no assistance from you since first joining the Army, receiving none, save £50 offered by you on my last departure for Cheltenham, and even declining that proffered in the year 1810 are arguments against my burthening you willingly. There may be means of decreasing the aid I might require of you to what you may find it convenient, and, (considering its importance to me) even pleasurable to accord; – or there may be means of avoiding the necessity of any aid whatever, to which I would as cheerfully resort as I have done hitherto – with the utmost confidence in my own industry and application added to some capacity (pardon my assurance) for attainments of almost any kind; my thoughts have turned upon husbandry and the clerical profession, but it is to obtain the help of better judgement that I apply to you. Stranger as I am in England, it is not to be expected that I could of myself decide upon an affair of this moment – I must necessarily rely upon the sincerity of an experienced Friend, – on the advice of greater wisdom than my own: – and where have I a more reasonable hope of the one, or a greater certainty of finding the other than in my own Father?

By my approaching absence from Vicar's Hill, I hope to shun verbal communication on a subject which interests me too deeply to ensure a perfect command of my feelings, and for the same reason I entreat the favor of a written answer: if decidedly inimical to my wishes here expressed accept this promise that I will never renew the subject to you in future. If favorable to me, why no time is to be lost in entering upon new speculations.

I hope this letter may be, at all events sufficiently intelligible, (however a severe head ache has operated to render it otherwise) to give you an insight generally to my views: I think more might have been written on the subject, and more to the purpose certainly at a less sudden occasion and more convenient season. Believe me, my dear Sir, Your affectionate Son, R. F. Purvis.

The Admiral's written reply, if he gave one, has sadly not survived but what is certain is that he was touched by Richard's advocacy and decided, not only positively but extremely quickly, to give him his full support, because Richard was admitted to Jesus College, Cambridge, to read Law with a view to the Ministry, on 25th January 1819, only one month after his Christmas Day letter.

There was never any doubt that Richard would do well at Cambridge: he had an excellent mind and was ready to apply himself to his studies with total commitment. He was still a serving officer in the Bengal Army and would receive his basic Lieutenant's pay, such as it was, for the full term of his furlough. This would take him up to the end of May 1820 when he would resign from the Company's service on a half-pay pension which would augment whatever miserably small stipend he might ultimately command as a country curate. He knew that he would never be rich by his own employment though, of course, he had expectations from his father.

## In January Richard heard from George Snodgrass in Paisley:

My dear Dick, — I have been a most miserably bad correspondent since I came to this Country and you will be surprised when I tell you, much to my shame do I acknowledge it, only two days ago did I send off to India my first dispatches to that Country since I came home. But I intend to mend in time to come. How do you get on my good fellow. I trust well and as happy as I wish you. I hope your father and all friends are well. I long much to hear from you with all your news and how you now like old England after a few months' trial.

Richard's instructions to Snodgrass to watch the newspapers for his engagement to Georgina had, perhaps, been a little premature; but Snodgrass had not forgotten:

By the way, I have been daily on the lookout in the newspapers for your name but as yet have seen no accounts of you, you may guess what I mean. I am only waiting for you to shew me the example, but indeed I have not yet managed to fall in love though I am trying to do so all in my power.

George Snodgrass, unaware of Richard's plans, tried to persuade him to come and stay with him in Edinburgh where his brother, a Writer to the Signet, would be happy to put him up. He was worried at the amount of money he was spending which he felt might force him to return to India earlier than he had intended:

How stands your purse Dick. I fancy money flees from you pretty quickly, I find it does so from me very expeditiously and in five months have got through £350 — which is just double what I intended, and find my calculations on board ship are all a pack of stuff, but I must just trip off the sooner and intend packing up my [tatters] after next summer and being off for old "Curry & Rice" again in the cheapest mode I can well fix upon. What say you to this. . . . Have you had any letters of a late date from India. My latest is April from Elphinstone at Patna — little news, poor James Rattray's death the most particular and interesting. Poor Griff Holmes was on the River in a very dangerous state — the Army all returning to Cantonments. If you have any news from Jack Home pray let me have it. Alas poor Ridge, his death no doubt would surprise and vex you much. Pray how is poor Johnson, I hope recovered.

Snodgrass intended to stay in Edinburgh for a few more months then a couple of months in London:

. . . and then set off for France notwithstanding our troops are out of that Country and people seem to think it will be unsafe. Going there afterwards I am of a different opinion. What do you intend doing Dick. I should like to go over to Dublin for a short time too, but have fixed on no time for that trip, but I must visit that place too.

During the previous August, Richard had written to George Homer as he had still received no note from him of the Mess Bill he had left unpaid when he transferred in a hurry from the *Thomas Grenville*. He received a reply in February:

Your last letter dated the 9th August last year I did not receive until my arrival in town the beginning of December and as I had to commence upon preparations for the present voyage immediately, I deferred writing being in some expectation of seeing you in town: but I was disappointed of that pleasure. To relieve your distressed mind about your large debt I give you an account below: balance of which, whenever it quite suits your convenience, please pay into the hands of Mr. Robert Waters, No. 3, St. Mildred's Court, London.

The sum that Richard owed was £4. 19s. 6d. — £3. 6s. of which was for soda water.

Now I have furnished you with all the pecuniary information, let me to chit chat. Capt. Alsager and myself are here in the Waterloo waiting a fair wind, our destination to Bengal and China. Passengers for Bengal are: the Marchioness of Hastings and 7 other young ladies all unknown to you. By the bye, one is married I forgot, and 3 of the other 6 are of the Marchioness's party. Major [Macrae], Major Stanhope, Capt. Conway in charge of the recruits, a free Merchant, three writers and eight cadets making a party of 28 at table. No doubt you will say with such a crowd, God help us!
  I should have been most happy if you were of our party had you been going out — but I am still more so to hear from Major Stanhope, your old schoolfellow, that you have sheathed the sword forever and are preparing for the Church: as I know well, you preferred almost anything to returning to India. May you succeed in all you undertake and enjoy health and happiness is my sincere wish. I have seen very little of our old shipmates — indeed I have never caught sight of Capt. Nicholson or Snodgrass. The former is living near Wanstead and as I understand in very good style. . .I must now close this and beg excuse for the hasty scrawl which is written at a seaport town Inn.

  P.S. Capt. A. desires particularly to be remembered to you.

In July 1819, while staying with friends in Cheltenham during his summer vacation, Richard learned of the death of his cousin George, of the 4th Native Infantry, who had died at sea aboard the Indiaman *Sovereign* in April during his passage home on sick certificate. George was the fifth of his poor Aunt Lucy's six children who had died early, leaving only Barrington, who was still with the 13th Native Infantry in India but was due home on furlough the following year.

Richard's (Blackbrook) cousin George had joined the *Rochfort,* 80, commanded by Captain Andrew Pellet Green and had sailed for the Mediterranean. John and Renira returned to England in July when the *Magicienne* was paid off and John came ashore. He was not to be employed at sea again for the next twenty-two years.

At the end of July Richard heard again from George Snodgrass whom he had asked, when in London, to check on the progress of a gun being made for John Home at Manton's and, if the gun was ready, to arrange for it to be taken out to India with a friend:

My dear Dick, — I am indeed very much to blame for not having sooner written to you respecting the commission you gave me about Jack Home's gun; but the real and true cause was my having been taken up entirely with my friend James Clark, who I was assisting in London to get properly fitted out for India, and though I did not write to you, as I confess I ought to have done, yet the principal part of my duty to you was not neglected — viz. calling upon Mr. Manton which I did and found every thing with him as I could have wished it. The gun was then in a state of forwardness though it could not be got ready in time for my friend James Clark to take with him. I left him on Sunday morning in London, his ship left the river the same time with my self, and he was to join it next day at Gravesend and proceed on to the East with all expedition. Dudgeon of the 10 N.I. and Capt. Sutton of our Artillery are the only two belonging to our Service that I know who go with him. He has sailed on the Rochester, Capt. Sutton, and pays only £200 Stg. for the half of the [Great] Round House which is very cheap in my opinion. . . . I wish you would write to me Dick like a good fellow. Poor F. [Airdrie] of our Regt. died in India lately, his brother Dick with Pratt of our Bn. have both sailed for Calcutta. — God bless you, my dear Dick, I hope your friends are all well.

I beg my most respectful compliments to your worthy father and remain, your sincere friend, G. Snodgrass.

Before returning to Cambridge, Richard visited Blackbrook to pay his respects to his uncle and aunt and, more importantly, to renew his suit with Georgina.

# 2. Ordination

*Jesus College, Cambridge. 1819.*

John had once written to Richard of his bride-to-be, Renira, that she might have benefited from staying at school a bit longer and Richard sometimes wondered if the same might be applied to Georgina. She was certainly very accomplished — she painted, sang and played the piano all with reasonable competence and could hold her own in conversation with any company to which she was likely to be exposed. Yet, thought Richard, there was little substance in what she had to to say, whether in conversation or in her letters, which seemed mainly to consist of talk of balls and belles and beaux and parochial gossip. Perhaps, Richard thought, another year at school might have encouraged her towards an interest in subjects of more consequence; but perhaps all young ladies were like this nowadays, he really had so little experience of them.

Her handwriting was beautiful showing great strength of character in its strong, even form — so unlike her mother's which was always written with such impatience that it was hardly legible and devoid of any form of punctuation. It was not surprising that George Purvis got Georgina to make the entries of Births, Marriages and Deaths, etc. in the Family Records. She had, however, inherited some of her mother's beauty. She and her sister Renira were strikingly good-looking with fine, classical features and dense, dark hair which they wore in soft ringlets. So alike were the sisters that they were often confused:

At Mr. Pulteney's, Mrs. Hall came up and said: — "how do you do Mrs. Purvis". I bowed rather coolly, not having seen her but once before, and she remarked to Julia how cold Mrs. Purvis was and then Julia undeceived her – and Captain Peyton talked to me for some time for Renira.

During their time in the East Indies, Renira had presented John with two sons — John, born in 1816 in Ceylon, and Robert born the following year at Port Louis, Isle of France. Georgina clearly loved her two little nephews and, suffering from that common delusion that tales of the charming ways of children and dogs must necessarily be of interest to anyone other than their parents or owners, related such to Richard with regularity:

Renira, John and the children came to us Monday; little Robert is wonderfully improved, indeed I love him as much as Johnny; he is become so affectionate and good, he is looking remarkably pretty; Johnny is improved in talking but I think is more riotous than when he left us; if I write and express myself badly it must be excused as Johnny is close at hand and never ceases talking. He told me the other day that Richard had "cut off all his ears".

Richard spent Christmas 1819 with his father, who had been made a full Admiral on 12th August, at Vicar's Hill and returned to Cambridge to resume his studies early in the New Year. Georgina and her parents spent a fortnight at Vicar's Hill in January before proceeding to Bath where they took lodgings at 34 Milsom Street. The Regency period had just ended with the death of King George III, the city was in mourning and all public amusements had been suspended. Georgina, as she had promised, wrote to Richard in February with her news:

My dear Cousin, — I never make promises without performing them and as I am now a little at leisure I will sit down and give you an account of our proceedings since we left Blackbrook. We spent a fortnight most agreeably at Vicar's Hill, my Uncle and Aunt were most kind to us and studied to our pleasure as much as possible, indeed I think I am quite in favor again for I was very happy there. I went to two Balls, one at Newtown Park where I saw my Friends Julia and Anne Fawcett. My Uncle stayed till half past four o'clock at the Ball. I went with Mrs. Peyton and Mrs. Armstrong to a Lymington Ball my Father not wishing to go and my Uncle confined with the gout in his foot. Several of the [Navy] were there but I think the Young Ladies have quite spoiled those Young Men, indeed I do not think the Belles there are so well behaved as those in our neighbourhood. Mrs. C. Roberts was at the Ball but I thought she was rather cool to me. I cannot tell why I do not think she is near so friendly as she was.

We left Vicar's Hill last Monday and arrived safely here that night; the next morning was employed in looking for lodgings and we have very nice ones. Wednesday Papa and I went to a party at Mr. Garrett's which was very pleasant, there are two daughters of Mr. D. Garrett's; very agreeable girls; we are become very sociable, I am to form one in their Quadrilles when we have any. We dine at Mr. Garrett's on Wednesday. What an excellent appointment Captain Garrett has – Renira will be delighted to have them so near and I hear the Young Ladies are very pleasant. I have to return you many thanks for the music you sent me; it is uncommonly pretty tho' I fear one song is beyond my abilities – I mean "Lo here the gentle Lark". I brought it with me as I have a piano and shall endeavour to learn it. Papa begins taking the Waters today, Mama tomorrow; they are both quite well; at Vicar's Hill we heard from George; he was quite well and perfectly happy; he desired to be remembered to you. We had a letter from Renira the day before yesterday; she had not been well, we hope to hear a better account today; the children are quite well. We left my Aunt much better; she has left off drinking wine and takes some spirits; we thought her much altered, grown very thin, she was very kind to us. We had a visit from Mr. and Mrs. Leman yesterday; I suppose we shall be invited to some of their parties. Everything looks very mournful – it is unfortunate the poor King should die just now as all public amusements are suspended for a time; people here wear very deep mourning; I shall be quite ruined as I have many things to purchase. The death of the Duke of Kent was indeed melancholy. Mrs. Ricketts has called on us and we on her but have not met. Sir Edward and Lady Thornbrough are here and have also called. Mrs. Ives and Arabella are here, they are old friends of ours which is pleasant for both parties and so are the Mackies; there you see we have plenty of acquaintances and Papa is gone out and taken our letters which has worried us as we are anxious to know how Renira is. We went to pay a visit in the Upper Crescent and in the mean time the letters came. We have just got our letters – Renira is much better she says, all her neighbours have been very kind to her. She tells us Mr. Delane's marriage is no longer a secret – he is to marry Miss Gage and Mrs. Delane is to reside at St. Margaret's. Papa is going to dine with Captain Maitland and we are going to Mrs. Jacks. Papa is in hopes to be able to get me a ticket to the York House Ball. Mr. Garrett is also going to use his interest so I think I should go. I shall write to you again when I have more to tell you. Papa and Mama desire to be kindly remembered to you and accept my best wishes believe me dear Richard, Your sincere Friend and affectionate Cousin, Georgina Purvis.

In April, Renira presented John with their third son who was christened George Henry Garrett and later in the month Richard heard from Daniel Garrett in Honiton advising him that his son, William, had arrived in India and had got a good appointment in the Bengal Civil as "Assistant to the Hon. Mr. Elliott, Collector of Burdwan". He also mentioned his two daughters who had been staying with his brother William in Bath — the "very agreeable girls" that Georgina had made friends with:

My two daughters are still at their Uncle William's at Bath, but on Saturday next we expect them home. Eleanor has been absent between 6 and 7 months and Emily between 3 and 4. They will enjoy the fresh air after being stewed in hot rooms. They have been uncommonly gay we hear, but Bath is thinning now very fast as the summer approaches.

He tried to persuade Richard to come and stay with him in

Devonshire during his summer vacation and recalled that he had not seen his father since the day he went to Court after his return from Cadiz. But vacation plans were far from Richard's thoughts at that moment. He had made up his mind that he wanted to be ordained a deacon at the earliest possibly opportunity. He had worked extremely hard in his first year at Cambridge, not allowing himself to be distracted by social activities or anything else, yet he doubted if he was sufficiently well prepared for examination by the Bishop. He was far ahead of his fellow undergraduates who tried to persuade him that he was more than ready. John Shillibeer, a friend who was also preparing for the Ministry, wrote to him from Plymouth in March:

Do you know a Mr. Woolacombe of Jesus? He has been Ordained by the Bishop of Exeter and has got many terms to serve but I do not think he has been in College since I joined — you perhaps may know him but I have been told he is very dull and his passing was noted down as a miracle; and I hear of so many below-par gentlemen having [gotten] through the fiery ordeal that really I think that if we could get a Bishop in the mind to examine us we might be eased of all our trouble and anxiety. For you, I should have no kind of fear because the knowledge you have already acquired of the Greek is much more than is at all necessary. On this [score] I am very different and if I was to offer myself I certainly must have recourse to some kind of stratagem which must be commonly practised.

The next opportunity for ordination would be in June, at Norwich. Richard had been aiming at this but was still in great doubt as to his state of readiness. Shillibeer again tried to reassure him:

I hope you do not give up thoughts of going to Norwich at the next Ordination, depend upon it if you do from any idea that you are not sufficiently prepared you have come to a wrong conclusion.

His friends were deeply impressed with Richard's dedication to his studies at the expense of any sort of social life; yet they were concerned for him that his resolution was perhaps too intense:

I hope you walk out occasionally — don't fag so much, you may depend upon it, it is unnecessary for what you have to go through.

By 28th May, George Snodgrass was preparing for his return to India and wondered if there was any chance of Richard coming with him. He was staying in lodgings in Duke Street, St James's and had

been to Manton's to collect John Home's gun but it had already
been sent out to him:

My dear Dick, — As I wish very much to hear how you are and to know what
your present intentions now may be, I will esteem it a particular favor your
writing me, as if you think of again bending your steps to India about this time, I
know no one I would be more happy to have as a shipmate than yourself. I am
now so far on my way to Bengal and am determined upon making myself as
comfortable as I can there as well as on board ship, and if you only saw my room
here it would make you laugh. It has the appearance of a Europe shop in India,
amongst other articles a bang up collection of music of the first rate composers
— Mozart, Haydn, etc. etc. so that we would have some good fun together on
board, but I trust you will find it to answer better your purpose to remain here, as
I know well your dislike to India. I confess to you that if I had my choice I would
prefer also this Country, but not having that in my power, I have made up my
mind to again going back and am in as good spirits as one in my situation well
can expect to be. . . .

Snodgrass had not forgotten the comfortable time he had spent at
Vicar's Hill and would no doubt have liked an invitation to spend
his remaining time in England at Lymington:

Make my best respects to your father if you please, I hope he is quite well. I
should like above all things if I could get the length of his beautiful place, nothing
like it have I seen either in England, Scotland or Ireland, but I fear I must just
remain in this smoky place and run daily to that black building of ours in
Leadenhall Street. Henry Cock will be home next spring as he could not get leave
of absence last cold weather. Jim has gone with his Corps to Bundelkund and our
Battn. gone to Allahabad. Great changes in our Army expected and an increase
of officers as well as Regts. etc. etc.
    Adieu, my dear Dick, Believe me ever, your sincere friend, G. Snodgrass.

Three days later, on 31st May 1820, Richard resigned from the
Military Service of the Honourable East India Company and on the
11th of the following month, despite his earlier apprehension, was
ordained deacon by the Bishop of Norwich.

Richard's cousin Barrington, of the 13th Native Infantry, arrived
back in England on furlough in June. His first priority had been to
return home to Beccles, in Suffolk, to be with his poor grieving
mother who had prematurely lost five of her six children; now he
was concerned with how to draw his pay from the Company during
his furlough. He wrote for Richard's advice addressing him, for the
first time, as "The Revd. Mr. Purvis":

My dear Cousin, — I lament much that I have not yet had the pleasure of shaking you by the hand: but sincerely trust you will favor me with a visit as soon as you conveniently can and I am sure my mother would rejoice to see you — thro' God's blessing she is much better and her mind is more at ease since my return altho' she has lost the use of her left side, but still I hope, if the sun will favor us with his enlivening beam, to see her again in her garden chair enjoying the pleasures of the summer.

Your kind offer and to convince you that I sincerely excuse you for not fulfilling your intended promise of a visit has induced me to trouble you with a job which is to inform me how we Indians are to draw our pay for the two and a half year's furlo' which I may be entitled to after 30th June to which period I am paid up. I wrote to Col. Salmond enclosing my Certificates of Service and leave; but did not personally report myself as I was in too great haste to see my mother first. My printed pay certificate I still have by me and I have not received any answer from Col. S. as to the receipt of the others. Now inform me how? when? etc. I am to get my pay. Is it paid in advance or arrears?

The Revd. Thomas Purvis, Rector of Melton, Suffolk, had been a first cousin of the Admiral. His eldest daughter, Amy Laetitia, had married Revd. Nathaniel Colville and had given him three sons and four daughters, the eldest of whom was called Amy Laetitia after her mother. Both parents were now dead and their children lived at Lawshall, near Bury St. Edmunds; Barrington clearly saw the possibility of a potential wife among the daughters:

I set off tomorrow (Tuesday 20th) to Lawshall near Bury St. Eds. where I intend staying 6 days and shall be back by the Tuesday following. I wish to see my fair cousins. Mrs. Colville was a daughter of our Aunt Mrs. T. Purvis: she is dead but has left 3 amiable daughters and 2 sons who are old friends of mine.

Like Richard, Barrington had no intention of returning to "Curry and Rice" to complete his service though he had not decided what career he was going to follow. As his parents' only surviving child, he was now heir to the estates of Porters in Essex and Beckenden Grange in Warwickshire so the need for a decision was not as acute as it had been in Richard's case.

I have not yet determined what line of life is befitting me. The Church I fear requires more study than I have inclination at present to undertake to make myself master of the Greek and Latin and the latter I have almost entirely forgot. I think I am more fit for an Esqr. than a DD or AM — but time, and after looking about me a little will enable me to inform you more about it when I have thought more seriously about it myself. I shall rub up my Latin and French in the winter at any rate by way of amusement and as Beccles is a quiet place it has many inducements to make me study.

A few weeks later, Richard saw the engagement announced between Barrington and Amy Laetitia Colville, the eldest daughter. They were married at Lawshall on 11th September 1820.

Richard spent his summer vacation at Vicar's Hill from where he made regular visits to Blackbrook to see Georgina. His stepmother had not been well and she and the Admiral intended going to Cheltenham to take the waters. Richard was somewhat torn as to whether he should accompany them or go and stay at Blackbrook. He would certainly have preferred the latter but felt that, in duty, he should probably go with his parents. His aunt at Blackbrook thought the same:

My dear Richard, — Your letter is this day arrived and I am glad to hear so good an account of yourself but was sorry you do not give a better of Mrs. Purvis who I think wrong not to go immediately to Cheltenham; in her last letter to me she said they only waited the arrival of a letter from the Physician for you all to set off and though I am sure you will believe how sincerely glad we shall be to see you for as long as you like yet pray do not let your visits to us prevent your accompanying them to Cheltenham.

While staying at Vicar's Hill, Richard heard again from George Homer who was at the Jerusalem Coffee House, Cornhill. He and Captain Alsager were still serving in the Indiaman *Waterloo:*

It gives me great pleasure to find you have so soon obtained Deacon's Orders and sincerely hope you will assume the Priest's Gown and become a Silly Villain (alias civilian) quite as soon as you look forward to. — I am sorry I was not in town when you were up. I should have been much gratified to have shaken you by the hand. However, from your avocations and mine I fear that will not take place till I can retire to my cottage which I hope will be after two more voyages. Then, I hope to renew some old acquaintances etc. I trust yours will be of the number. . . . My voyage has been quite agreeable to me in every way, excepting pecuniary emolument: never were things in our way so bad but as I do not suffer more than my neighbours I continue to bear up with my ill luck. My health is not of the best I am sorry to say I had nearly left my bones at Calcutta. Yours of course cannot improve much while under such confinement but as you say: "it is an easy compound for final establishment in this blessed land". I have missed seeing Nicholson and Snodgrass being in the country. I believe they are by this time in blue water. Being good fellows, I say God send them safe back again, this which I am sure you will join. I am sorry you gave yourself so much trouble about the £5. Mr. Waters fully explained. We have not succeeded in getting our former voyages which we much wished but are stationed for St. Helena, Bombay and China which promises very little sport and a very tedious trip.

Richard's next task was to try to persuade the Court of Directors of the Honourable East India Company to pay him a Captain's pension instead of a Lieutenant's which was all, strictly speaking, he was entitled to. He had left India a Brevet-Captain but, during the course of his furlough, there had been deaths and promotions in the Regiment which would have meant that he would have been a full Captain had he returned to India. John Home, one place junior to him in the Regiment, was promoted to Captain on 31st May 1820 — the day that Richard had resigned from the Service. He was not too optimistic of his chances but his was, surely, a borderline case and the Company had been known to show indulgence in similar cases — especially where ill-health had been involved:

Sir, — Herewith I have the honor to forward the prescribed final certificate from Doctor Chambers, Physician to the Honorable East India Company, for submission to the Court of Directors, and request the favor of your causing it to be accompanied by this solicitation for retirement from the Army upon half pay.

Rightfully, I believe, as having quitted India Brevet Captain, and only Regimental Lieutenant, I am but entitled to half pay of the latter rank; tho' being a Cadet of the season 1803, I am induced to hope that the Honorable Court would kindly take into consideration the singular tardiness of my promotion, which gives me but to claim so inadequate a compensation for a service of seventeen years and its consequent loss of health. The deaths of Major Castro and Captain Boyen, the promotion of Major Latter, and resignation of Captain Johnson, have elevated me to the rank of Regimental Captain since my return to Europe. Would then the Honorable Court under consideration of my peculiar circumstances bountifully grant me to retire upon the half pay of Captain, which rank in the common course of events I should have attained with those of my juniors who now stand fifth Captains in their regiments? However, since [the record] has abundantly shewn how readily my Honble. Employers have hitherto generously consented to ameliorate by their munificence the situation of many of my fellow sufferers in their service, I hope the importance of the affair to my future comfort and happiness will plead for me with the Honble. Court for intruding upon its time with the following candid statement of my pecuniary circumstances in aid of my request for the above indulgence.

The first six months of my residence in England having been wholly, but I regret to say vainly, dedicated to the search of health by trial of mineral waters under the best, and at the same time most expensive, medical advice procurable [during which] I despaired of ever obtaining the re-establishment of health for Indian service I sought. Wherefore having entered at the University of Cambridge, and there residing at charges considerably beyond my means, I turned my mind to the studies of a new profession which have already placed me in Holy Orders; so that the door is now closed upon my return to India whether my Honble. Employers be [sympathetic] to my designs or not. In my clerical profession I may possibly obtain a curacy yielding from £80 to £100 a year; and I gratefully acknowledge myself already indebted to the service of the Honble.

Company for about £1,000 (now in India) saved in my capacity as Interpreter for which office I was selected both in the 21st and 30th Regts. — yet do I humbly trust that a final relinquishment of a profession in which I have so irreparably suffered and so faithfully served, the recompense of half a crown a day will be accounted to fall something short of my just deserts. A long enumeration of services should [.....] be wanting if I could imagine such likely to promote my object without seeming to claim what I do but entreat; and even under present circumstances a sense of the pride of my military profession denies me to suppress that my duties in the field concluded under Sir David Ochterlony's command: and that in the capacity of Quartermaster to the 4th Brigade of his army, I first penetrated the Chooreea Ghattee Pass in the mountains of Nepaul, being there in charge of the Guide and Intelligence Department by which that object was secured — a service for which my immediate Commanding Officer, Brigadier Bennett, was deemed by the higher authorities worthy the Companionship of the Bath

A few weeks later, Richard heard from the Secretary that the Court of Directors had considered his request but were not prepared to offer him a pension other than the 2s. 6d. per day to which he was entitled on retirement from their service in the rank of Lieutenant.

# 3. Georgina

*Blackbrook Cottage, Fareham, Hampshire.*
*10th November 1820.*

Now and again Richard would succumb to the petitions of his friends to join them in a day out. On one such, to the races at Newmarket, he chanced to meet his old friend Thomas Thornhill, who had been Judge at Bareilly. Thornhill had resigned from the Bengal Civil in 1811 and, for the past nine years, had devoted himself to horseflesh which had always been his principal passion. They had much over which to reminisce but conversation was difficult in the middle of the race programme and Richard did not wish to distract Thornhill from his sport. He had received a letter from him a few days later:

My dear Purvis, — I calculated on seeing you again on the Heath or should have said more to you on Monday. I go to town tomorrow and home about Wednesday where I hope to see you as soon as you can be spared from your studies. I lie nearly in your route from Cambridge to Hampshire and the Oxford coach will take you to within nine miles of my residence. Should you come by that conveyance go to the Roebuck at Oxford and the people there will direct you to my house — my junction is Woodleys near [Wandstock]. Charles Ridge is in town and about to sail. Very truly yours, T. Thornhill.

Richard and Georgina were, by now, regular and intimate correspondents — Richard learning all the gossipy Fareham and family news from her and imparting all the, somewhat less interesting, university news in return. Georgina's letters were one of the few intrusions he permitted into the harsh learning discipline he had imposed upon himself. During his vacations, he saw her as frequently as he could and she always seemed to take pleasure in his company. Although nothing had ever been said between them, other than the most proper civilities, Richard felt that they had a growing understanding and that, when and if he should be in a position to ask for her hand, he had reason to hope that she would not be unreceptive.

Georgina, for her part, had been flattered by Richard's obvious interest in her when he had first returned from India — he a dashing officer with a bushy moustache and a twinkle in his eye, home on leave from the Indies, and she a young girl just out of boarding school with little experience of other admirers; but Richard had changed in the intervening two years — his studies had made him very intense, almost saturnine, and, although he was always very charming to her, the affability of the officer had been replaced by the gravity of the clergyman which, if more suitable to his new profession, was certainly less attractive to a twenty year-old girl whose chief pleasures were dancing, which Richard hated, and socialising, for which he had little available time.

If, in 1818, Georgina might perhaps have regarded Richard as a possible future husband, she certainly had no such thoughts now and it concerned her that she might, by her friendly behaviour towards him, have led him to believe otherwise. She enjoyed his company and correspondence and did not wish to cut herself off from him but perhaps some little hint to discourage him from expecting too much of her would be prudent. From now on, she decided, she would sign herself "your sincere friend" instead of "your sincere friend and affectionate cousin".

My dear Richard, — Having just finished a letter to my Aunt I feel I may fill up an hour in addressing myself to you and trust that neither my time or pen are ill employed, at any rate, I can draw this conclusion, that in a little time I shall receive an answer from which I always derive pleasure and for your last favor pray accept my best thanks and for the friendly advice it contained; my eyes have been a little opened since I heard the news of my Friend's intended marriage and I have quite determined never to express myself too warmly on any such subject as I cannot but suppose should Emily and I ever meet we should both feel awkward which feeling we might have been spared had we been less explicit, and I may add, less warm. . . . Captain C. Stanhope was to be married yesterday from a letter Mrs. S. received from her daughter, who returned to England in February with the Bride and Bridegroom. Papa had a letter from Barrington in which he mentions his being perfectly happy and my Aunt Timms saw Captain Kidd, who spoke of Mrs. B. P. as being a very nice young woman; they are living with our Aunt Richard, who, Barrington says, required their presence and attention. Major Sackville has paid them a visit and I see by the paper he is arrived in London as soon as the Lemans left us. Caroline Hay came to us; she is an agreeable little personage and you would have enjoyed hearing her play and sing: she took a second and our voices are well adapted to sing together. Captain Barrington spent three days with us and we all went to the Fareham Ball; Papa was Steward and we had an excellent Assembly; there were 120 people and I spent a most delightful evening. Admiral and Mrs. and Misses Scott were so much pleased with the last Ball that they have promised to come and dine with us and attend the next. They reside at Southampton; did you read the planning paragraph that appeared in the London, as well as in the Portsmouth, paper? Renira, John and Robert are now staying at [Swainston]; they went this day week and I hear they go to Vicar's Hill from the Island; we have not heard from Renira since she went, therefore we know nothing of their movements, but Arnold had a letter Sunday. Little George is grown quite a beautiful boy, Johnny looks extremely well; we could not have him here, as the children at our farm have got the Whooping Cough, and this is not a desirable time of year to allow a child to catch it. The Nashes are just returned from Scotland, being truly delighted with their trip; I saw Mary Lessing Saturday, she is grown thin which is an improvement to her. . . . My Aunt tells me there are to be no Balls at Lymington therefore I daresay our Assemblies will often be honoured by some of those Lymington Belles and Beaux. We took Elizabeth Garrett home last Thursday, she spent three days with us, as John brought her from Southampton, and they were on the eve of departing for the Island, so she came to us; we saw Sir George and Lady Garrett, Louisa and Mary Anne; Sophy was to return on Sunday; I must own I think her the flower of the flock. Mrs. Henry Garrett was better: Captain G. is laid up having sprained the tendon achilles. Mr. and Mrs. Garrett are at Cheltenham and will not I believe leave that place till summoned into Devonshire to attend their Niece's Marriage which is fixed for the 28th of this month; I am to have a piece of Bride cake: Louisa and Sophy after declaring nothing would induce them to go to Bath, as it was exactly like going out to India, have accepted their Uncle's invitation and go in January; two more examples of changing their minds – I wish I had the option of going – I would not hesitate for a moment.

I shall not seal this tonight but I must now finish as the clock has struck seven – Adieu! Papa and Mama join with me in kind regards and best wishes, and believe me my dear Cousin, Your sincere Friend, Georgina Purvis.

The Cambrian sailed this morning to relieve the Glasgow.
Thursday evening 9th November.

## Her father added a footnote from which Richard gathered that all was still not well between him and Renira.

My dear Richard, Georgina having left me a little bit of her paper I cannot but use it to thank you very much for your last kind letter. I know you are always pleased to hear we are well and happy and I am able to say we are quite so and looking to the New Year with no small degree of pleasure as early in it we expect to see our beloved George who I am happy to say continues on excellent terms with his Captain etc; his last letter was dated September 11th. Renira and John are I hear going to Vicar's Hill but Renira never says much to me. . . . I am your affectionate Uncle, George Purvis.

## Richard was not prepared to accept the Court of Directors' decision on his pension without a further attempt to obtain satisfaction in

what he strongly felt to be a just claim. He therefore wrote to a Stanley Clark who was obviously a man of public influence (he may have been a Member of Parliament, or a Director of the Company) to solicit his support. However, Mr. Clark, whoever he may have been, did not read the correspondence thoroughly and, to Richard's unconcealed irritation, entirely missed the point of his protest:

I acknowledge with many thanks your favor of the 19th Inst. in which, as it were in partial compliance with the contents of my former letter you are so kind as to express a "trust that the result of my official application may have proved satisfactory to my expectations" which however had you referred to the contents of that official application, I had not now need to acquaint you is by no means the case: and it was to procure your so referring and your favorable consideration on my behalf in your public capacity that I before took the liberty of addressing you. The 2/6d. per day which the Court seems to have adjudged a sufficient compensation for so long a service in such an injurious climate is no more than what I claimed upon rights and is, allow me to say, 2/6d. per day short of the sum a Lieutenant of H.M.S. may claim after the short period of seven years service, although he may not have served beyond his native climate. I am now induced by two powerful motives to trouble you with a duplicate of my letter to the Court. The fact is that I draw a favorable conclusion from the sentiments of apparent kindness conveyed in your letter: and the second, that I draw from that of Mr. [Abun] this unfavorable one, namely that from his [expression] "I am informed that the Gentmn. in question is now a [clergyman]" as if he had [wished that] you might have supposed me to have procured my ordination clandestinely and then deceitfully endeavoured to extort from the Honble. Company their further aid from motives of mere avarice but the case is not so. My circumstances are candidly stated to them and but for the sacrifice of my constitution which I have made in their service, I should have the honor of serving them still. Such Sir is the statement upon which the Honble. Court has [granted] to me the allowance of 2/6d. per day but I am still under confidence that a slight execution of your influence would procure its being reconsidered, when a comparison of my services with those of officers in His Majesty's [army] of the same standing would doubtless obtain for me an amendment or, if the Honble. Court should decline such consideration, might I entreat your interest with some of the principal proprietors of India stock to the whole bulk of whom I hereafter contemplate a circular memorial [prosecuting] a comparative view of my services and other documents for their benevolent consideration.

Strong stuff indeed! As the Company's pensions records for this period have not survived, we shall never know whether Richard succeeded in getting a Captain's pension. It is unlikely. It is also unlikely that he carried out his threat to circularise the shareholders if only on the grounds of the expense and time such a course of action would have involved.

Richard intended spending a few days at Blackbrook before Christmas and received a letter from his aunt dated 9th December confirming this:

By your letter to Georgina I understand you intend to come to us before Xmas provided we could receive you. I assure you it will give us much pleasure to do so any day after Thursday the 14th. Your Cousin has written to the Garretts to tell them you intend paying them a visit both at Haslar and Portsmouth if they are disengaged and she desired they will write and let you know. Sir George and Lady Garrett told me the last time I saw them they hoped you would fulfil your promise and come and see them so I think they expect you. Georgina only left them Thursday last she having spent ten days with them which has done her good as she was about [four] weeks ago very ill with a violent nervous fever; you will see her a little pulled down.

No letter ever written by Richard's Blackbrook aunt and uncle failed to mention their beloved son George. As their only son in an age of large families, he had a special significance to them and their devotion was absolute:

I had a charming letter from our dear George last week the post dated November [11th] from Gibraltar – so far on his way home but you may suppose he suffered no small disappointment on arriving at the Rock to find instead of proceeding to England they were to return to Naples Bay and join the Admiral. I think it is now very uncertain when we shall see him but we must not repine and thank God he is well and happy and assures us is on the best of terms with his Captain and all the other Officers. We are led to expect him early in the next year.

The tenant of the Blackbrook Home Farm was one James Mansell whose children had contracted whooping cough:

Renira and John are at Vicar's Hill with little Robert and have been there three weeks; dear John and the sweet baby are at home as we dare not bring John here the Whooping Cough being at James Mansell's very bad, which is too near. Let us have a line to say what day you will come to us . . .

During his stay at Blackbrook before Christmas, Richard asked his uncle for Georgina's hand in marriage. Somewhat taken aback, George Purvis seemed concerned about two things: firstly, what did Georgina think about it? Richard explained that he had not yet proposed to her so did not yet know her feelings himself. Secondly, what did Richard's father think about it? He had not yet mentioned the matter to his father, he explained, preferring to wait until he had Georgina's answer. This seems to have displeased George Purvis the most. Did Richard not realise, he asked, how hurt the Admiral had been when he learned that John had been concealing from him his understanding with Renira for so long, and only told him about it after the arrangements for his marriage had been made? Did he not feel that he should have no secrets whatever from a father such as his? And did he not realise what an awkward position this placed him in with his own brother from whom he had never concealed any confidence throughout a lifetime of fraternal trust and harmony? Though this was the first intimation he had had of Richard's intentions towards Georgina, so correct had Richard's behaviour been, the Admiral was bound to think that his brother had prior knowledge of the affair, or at least a suspicion of it, and had betrayed the trust which had always existed between them by keeping it from him. Whatever the outcome, his uncle told him, Richard must make a full disclosure of the matter to his father at the earliest opportunity and must make it quite clear that he had not at any time until the present been party to the knowledge.

When Georgina received Richard's proposal, she realised that her earlier fears had not been unfounded. She was also dismayed to hear that he had spoken first to her father which made his proposal "official" and precluded any chance they might otherwise have had of the matter being dealt with kindly and confidentially between the two of them. She had hoped this moment would not arrive and had not prepared herself to refuse him in a way which would do the least possible damage to his feelings and his dignity. She therefore played for time telling him that she had not been expecting such an honour and must consider his proposal carefully. She would give him her answer before he left Blackbrook the following day.

Richard was hurt and disappointed that he had not received an immediate and enthusiastic acceptance but it did, to some extent, prepare him for the interview the following morning at which Georgina told him, with as much tenderness and sympathy as she could, that, though she loved him as a special cousin and a very dear friend, and deeply flattered and honoured as she was by his proposal, her love was not of the kind which would allow her, in conscience, to accept it.

Richard returned to Cambridge after Christmas determined, initially, to have nothing further to do with the Blackbrookites. He was certainly not going to reveal his humiliation to his father as his uncle had insisted. In January he wrote to Georgina in a style which, if not wholly frigid, left no doubt that their relationship had changed. He enclosed a music chart he had promised to send her. Then, early in February he received her reply — friendly, vivacious, gossipy as ever — as if nothing at all had happened between them to threaten their friendship:

My dear Cousin, — I am happy in bestowing an hour to answer your letter, and to thank you for the chart, which will be useful and informing to me in that style of singing to which, at present, I am quite a novice. I doubt not I shall meet with many difficulties, however I will endeavour to surmount them as far as I am able. My others I have lent to Jane Garrett, she having expressed a wish to copy them and I, in return, am to have some of hers; she sings, I think, with taste, but in my opinion, she wants instruction; we are all quite delighted with her, she is, indeed, a superior young Woman, and one whose society I am anxious to cultivate, knowing I should from it derive pleasure and improvement; I only regret we are not nearer and could have more opportunities of meeting; the two girls came and accompanied us to the Assembly; their Brother went to Renira's: it was an excellent Ball and our young Friends were much pleased; indeed it was the best and [smartest] Ball we have had this Season; there were 150 people, and a happy mixture of Army and Navy – Capts. Brace and Bligh, by their attention and politeness, gained universal praise; the former paid himself an additional Guinea so that we were enabled to dance till a later hour than usual, which I assure you, we did not dislike; the Guards honored us with their presence, and I had the extreme felicity of Quadrilling with one; two Capts. in their uniform graced the Assembly, with one I danced and Mary Ann the other. Capt. Carry (my partner) was both handsome and agreeable, being a true sailor, which you seldom meet with now a days, as Sailors as well as Soldiers, are become Dandies and Figurantes.

No tidings of George's return, we received a letter from him a few days ago, in which he mentions the report that Glasgow is not to return to England till the latter end of March; he says he is perfectly well and longs to see us all. . . . No doubt you have heard of our Port Admiral Sir George Campbell having put an end to his existence; I have learnt he was a most nervous man, and that any trivial circumstance, which in any other person would have passed by unfelt and unnoticed, worried him beyond expression. The reason given for this dreadful act, is that the Iphigenia, before she sailed, was in a state of mutiny, and that Sir George had received a reprimand from the Admiralty for not sending her to Sea; it is needless for me to enter into further details, as you will have read a full account of the whole business in Motley's Paper.

I had a long letter from Louisa Garrett about a week ago. I am sorry to say that neither Louisa or Sophy like Bath. No! They tell me they are much, very much, disappointed. I pity their tastes and wish I could change places with them; it seems extraordinary to me that surrounded by kind friends, partaking of all sorts of amusements, having their wishes gratified in every way, that they can not be happy; I must confess, I think they do not deserve so much attention and kindness, but I believe there are some who will never be happy though surrounded with every thing calculated to make them so – they are not to return till March; Louisa says Capt. Johnson and Major Sackville are at Bath. We expect Lady Garrett here on Friday, as she takes Harriet and Amelia to Southampton, and will return here to dinner and stay to sleep. Miss Barney spent two days with us, she has promised to come to us when George returns. You will be surprised to hear Mrs. Brett is going to be married to Mr. Charles Blatherwick, it is quite true, and the wedding is to take place immediately, much to the annoyance of Mr. and Mrs. Anderson – Mrs. and Miss Brett have behaved in the most ungrateful and shameful manner to them, I believe they do not now speak. Mr. Charles B. is 13 years younger than his intended, every body is up in arms about it, and can but have a most despicable opinion of the Lady. We dine at the Andersons tomorrow and shall hear more about it. Capt. and Mrs. Carter are at Vicar's Hill, Mama had a letter from my Aunt the day before yesterday, in which she gives a most excellent account of herself and my Uncle – Mama has been suffering with dreadful head aches but my Father is looking remarkably well. And now, I am sure, I have exhausted your time and patience enough and will only add that all here unite in kind regards and best wishes, believe me, as ever, Your sincere friend, Georgina Purvis.

P.S. My Father is not to be Sheriff this year, the Duke of Wellington has let him off for this time but I believe not ultimately.

Then in March he heard from his Blackbrook aunt, intoxicated by the return of their beloved George and, again, quite normal and friendly as if nothing had happened. Perhaps, thought Richard, it would be petty to remain aloof from them when it seemed clear that all they wanted was to return to the happy and easy relationship they had enjoyed before he had made a fool of himself:

My dear Richard, — I feel quite ashamed at not [formerly] writing to you but ever since George arrived I have hardly had a moments time, what with going to Portsmouth etc. I am happy to say he is every hour improving in looks as on his first arrival we were hurt to see how very ill he looked; he is grown very tall and thin otherwise not altered except not [in such] high spirits; he has been down almost every day at Portsmouth and today is gone to be paid off for the present; he is appointed to the Tyne, Captn. White, but his kind friend Captain Maitland is going to give him letters to a particular friend of his who is going to have a ship on the Mediterranean Station and George is very much pleased with the idea of it, but by going into the Tyne for the present he will get a little [time] at home.

Renira has not been well but is quite recovered now. I wish both she and John found more happiness at home, as Mr. Blatherwick told your Uncle yesterday, she did enough to ruin the best constitution in the world but they are never happy, but visiting about; I cannot think how they can feel comfortable leaving those sweet children to Irish servants as they generally have, but I never give advice, I know it will not be attended to. Dear little John has been with us for the last month George had a letter from your Father today, and well written so his gout must be much better. Your dear Uncle, I am happy to say, keeps quite free and I hope with proper care will do so. You must excuse this [messy] journal as my pens are bad and I am hurried for time. Your Uncle George and Georgina unite in kind love to you with Your sincere friend and affectionate Aunt, Renira Purvis.

P.S. George will write to you very soon and hopes he shall see you before he leaves England again.

By May, Richard had hopes that his relationship with the Blackbrookites might just return to normal with, perhaps, just a little bit of very proper frigidity on his part towards Georgina, and that his uncle would forget his direction that Richard must disclose the affair to his father. However, his hopes that he might be spared this embarrassment were shattered by a postscript from his uncle to a letter of Georgina's which he received in May: he hoped Richard had remembered his agreement that he would make a full disclosure to his father. He would be staying at Vicar's Hill early in July and would feel it his duty to apprise the Admiral of the affair if Richard had not already done so.

This, Richard thought, might be the very best thing; he could take a circuitous route home at the start of his summer vacation, visiting a few friends on the way, thereby delaying his arrival at Vicar's Hill until after his uncle's visit. He would then be spared the embarrassment of relating his humiliation to his father and, with luck, his father might have the delicacy not to raise the matter with him at all.

# 4. Priesthood

*Vicar's Hill, near Lymington, Hampshire.*
*1821.*

On 17th June 1821, Richard was ordained priest at Norwich. He then began his "circuitous route home" to delay his arrival at Vicar's Hill until after the Blackbrookites' visit during which he expected his uncle to have made the disclosure to his father regarding his affair with Georgina. He stayed for a time in Yarmouth, London and Bath before arriving at Vicar's Hill only to find that his uncle had postponed his visit and he was therefore left with no alternative but to tell his father and stepmother himself about the events at Blackbrook last Christmas. His father showed little interest one way or the other, his only admonition being that, whatever Richard's relationship with anyone at Blackbrook had been, or would be in the future, it must not in any way prejudice his own relations with his brother. When Richard told them that he now wished to return to the same amicable footing with Georgina on which they had been prior to this business, his stepmother had cast her eyes to heaven and said in an exasperated tone: "You Purvises are strange lovers". Richard wrote to Georgina the following day and inscribed the copy he kept — "My last letter to Georgina":

My dear Georgina, — So shamefully am I in debt to the Blackbrook family in the writing way that I know not where to commence the ceremony of liquidation till I consider that you were my greatest creditor, and since the subject now chiefly occupying my thoughts respects yourself, it may be as well that the communication is to you. Know therefore that I yesterday made an impartial disclosure to my Father and Mother, of the whole affair which was the subject of my Uncle's laconic postscript on the 19th of May last: and this will I trust reduce the understanding between us to that same friendly footing which on your part existed prior to the last Christmas, but which on mine had been trespassed upon by one incautious step. I had expected your visit to my Father would have taken place before I should reach home, and in fact originally projected a circuitous route hither . . . in this case the disclosure I allude to would have been made, as I before desired and expected, by your Father; . . . I have done what your Father seemed to expect of me, and I hope it will now meet his approbation, although I must confess that howsoever desirable may be the [evincement] of unclouded confidence between Brothers in matters of importance, I do not conceive that silence upon the affair between us was in any way culpable concealment – on the contrary I should have apprehended revealing to a Father the unsuccessful amour of his Son, when that Son had acted honorably and openly, was not by any means a conciliatory measure, nor, for the very reason which my Uncle stated, altogether prudent. But let it now pass: I can observe nothing from my Father's conduct or conversation which bespeaks emotion either one way or the other, and all my Mother says is that the Purvises are strange lovers – alluding to terms of friendship between you and me remaining undisturbed.

Richard knew that a ball was being planned at Blackbrook, in honour of young George before he sailed, and was anxious to ensure that he did not receive an invitation:

It is time I accounted for [my absence and my] silence because my Mother mentions my Aunt's kind enquiries after me, and talks of a Ball and the like at which you are about to [preside]; but I hope you will do me the favor to [regard] this as a caveat against all kind of invitation, because you know my antipathy to dancing and that I would be but a living burthen upon your party, neither would I quit my Father's house so early on what might appear (but is not really so to me) a pleasurable pursuit after so long an absence from it.

He then described his "circuitous journey":

From the Ordination at Norwich I proceeded on a visit to a friend of my Mother's in the neighbourhood of Yarmouth . . . Then I proceeded to London – not upon an errand of pleasure for the time passed in the misery of executing [various commissions] for India and taking leave of friends bound to that hateful climate whom I may never meet again. I [indulged] myself here with [visits to some] of the principal exhibitions which were for the moment gratifying. After London I visited Bath, where the Garretts would not hear of my residing in an hotel while I paid my respects to themselves and the different [relatives and] friends residing in that vicinity, I therefore removed into their magnificent and hospitable mansion and stayed with them a week – they desired their regards to all your family when I should see you, more especially to yourself being that you are a favourite with them both.

The 6th July 1821 was the 30th wedding anniversary of George and Renira Purvis at Blackbrook. Richard's stepmother had sent a present to her sister-in-law which Georgina acknowledged on the same day:

My dear Aunt, — Your pretty present to my Mother arrived this day the anniversary of our Parents wedding day and we all admired it extremely, it is something quite new, and we are of opinion that you have shewn great taste and judgement in the device and shading etc. etc. I began to think I should never hear from you again and was therefore agreeably surprised in receiving yr. note. You say no one writes you any news, I shall have great pleasure in telling you all I know though I fear it will be but little. — I spent a fortnight very pleasantly in Penny Street and we had several very pleasant parties and dancing in the evening. You need not be afraid of my dancing now too much, I am quite a different person to what I was before my illness, I am thinner and feel stronger than I was. The two Garretts spent ten days with us and accompanied us to the Fareham Assembly, we had also Mary Ann and Jane from Haslar. We were all dressed alike in white silk net dresses with finishings composed of white velvet and beads and being in uniform, I assure you we were considered a smart Quadrille. We were very much disappointed that the party on board the Athol was put off as we began to assemble. Lest it should never take place however Capt. Clowes of the Rose (to which ship George is appointed and is intended to wait on the King) has promised us a Dance. Capt. Clowes is a pleasant gentlemanlike young man, and George goes down tomorrow to join him. We are going to have a Quadrille party on Friday next and we wish we could prevail on you and my Uncle to join us; you thought [it too much] exertion to come to Mrs. Carter's wedding – fancy then you are coming to mine, as you promised us to do, should such an event ever happen, we should be delighted to see you and my Uncle. We mean to dance in the dining and drawing rooms, safe in Papa's, though we do not mean to have a grand supper. I hope this will give as much satisfaction as the last, we have bespoken three of the Marine Band, you have no smart Beaux to send us from Lymington, we have plenty of Belles.

I am very glad to hear so favourable an account of Mrs. Carter and her Baby – I shall go and see her as soon as she will admit me. Renira and John are staying at Haslar as soon as they return I am invited to go there. Little John breakfasted with us on the twenty ninth, and dined and went to the Fair with us; he is grown so tall and thin, but looks uncommonly well – the baby wonderfully improved, though very backward in walking. Robert looks in very good case. Renira and John both grown very stout. People tell us Papa is looking well, but I do not think he has gained his strength so well as we could wish. Mama enjoys her ride in the Pony Chaise and has no reason to be the least alarmed, she says she does not feel any. [Martin] I fear will never recover his strength I forgot to mention we were all delighted with the Assembly, and Jane and I danced every Quadrille and Country Dance till far past three o'clock, the rest were not as frisky; there were 130 people and an abundance of Navy though John was disappointed of Capt. [Bennie] who did not like to come having a Court Martial pending over him, and Capt. Hay who sailed the day of the Ball. Miss [Tonge] did not look so well as usual, she was badly dressed and was the only person in black shoes. Mama begs I will leave her room enough and really I have written so many cards of invitation that my hand is now quite fixed out and I fear you will find this illegible. Pray remember us most kindly to my Uncle and with our devoted love to yourself – Believe me, my dear Aunt, Your affectionate Niece, Georgina Purvis.

## Her father added a note:

Pray thank my Brother for his very kind letter and say Madam [Vereloh's] Coachman is settled here, as Minchin with whom he lived some years gave me a good character of him. I am just returned from the Bursledon Bridge meeting: it is still under substantial and I trust permanent repair, which will cost us £1200. I go to the Sessions at Winchester on Tuesday to swear many oaths with my Brother Magistrates of this Division. Fare you well says Geo. Purvis.

And her mother:

My dear Sister, — Accept my best thanks for your very pretty present which I admire very much and shall value for your sake. Georgina has told you we have made up our minds to give a little Dance before our beloved George sails as he is deserving of any kindness we can show him as well as his sisters and tho' it will be an expense we must not mind it for once. I fear you will not be persuaded to come to us but we could give you a bed and on such an occasion you would not mind sending your Servants to the Inn. Think about it. Where is Richard? I wish to write to him but know not where he is. Let me know.

Where indeed was Richard? Skulking somewhere to avoid an invitation to the Blackbrook quadrille party, resentful of the fact that everyone seemed to be behaving so normally while he nursed a broken heart? He was certainly back at Vicar's Hill by the middle of August where his uncle wrote to him enquiring after his father's health and inviting Richard to Blackbrook to see the beloved George before he sailed in the *Prose:*

My dear Richard, — A report yesterday (which I most sincerely trust has not the smallest foundation) reached my ears that your excellent Father was not quite so well as we had flattered ourselves from your Mother's reports of him: do me the kindness therefore to set my mind at ease in confirming this mistake; and as the Prose is ordered for foreign service, and will go out of the harbour to-morrow; and knowing your inclinations to see George ere he may depart, suppose you were to take a trip hither for a day or two for that purpose: we are ignorant of his destinations, but hope it may be the Mediterranean: if South Sea or West Indies, we must remove him, which I shall much regret as he is so very desirably fixed, but he must be in England the beginning of July next to pass at the College.

Richard had not seen Georgina since the affair at Christmas and dreaded their first encounter. He realised, however, that he could not put it off indefinitely — the Blackbrookites were close family, after all, and, apart from any other consideration, he knew his father would not countenance any protracted sulking with them. He therefore accepted his uncle's invitation to spend a weekend at Blackbrook, ostensibly to bid farewell to George.

His first meeting with Georgina was not as bad as he feared it might have been. Her behaviour towards him was the same as it always had been — animated and friendly. Her conversation was punctuated with smiles and little humorous asides, directed at him, and gossipy confidences delivered at his elbow in a stage whisper. It was as if nothing had happened between them and Richard found his heart beating a little faster as it always had done in her company. He knew, however, that a degree of circumspection was necessary on his part and was at pains to avoid any situation where they might be left alone together in the same room and was careful to address his conversation to the company in general rather than directly at Georgina.

On Saturday night, when Richard had retired to his room, his uncle knocked on his door and joined him for a talk. Remembering how hostile he had been towards John over his attentions to Renira years ago, Richard was surprised at the kindness and sympathy he now so obviously wanted to extend. He told Richard that he had some idea of what he must have suffered and that he had been observing Georgina's behaviour towards him during the course of the evening and considered it reprehensible — implying that he believed she was again leading him on to expectations which she knew she could never gratify.

Richard asked for his uncle's advice: he had planned to attend the Salisbury Music Festival in a couple of weeks' time where he would stay with John and Renira, part of the Garrett family and other good friends. It was a jolly event to which he was greatly looking forward but had learned this evening that Georgina would also be going as part of John and Renira's party. Would it, he asked his uncle, be imprudent for him to attend in view of the circumstances. His uncle told him that it must be entirely up to his own discretion but urged him, once again, to keep nothing from his own father from whom he would always receive wise and sympathetic counsel.

On his return to Vicar's Hill, Richard wrote to his uncle:

My dear Uncle, — I have explained to my Father all the conversation which passed in my bed-room on Saturday night, but it terminated, as I predicted, in a lost, or at all events little profitable labour; for he declares himself perfectly indifferent to every circumstance connected with that subject, both in reference to the past and future; but only cautions me that it be not a cause of dissension between you and him.

It rested then, by your own permission, with my discretion, and the result of mature deliberation is that I shall go to Salisbury; for altho' I did feel prospectively, as before explained, but little relish for the first rencontre with my cousin, and endeavoured to avoid it by divers unavailing expedients – as for instance by a delayed and circuitous route hither from College, giving place to your proposed visit, declining Mr. Radcliffe's duty, abstaining from an interview with George, etc. etc. – Still by the ice being once broken I seem to have lost that repugnance – or at all event to such an extent as that it may not operate to the forfeiture of my Brother and Sister's company and the delight of much good music at Salisbury.

It has been always my purpose to avoid what is too commonly the case, the generating of enmity between parties situated as Georgina and myself, and we have a fatal instance of its consequences in Eastwood's case. Let ours therefore be resigned to a gradual and natural subsiding, which like a sediment in liquid cannot be thrust down, but any attempts at force, on the contrary, tend but to increase and continue the agitation. I would add to this that the evil consequences, (if we need apprehend any) are all on my side – since you now profess to think Georgina's conduct reprehensible, as being fraught (I suppose you mean) with too great kindness and encouragement towards me: but it is no other (if even half as friendly) as she practised prior to Xmas last; and had you then been of that opinion, I most probably had never been made a fool of: but now I may be upon my guard.

I still entreat you to deliberate upon this business and if you should be of opinion that we ought not to meet at Salisbury, your letter may find me at the Spread Eagle on Wednesday, whence I will readily pack up and return upon some frivolous pretence or other before the Titchfield party can arrive.

I am desired by my Mother to acknowledge with thanks my Aunt's note and to mention that she as well as my Father look forward with pleasure to your coming over after George's departure, an event which though for your sakes they would not desire to hasten, they are happy to congratulate you on its being for so favorable a climate and in every respect so correspondent to your wishes.

Now that Richard was an ordained priest, his father, as ever anxious to serve him, intimated his willingness to purchase an advowson — the right to appoint a member of the clergy to a specific benefice — if one such suitable to Richard's requirements should become available. The system of patronage in the Church of England was every bit as entrenched and inviolable as in the Armed Services and, indeed, as in most other professional areas at that time. The Admiral had suffered from not being able to advance Richard's interests in the Bengal Army but now, though he had no influence in ecclesiastical circles, he certainly had the money to buy an entrée for his son.

From this privileged position, Richard was still anxious to obtain a position by his own efforts, if this should be possible. He had acquired plenty of practical experience in chasing after patronage during his latter years in India and now he set about trying to attract interest for presentation to a curacy. There was a pleasant village called Bransgore, roughly midway between Ringwood and Christchurch, where a new church was being built which was due for completion and consecration in the autumn of 1822. Having established that the first curacy would be in the gift of a Mr. John Proctor Anderdon, of Beech House, Ringwood, who was obviously a person of some local influence, he called on him and made known his interest in the appointment.

When he returned to Vicar's Hill on his Christmas vacation, Richard announced his intention of calling again on Mr. Anderdon and preceded his visit with an explanatory letter:

Dear Sir, — As I intend to have the pleasure of calling on you tomorrow, it appears expedient that I should first prepare a written explanation of the circumstances which now prompt this second unsolicited visit lest per chance your absence from Beech House should render it entirely nugatory.

Accustomed as I now feel myself to be with you, there are those peculiar points of delicacy, both on the one side and on the other, I apprehend, calculated to place a restraint on the conduct of us both which is liable to misconstruction therefore I shall prepare the business now in hand with the sincerest declaration of candour, and a [determination] on my part to arrive at that elucidation of my future hopes, or the contrary, with respect to obtaining the curacy which is in your gift and anxiety, at the same time, lest my profession and requests, or even the cause itself of this address should appear brash or ill-timed, and lastly to express that if such should appear [the case] that it should be attributed to the urgent necessity on my part, from existing circumstances, of writing at [this time].

It were [superfluous] to say that I had not derived hope from the nature of your conversation during my last visit that you would immediately enter upon that investigation of my character and conduct as well from my college as from numerous mutual acquaintances here and elsewhere which would induce you at all events to consider me the candidate [next] in order after the gentleman recommended (I think you said) by Mr. Casemajor, provided your references were assured agreeably to my expectations and the confidence I there expressed. With respect to my private views, I believe I fully explained to you that [exclusive] preferment was by no means my object but that I sought a retired and quiet professional office in this county particularly, to which from birth I have been [attached], where my time would be devoted to those pleasing and interesting duties of a clergyman . . .

As Mr. Anderdon had only the first presentation to the curacy in his gift, he naturally viewed Richard's prospects from his father with some concern. Were Richard appointed and then move to some living acquired through his father's gift, or other influence, there would then be a vacancy for a new curate at Bransgore in whose appointment Mr. Anderdon would have no say. Aware of this concern, Richard was anxious to reassure him:

I mentioned that my father was anxious to forward my establishment in a living by purchase, of which he had given ample proof by the several negotiations he had contemplated but which either from situation, nature, title, neighbourhood or other circumstances, had been hitherto broken off. I further, I think, explained that I was prepared to relinquish all such expectations of preferment if I could only succeed in so impressing you in my favor as to expect the nomination in question. Moreover, to certain objections which in the course of conversation you advanced, I stated that no advantageous [marital] connexion, no acquirement of fortune, nor any further purchase of advowson or presentation by my father were likely to cause my vacating the cuaracy and depriving you of the advantage you now enjoy of nomination which for the sake of neighbourhood and [peace of mind] is to you a matter of so important interest These are I think the chief of my own prospects and intentions which I have already disclosed to you and which in confirmation I here repeat with this one addition that I do not proffer myself as one who is to be dependent upon the situation now in your gift but as one who would enter upon it with its concomitant duties either as instigator so far as my means may permit, or coadjutor by your means with a zeal by no means inferior to your own.

Though Anderdon clearly liked the idea of Richard having the curacy, he was still nervous that he might leave it if something more advantageous should be offered. There were other considerations, too, which prompted a cautious reply on 29th December:

Dear Sir, — Allow me to express my acknowledgements to you for your letter, and to assure you that I will not withhold an equal degree of candor on my part in answering it. The subject of it, indeed, is to me of the highest importance, and ought to preclude all reserve.

When I had the pleasure of seeing you (which I did, you will remember, without any sort of introduction but your name and personal pretensions) I detailed my views with a degree of frankness which, perhaps, the circumstances scarcely justified, and which I certainly should not have done but that I felt myself to be in the hands of a gentleman. This detail must, at once, have developed to you how indispensable it was that we should be far better acquainted with each other than it was possible we could be through the means of a single casual interview, and a, more or less, desultory conversation. You will recollect too the diffidence I expressed on the score of your change of profession, the probability of your making such a connexion in marriage, or obtaining such an accession to a paternal estate, as would occasion your removal. And you acquiesced in my representation that any change would be destructive to my views, as my patronage extends only to the first presentation to the curacy. I think I also mentioned to you that the church, now building, could not be consecrated earlier than Sept. next, and that the expected stipend (£110 a year) must be consequent on that ceremony.

   Superadded to all this, the treaty with the gentleman so strongly recommended
by Mr. Casemajor (who is represented as possessing pretensions peculiarly suited
to all our objects) remains precisely as it did when I had the pleasure of seeing
you, and I fear can only be put again in motion by my personal presence in
London: – This cannot occur till I take my family to town the first week in March.
   Under these circumstances, I have, from motives of the purest delicacy towards
you, not only withheld in the enquiries you so much encouraged, but have never
mentioned to a single individual, that any intercourse whatever on the subject had
taken place between you and myself.
   I confess that I have frequently contemplated the means of obtaining for Mrs.
Anderdon the pleasure of your acquaintance (for she and I have but one feeling,
and one wish, on this my important subject) and nothing but the peculiar
inclemency of the weather has prevented us from returning Admiral and Mrs.
Purvis's visit at Vicar's Hill. The same cause has, more or less, restrained me
from asking the favor of you to spend a day or two with us here: – for though it
may not be so important to you that you should find our habits and our views
congenial to your's, yet it is indispensable that you should find them similar to
your own, as no inconsiderable share of your comfort would be likely to spring
from this cause in case the suggested alliance between us (if I may call it so)
should ever take place. Indeed, it is gratifying to us to observe from your letter
how considerably you partake with us in the zeal by which, I have no scruple to
acknowledge, we ourselves are influenced.
   Thus, you will see, my dear Sir, that I am in no condition, at present, to say
anything definitive to you; though I am prepared to move in the affair by such
rules as it is quite as important for your sake as for our's should be our guide. I
consider that, at present, we are almost strangers to each other – that we may
become friends and coadjutors in promoting the welfare and happenings of many
others.
   But, I assure you, that it would afford me sincere pleasure to learn that your
father has made for you a provision, otherwise, in the church, far more
advantageous, in a pecuniary point of view, than that which it may be in my
power to propose: and I entreat you not, in any respect, to allow what has passed
between us to interpose against any such arrangement if it should offer.
   If you should be disengaged on Thursday next, we shall be happy in the favor
of your company at dinner, and hope you will be induced to stay till Saturday.

Richard never acquired the curacy at Bransgore though John
Anderdon invited him to the Consecration in October 1822:

. . . on Wednesday next at 11 o'clock, in your canonicals, though I sincerely
regret that the bishop's suite and a necessary invitation to all the magistrates in
our immediate neighbourhood preclude me from asking you to dinner. You shall
not, however, be turned away hungry.

He also consented to undertake duties at the church *pro tempore*,
pending the appointment of the new curate.

Our very extraordinary vicar will be happy (and I need not say how much we shall be so) to profit by your kind services for, probably, two or three Sundays, until he shall make a regular appointment of a curate. Should you be disengaged, and disposed to render us this important assistance, we would stipulate for your favoring us always with your company here till the mornings of Monday, which will be very acceptable to us, and we will endeavour to render it not disagreeable to you.

Richard accepted his offer and, during his spells of duty at Bransgore, always stayed at Beech House with the Anderdons with whom he formed a firm and lasting friendship.

# 5. Whitsbury

*Jesus College, Cambridge. 1822.*

Not all Richard's fellow undergraduates shared his industry and commitment which, later in the year 1822, would be rewarded by his achievement of a First Class Bachelor of Law degree. John Earle, not fancying the winter mud between his lodgings and Hall, decided he would skip a term and wrote to Richard from his house in Harley Street asking if he would dispose of the tenancy of his lodgings:

My dear Purvis, — I have some thoughts of not reading at Cambridge this term: — It is by no means agreeable in winter to splash backwards and forwards thro' the mud to Hall and Chappel — and during the only two winter terms I have resided there, I have been attacked with the same kind of mess; besides this, my good friend, Hustler will be absent from thence. On the other side of the balance come the lodgings and the necessity of paying for them. If I could get a tenant for them, it would decide me. — Pray be so good as to assist me in this; see if you can dispose of them for me, and let me hear from you speedily on this subject. Speak with Mrs. Langton about it; if she could get a tenant for the whole year it would be better for her as I have only agreed to take them for this term: — or if she could let them for this term, I will take them for the two next instead. Make some arrangement about this as soon as you can. Excuse this hasty scrawl and believe me, Yours most sincerely, J. H. Earle.

If I succeed in disposing of them, I shall come down for a day or two to move my things which at present occupy some of the drawers etc. — wch. may be wanted by a new tenant.

His studies at Cambridge completed, Richard continued his search for a curacy while at the same time taking temporary clerical duties when and where he could find them. He had acquired a reputation for reliability among his friends and was ever ready to help them out. The Revd. J.K. Greetham had a living at Petworth, Sussex, and needed to attend at Cambridge for a few days; but there was nobody to take over his duties. Richard offered to stand in for him while he was away.

My dear Purvis, — I have been anxious to write to you for the last ten days, but my occupations have been lately so numerous that I have scarcely had a moment until the present so to do. Your very generous offer of assistance I am compelled to accept. I regret it for your sake particularly as it will divide you so far from the society of Vicar's Hill and all the comfort and luxuries attending the same. The consequence of being a man of sincerity has got you into this scrape, for most certainly I should not have availed myself of your offer if I had not been most fully satisfied long ago that your actions always follow your words. . . I propose to be at Cambridge on the 15th or 16th therefore can take my duty on the 10th but I should wish to see you a day or two before I depart if you can conveniently manage it, as there will be a few professional matters to arrange — perhaps you will let me know when you will fix to arrive at Portsmouth and I can plan to meet you there. I found on my arrival friend Benson had been preached at Petworth during my absence.

Nor, at the time, was it considered unseemly for one clergyman to ask another to investigate the class and background of one of his parishioners:

Well knowing that you are well pleased when you can serve others, I am induced to ask you to make further enquiries about a young man of the name of Lavington, of whom I spoke to you about when at Cambridge. . . I wish however further to know whether Mr. L.'s parents were in trade or profession, or what they were, and whether the family is now respectable and with what class associated. — What time the father died and his Xtian name — you will find this on his tombstone and if any further information as to the character of Mr. Lavington can be obtained I should be glad. I know I am imposing a troublesome task on your shoulders but my impudence does not stop here for I have in addition to request your earliest convenient attendance to this matter as I am much in want of the information. — J.K.Gtm.

In April Richard learned, to his great distress, of the death of his cousin Barrington, less than two years after his marriage to his cousin, Amy Colville, and before his furlough from India had expired. Amy had given birth to a little daughter, Frances Laetitia Philippa, the previous October which may have been some small comfort to Richard's Aunt Lucy who had now lost every one of her six children and had seen the end of the male line of her late husband's branch of the Darsham Purvises. In November there was more sadness when John and Renira's eldest son, "Little Johnny" died aged just six years.

In October 1822, Richard heard of a temporary curacy which would become vacant the following summer at Irchester, near

Wellingborough. He asked John Shillibeer to have a look at the place and send him a report.

> . . . I just write a few words to say that I sent a letter to you from Wellingboro yesterday week last, giving a hurried account of Irchester — but if the letter has not reached you let me say that I think it will answer your purpose extremely well but I will give you all particulars if I find that my last has not gone safe.

While serving as temporary Curate at Irchester during the summer of 1823, Richard found himself, perhaps for the first time, in a position of sacerdotal judgement when he had to chose between acceptance of an attractive invitation to Wollaston Hall, just outside Wellingborough, or the censorship which he knew his refusal must imply. It seems that the proprietor had been in some trouble with the law over his debts and Richard felt that, not only must he refuse the invitation, but must state his true reasons for so doing:

> My dear Sir, — Altho' perfectly sensible of the kindness towards me individually which has procured me the honor of an invitation to Wollaston Hall tomorrow, still it has thrown me into a perplexity of thought that is better understood than described; and my positive intention to decline that honor I have postponed to this late period mainly hoping that some unforeseen circumstance might incidentally call forth my purpose in a more conciliatory and less embarrassing shape than that in which I am now compelled to offer it. What the world denominates a polite excuse (if I were inclined to offer it) would by no means answer my end; because as I must appear in the discharge of my ministerial functions . . . no plea of casual indisposition would be accepted. It remains only then candidly to state that a conscientious view of unpleasant proceedings against you which occurred on this day fortnight past and once before in that same week forbids my receiving any attentions from you which would seem to increase your pecuniary embarrassments. I may add not only that it is repugnant to my private religious feelings, and that it is a self denial due to the sacred office which I bear; but also that it is incompatible with the Christian example I am called upon to prove myself before them amongst whom the circumstances of your arrest are as notorious as all such transactions commonly are relating to the conduct of their superiors.
>
> I trust entirely to your good sense that this candour and conscientious feeling of mine which has for its foundation your profit and advantage rather than any sentiments of [severity], and however humiliating it may be to our human pride, (of which I in common with other [mortals] confess myself a [liberal bearer]) I do trust, [and say], that this sacrifice on my part of great happiness to the imperious call of duty will by no means render you an enemy either to myself personally or to the interests of the Church in which, by God's grace, I serve, but that you will believe me still to remain, my dear Sir, Your most obedient servant, R.F. Purvis.

On 29th May 1823, Richard's Aunt Renira died during a visit to Vicar's Hill. She had been ill for some time and her husband had hoped that a change of air at Lymington might have been beneficial to her. She was only fifty-one years of age. Georgina thus became the mistress of Blackbrook.

Then, towards the end of the year, Admiral Purvis had the offer of an advowson for the church of St. Leonard's at Whitsbury, a small village near Fordingbridge in Hampshire, which would give him, and his heirs in perpetuity, the right to appoint the vicar. This was the opportunity for which he had been waiting: he bought the advowson and presented Richard to the living on 10th March 1824.

On the occasion of Richard's "circuitous route home" from Cambridge in 1821, when he had been trying to avoid the Blackbrookites at Vicar's Hill, he had stayed for ten days with friends of his stepmother near Great Yarmouth, in Norfolk. The Revd. Thomas Baker had been Rector of Rollesby for the past twenty years and lived with his wife Ann and their ten children in a rambling rectory at the nearby village of Little Chessingham.

. . . where I passed ten as pleasant days as perfect hospitality and kindness could possibly make, and had difficulty even then in escaping from the friendly persuasions of a family not less urgent in their attentions than I have ever found those who come within the circle of my own connexions.

He had been particularly taken with Elizabeth, the eldest daughter, then aged twenty-five, and with the calm and capable way she supported her father in his parochial duties, and her mother in the control of domestic anarchy in their institution-sized household. He had marked her then as an ideal clergyman's wife and, two years later, on 19th January 1824, they were married by Elizabeth's father at Rollesby Church. In March the couple moved into the Parsonage House at Whitsbury.

Sebastian Land, Richard's old Adjutant in the 1/30th Native Infantry, had returned to England on Sick Certificate in 1824 but had not had much success in recovering his health. He wrote to Richard from London in January 1825:

My dear Purvis, — It is so long since we parted that I am become anxious to hear something of you, to know if you still continue to enjoy as much as once the new life you have marked out for yourself and that you are well and happy. As for myself, my engagements in this Country have been much broken in upon by frequent returns of sickness, and as yet I have made little progress in improvement on the score of health. The weather to be sure has been very unexpectedly damp and wet and has been all against me. I was fortunate in having it fine during my stay in Devonshire, which I left early in September for Cheltenham but my pleasures there were very circumscribed owing to an attack of my old complaint on my first arrival.

I met Johnson at the latter place and was much pleased to find him looking much better than I expected. He went from thence in to Hampshire, therefore I conclude you saw him subsequently. I have heard nothing of our friend Home since I left India, we have neither of us benefited by the late alterations and our ill luck still hangs to us . . .

On 23rd February 1825, Admiral of the Blue John Child Purvis died at his home, Vicar's Hill House, aged seventy-eight years, and was buried in Boldre Churchyard four days later after a ceremony conducted by the Vicar of Boldre, the Revd. C. Shrubb.

Good to his often repeated promise, the Admiral had made equal provision for John and Richard. His widow, Elizabeth, received all his household goods, the income from £20,000 capital and the right to remain at Vicar's Hill for her lifetime. To his sister Emma, Richard's "Aunt Timms", he left a continuance of the allowance he had been making her for some years past. To Richard he left his farms at Upminster in Essex and to John his farms in Ringwood and Wootton-under-Edge, in Wiltshire, and at Edwardston in Essex. After Elizabeth's death, or at such time as she no longer wished to live there, the Vicar's Hill Estate would pass jointly to John and Richard to dispose of as they thought best. A codicil added the previous year, relating to the Whitsbury advowson, was worded ambiguously which was to cause problems at a later date:

Whereas I have settled on my son John Brett Purvis and his wife Renira Charlotte Purvis the sum of £5,000 stock in the 3% Consols and appointed Sir George Garrett of Portsmouth and James Halford the younger of Norfolk Street, London, Esq. Trustees of the same, I have since presented my son, the Rev. Richard Fortescue Purvis, to the Rectory of Whitsbury in the County of Southampton (or Wiltshire) which I consider equal to the settlement made on my son John Brett Purvis the advowson of the said Rectory of Whitsbury for the benefit of any son of his which may be brought up for the purpose of Holy Orders, and if there should be no such son then to any son of my son Richard Fortescue Purvis either by his present or any future wife.

John Scott, his special protégé, in whose career he had always taken a particular interest, was also remembered in the codicil to an extent which must have surprised the Admiral's relatives:

To Captain John Scott of the Royal Navy now living at Bishop's Waltham in the County of Southampton, £2,000 sterling as a legacy from me.

One month after the Admiral's death, Richard's first child was born at Whitsbury at 2 a.m. on 25th March 1825. She was baptised Elizabeth at a private service conducted by her grandfather, Revd. Thomas Baker. Richard's brother John was her godfather and his stepmother and Georgina her godmothers.

Early in 1826, George Purvis of Blackbrook became ill and Georgina sent to Colchester for his sister Emma to be with him. Emma, "Aunt Timms", had a great deal of experience in nursing the infirm having spent most of her married life caring for her husband, Captain Richard Timms, an invalid of the 2nd Garrison Battalion, who had been in a very bad state of health for many years before his death. Despite his sister's attention, George Purvis became progressively weaker and died at Blackbrook Cottage on 2nd May.

If his brother's legacy to John Scott had raised some eyebrows, it was nothing to the furore which George Purvis's last Will and Testament raised in the family. Blackbrook Cottage, its contents and land amounting to about 12 acres, was left jointly to his son George and daughter Georgina. Blackbrook House, Blackbrook Farm and all his other land and properties in the Parishes of Fareham and Titchfield, were left in Trust, with George and Georgina as Trustees:

to divide the same between themselves and my dear daughter Renira, wife of Captain John Brett Purvis, to whom I gave £5,000 at the time of her marriage.

But the real bombshell was contained in the codicil he had added on 10th April, less than a month before his death:

This cancels Renira's portion as a "free gift" and places it in Trust for her, with explicit instructions that no part of it shall be handled in any way or at any time by her husband

John and Renira were stationed in Falmouth at the time and received a copy of the Will on 12th May. The following day Renira, predictably incensed, wrote to Richard at Whitsbury:

My dear Brother, — Yesterday's post brought me a copy of my Father's, I must
say unjust, Will both as it concerns myself my dear John and Brother — that most
undue influence was exerted over him at a time when his mind was weakened by
illness is to say the least of my suspicions. I have now two requests to make of
you, my dear Richard, one of which is that you would be my Trustee and
endeavour to see some little justice and fair play done me, for the sake of my
children, for believe me when I say I would much rather my father had not left
me a sixpence than have outraged my feelings by making me dependent on my
Sister and insulting my beloved Husband. My second request is this, Richard, that
you would immediately, if you can, come down to your Brother here allowing us
to pay your expenses on the journey (do not be hurt at my mentioning this but it
must be). His mind is so irritated and hurt that you know not what a favor you
would be doing me by complying and it is, I well know, the first wish of his heart
you would, with your cooler judgment, be able to put us both in a way how to act
and really we both need a counsellor. Do pray if possible come; he may do
something rash but do not mention that I have hinted at it; he knows only that I
am wishing to beg you will come to us. If Bessie could and my little Niece
accompany you I cannot say what additional pleasure it would give us. A
thousand thanks for all your kindness to Arthur. God bless you both — pray
come, Your ever affect. Sister, Renira C Purvis.

Richard showed great wisdom, both in the advice he returned to his
cousin and in his refusal to become involved in what might turn out
to be an extremely unpleasant family brawl:

My dear Ren, — I can readily enter into your feelings of trouble and vexation
upon the subject of your Father's Will, and most sorry am I that it was not of a
more satisfactory construction to you, and more conciliatory nature to John: but
I can do nothing in it, nor he, nor you, nor any of us. If it were ever so urgent I
could by no means leave Whitsbury at the present time, because George is absent
leaving his Parish in my charge, at all events to next Sunday week, perhaps
longer; but there is no reason why John should not come up here; the journey will
divert his thoughts and I think I could persuade him, and guide you to put on such
behaviour upon this distressing occasion as would avoid all open quarrel with
your Sister. Think within yourselves that no good could come of such a quarrel,
but on the contrary, harm. Georgina has nobody at present nearer to her than you
or your children and it is within the bounds of possibility that she may rectify the
grievances you have reason to complain of, whereas throwing out any hints of
undue influence and the like would only separate you in minutes for ever. For my
own part I should say no such undue influence could have been exerted by her,
because, as you know, our Aunt Timms was in constant attendance, with whom
both John and you being favourites, she would have deprecated any such
proceeding. I would therefore smother all suspicions (of which you mention the
above as being the least) — to say the most of them they are only suspicions,
which could never be brought to proof. Do not, my dear Ren, think I am taking
part either with one side or the other. My silence upon the subject of the Will
while [back] at Blackbrook, and my happiness in washing my hands of all
interference in the management (which I offered my services to undertake) must

convince you that I have studied to keep clear of family broils, and with the same view I must certainly decline becoming your Trustee. We have a sad instance in the trust of my Mother's fortune, and since disagreement in such cases seems almost to be unavoidable, I should certainly recommend you to fix upon some person to whom quarrels or agreements would be matters of perfect indifference, but with me it is certainly not consonant to my feelings, nor is it consistent to my profession. I have heard John mention Mr. [Manacke] for instance as being a kind friend, and if he would undertake it, no one I should think more capable, or as I should interpret from John's opinion, more honourable. And your Brother you know is your friend, with these and another of your own selection I am sure you can easily dispense with my services and spare me the disquiet in which such an undertaking would involve me. Let my advice however in the other respect guide you — keep God's peace and a good understanding if you can. I have been expecting John by every mail since he returned, and my instructions were to take him at once without any notice or ceremony to Vicar's Hill where Georgina is. This demonstrates that no enmity is entertained in that quarter. Georgina will return home next week, and afterwards come to make a visit of some length at Whitsbury. Let me therefore persuade both of you to keep your feelings under, and let John be here to meet Georgina with as much self command as he can exert, if not for the sake of peace and quietness among yourselves, still for the sake of your children . . .

John and Renira's second son, Robert Brownrigg Arthur, known as Arthur, was living with Richard's family at Whitsbury. The third boy, George, was with his parents in Falmouth and on 12th June 1826, Renira had her fourth son whom they christened simply Richard Purvis. On 21st November Richard's wife Elizabeth, known as Bessy, gave birth to a son at two minutes before 2 a.m. He was baptised privately by his father in Whitsbury Church and was christened Home Purvis which Richard explained on the flyleaf of the family Bible:

. . . the name "Home" being commemorative of a most sincere friendship of long standing with Captain John Home, Major of Brigade at Cawnpore in the East Indies.

# 6. Hatches & Matches

*Whitsbury Parsonage, Hampshire.*
*1827.*

Richard's parish at Whitsbury comprised some 140 souls, including masters, servants and children, and his church would hold 100 of them which he considered to be sufficient accommodation for those who usually did, or could, attend Divine Service.

The church was situated on the top of a steep hill above the village which was a major deterrent to attendance by the aged and infirm and a herculean challenge to those unfortunate enough to be required to carry a coffin on their shoulders to a Service of Committal. Richard undertook the whole duty of the parish, without the assistance of a curate, and held one service on each Sabbath Day, morning or evening alternating with Rockbourne, one mile distant. Morning Service commenced always at 11 o'clock and the Evening Service at half past 2 in winter and 3 o'clock in summer.

It was a poor parish consisting of the Vicar, five farmers and the inhabitants of twenty-six poor cottages. Richard found on his induction that no church offerings were made and did not consider it appropriate that any should be introduced. A school for poor children was maintained at the Parish Clerk's house at the Vicar's expense and two small charitable trusts, administered by Richard and the Churchwardens, provided limited medical aid to industrious tradesmen and some winter clothing for needy cases.

Asked by his Bishop to report on the form of Psalmody used, Richard expressed his fear that he might lose most of his congregation if he instituted any change:

The Psalmody has remained untouched during the incumbency lest in my endeavours to reform it the choir might entirely withdraw and so there might be none. The Choir consists of the journeymen, tradespeople and better sort of labourers in dispersing whom, as they are numerous, might give offence to the second rank or order of my congregation and perhaps the majority. This consideration I have weighed against my secret desire to reform the Psalmody and bring it to the old established times instead of fugues, solos, etc. which I do not altogether approve of. †

Richard found that the farms at Upminster which he had inherited from his father were a source of much annoyance. At such a distance, it was impossible to ensure that the tenants maintained the land and buildings in accordance with the provisions of their lease and, on a visit to Upminster to have a look at his property, he was shocked to see how run down the farms were with broken, unreplaced windows and peeling paintwork.

One of his tenants, Mr. Giblin, was not only behind with his rent but had neglected to send a goose to Aunt Timms on Michaelmas Day which was a part of his contract:

By a letter received this morning from Mrs Timms I am informed that you have neglected to send her the goose which was due to her on Michaelmas Day. I am at all times sorry to write to you in the language of complaint and I should be more sorry to put you to the expense of a correspondence through my solicitors in London but if more punctuality be not observed on your part you will drive me to that necessity. Messrs Cooke & Halford had not received your half year's rent last Lady Day when I last heard from those gentlemen which was on the 28th July. I have now written a second time to know if it be yet paid and if not what can I do in justice to myself and family but have recourse to those measures which are open to us all for the recovery of our just rights. †

On 28th September 1827 little Home died of convulsions while cutting his teeth. Richard received a letter of condolence from a former fellow undergraduate, the Revd. I.M. Edwards, who had chosen the life of a naval padre and whom Richard had introduced to his brother John's patronage. The year before, John and Renira had bought Bury Hall in Alverstoke, a magnificent mansion surrounded by a classical colonnade with seventy acres of gardens and pasture lands overlooking the Solent. Edwards was serving aboard the *Galatea* which was at Spithead awaiting sailing orders and had dined with John at Bury Hall the previous week:

My dear Purvis, — You will be pleased to hear that your brother and myself have at length come in contact. I dined with him on Saturday last and my reception was marked by as great a degree of kindness and attention as if I had been at Whitsbury. The same note which brought me your brother's invitation brought

---

† From a letter-book of Revd. R.F. Purvis in private ownership.

me also an account of the sad event which has befallen my kind friends at Whitsbury. I shall not attempt to describe how my own feelings were affected by this intelligence. To Mrs. Purvis and yourself it must have been a bitter affliction but more particularly to her. Capt. Purvis indeed told me that she has been exceedingly affected by it. – But let us hope that as time, which changes all things here below, wears off the vivid recollection of the beloved object so the grief which is felt at its removal will gradually subside and at length entirely die away. It would be almost presumptuous in me to point out to one like yourself, impressed with a deep sense of religion and possessing a well regulated mind and affections the good that may and generally does result from this kind of evil. I shall therefore content myself with observing that nothing is more prejudicial to our highest and best interests than an uninterrupted state of prosperity and happiness. – It disposes our hearts at all times but too much attached to the world, to be still more fond of it and to think it good for us to be here: whereas afflictions, and more particularly afflictions of the description that you have recently experienced, shew us the instability of every earthly enjoyment and that lasting happiness is to be expected only in the mansions of the blessed and in the paths of religion and holiness that lead to them.

If Richard derived any comfort from Edwards's letter thus far, one is forced to wonder how he reacted to that which follows which suggests that Richard and Bessy should not become too fond of their little daughter lest she should be destined for the same fate:

I do not know whether the affection of parents for their children can be carried to too great an extent; but if ever a child was calculated to inspire it to that degree it is your lovely little daughter. For some weeks after my first visit to Whitsbury I could not help continually reflecting how dreadful a visitation it would prove if it should seem good to Divine Providence to take her from you and had frequent thoughts of writing to you for the purpose of cautioning you against suffering your hearts to be too much set upon her. I hope that her health and spirits are so good as to give no foundation for the expectation of such an event, but still that what I have said will not be deemed inapposite. I beg you will give my best love to her if she has not entirely forgotten me.

We have at length done with the experimental squadron and Sir Thos. Hardy has struck his Flag. We are now ready for sea again but without orders and it is quite uncertain where we may be sent next. Report says to the Mediterranean. I will take care to inform you as soon as I know for certain and should it be a place where I can render you a service in any way whatever you have only to make your wishes known and they shall be complied with to the utmost of my power. – The Lord High Admiral was twice on board our Ship during his recent visit to Portsmouth and looked very closely into every thing about her. We had orders immediately after our return to prepare to carry him down to Plymouth but they were afterwards countermanded.

William Cobbett, the Admiral's old neighbour at Wickham, whose investigative zeal had exposed the sale of Writerships in the East

India Company and undermined Richard's attempt to obtain one, is perhaps best known for his *"Rural Rides"* an anthology of travel essays written originally for his newspaper *"The Political Register"* and published in book form in 1830. In the course of his journeys in 1825, he visited the village of Trotton, in Sussex:

From Rogate we came to Trotton, where a Mr. Twyford is the squire, and where there is a very fine and ancient church close by the squire's house.

A younger son of the squire, the Revd. Charles Twyford, had been Rector of this church since 1813 and, in 1827, Georgina announced her acceptance of a proposal of marriage from him. The family was naturally concerned and protective: since her father's death, Georgina was a very rich young woman and would be more so if the Blackbrook estate were sold, which was under consideration. Richard and John were far from happy that Twyford's financial contribution to the marriage was as he had represented it to his bride-to-be or, at the least, as she had understood it.

On 31st December 1827, Richard, who had just returned from his first visit to Bury Hall, wrote to his stepmother to solicit her assistance in trying to make Georgina see sense:

My dear Mother, — We returned from Bury Hall to dinner on Saturday where we passed as pleasant a time as the weather would permit. Everything was made agreeable enough in-doors, but, as you will have remarked wherever your residence there was, immoderate rain was a great obstacle to viewing the external beauties of the country. The house is a most excellent one and Renira is furnishing it quite in a style correspondent with the elegance of the apartments. Much family matter is in agitation by reason of the approaching union; and you will be sorry to hear that Georgina's prospect of fortune from her husband elect is, by every account I could hear, dwindled away, and worn down, almost from the noble to nine pence; and it is in order to ask you to use your eloquence in opening my fair Cousin's eyes a little to her own interest that I begin seriously with a little explanation of her lover's inconsistency.

Twyford, like Richard, had a Bachelor of Law degree and therefore fully understood the implications of the proposed Marriage Settlement about which Richard had questioned Georgina when they had met in Southampton the previous month.

When I met Georgina in Southampton, I questioned her by hints as to her prospects of a fortune to match her own, which we know to be very handsome. She told me that £20,000 were to be settled on her. I said – "Then I suppose you mean the amount of your own fortune." "No" – said she – "my own fortune is uncertain till Blackbrook is sold, but I shall have £20,000 whether my fortune be that or no, and if I survive Mr. Twyford, my settlements will give me £40,000." This is most probably the same account as you have received, and you were doubtless as satisfied with it as I was. Not to trouble you with the gradation by which Mr. Twyford's fortune appears to have decreased, I shall tell you at once its full amount. Viz. his benefice which is said to yield him no more than £400 pr. annum, and a bond upon his Brother's estate for £10,000 in cash. The advowson for his living is the property of Mr. Twyford senior, therefore the utmost that could be done for Georgina, and everything turning out most favorably her expectations of £40,000 could be never realised. But this is not all I have to describe.

The proposal was that Georgina's fortune should be calculated and one half of it, matched with a like contribution from her husband, to be settled in a Trust for her and her children's benefit; but, as Richard pointed out, the balance of Georgina's money would become Twyford's property:

None of the foregoing could be rectified by your remonstrances, but what I have now to say, I think from your influence, and I may say your authority over the fair lady, might. Mr. Paddon is directed to calculate the amount of Georgina's fortune, and the half only of what it may amount to, Mr. Twyford is to match with a corresponding sum, and these sums are to be put together to make a joint settlement for their mutual benefit and that of their children. Whether Georgina's fortune is to be calculated before or after the sale of Blackbrook I do not know – this would make a material difference. But whether or not you know enough of Law to be aware that the remaining part unsettled of Georgina's fortune will become the property of her husband, and will be at his command to spend, to be settled on another wife, to be alienated from Georgina's own children, or to support the extravagance of another woman's. Georgina would answer to these objections, her confidence in the man she loves; but who can look into the future and say such confidence shall not be abused.

If Georgina's entire fortune were to be settled upon herself, it would safeguard her and her children's interests and would preclude a great deal of complicated legal work.

What a simple and easy thing it would be, and how much saved in stamps, parchments and lawyer's bills, to have Georgina's own fortune settled on herself (whatever it might prove to be) instead of taking ten from here and replacing it with ten from there, besides a parcel of unintelligible mystery which nobody can understand? – I have reason to think, moreover, that Georgina's fortune will be divided in two parts for the proposed arrangements rather earlier than will be consistent with her interest; which I judge from this circumstance: the cottage is not to be paid for till after the marriage. If George's contract for the purchase alone be inserted in the settlement, (without the future division of the Blackbrook property, besides the whole description of Mr. Twyford's based upon his bother's estate,) it will make a very long addition to the "whereases" and add very much to the complication with which marriage settlements abound And this £2,000 not included in the settlement, places so much ready money in Mr. T's hands at his own disposal. If some, or all these things had not been pointed out to Mr. Twyford, I should not have been so correct in complaining of the measures, but I believe Mr. Paddon has not only recommended a different arrangement to that gentleman, but has intended to write, or has written to you also upon the subject.

Remembering how obdurate George Purvis had always been in any matter relating to the interests of his children, Richard felt that the family must do something; but it could not come from him:

I am too delicately situated with Georgina to offer an interference, but she has professed always to look upon you as her best friend, and in truth you are her nearest relation privileged to assume any authority in such subjects as this. I would therefore certainly advise you to enter a protest as a parent would do, (hers, especially,) against any proceeding that was unfair; and if I have pointed out anything in this letter which is contrary to the fact (all which might be ascertained from Mr. Paddon) or made any unjust surmises against Mr. Twyford, I heartily apologise to him for having been misled to do it; but still upon the information I have received, my conscience bears me out in desiring to see justice done to so near a relative. This bond for £10,000, we know that Georgina's father and mother would never have permitted her to match with her own ready cash. Mr. Twyford senior pays 4 pr. cent – the fairest way for Georgina would be to stipulate that when consols fell to 75 this money should be demanded and invested in the funds, which would not reduce their income. This subject has filled all my paper, which I hope you will excuse. The elder Bessy is complaining of what she supposes Rheumatism caught in travelling Saturday. The younger is merry as the Greeks were before the Turks came and cut their heads off. All the rest of the establishment are well as we left also John's party and all the Garretts. My little Godson is one of the finest children I ever saw. Yrs. affect. RFP

Richard added on a separate slip of paper, which could be detached from the main letter and burned:

This letter was written over again to omit this paragraph. This is most private. — The loves profess to have but one purse. Georgina displayed to me what she called presents from Mr. T. – a dressing case value 30 guineas, – handsome, heavy chain and cross value unknown, – watch with etceteras, all which Georgina's money paid for. Mr. Halford may know these things to a better certainty than we do; but if half of what I have described to you be fact, I think some endeavour should be made to open her eyes – if afterwards wilfully blind, there is no help. – The one purse, in true generous feeling, ought to be the gentleman's.

Whatever pressure her family may have brought to bear upon her,

Georgina had made up her mind and could see no wrong in Charles Twyford. In January 1828 she and her fiancé spent two weeks at Vicar's Hill during which her aunt, no doubt, took her aside and tried to explain to her the reservations which she, John and Richard had about the Marriage Settlement. Georgina, aware of their disapproval and anxious to lobby some family support for "the best and most excellent of men", wrote to Aunt Timms on 13th January hoping that, after the wedding, she could bring her husband to Colchester to meet her "in unprejudiced surroundings":

My dearest Aunt, — I flatter myself you will like to hear of my future plans and present arrangements. We have been staying at Vicar's Hill and spent a very agreeable fortnight with my Aunt. Mr. C. Twyford was with us which constituted my happiness and I every day discovered more to admire, to love and esteem. He has behaved in the most handsome manner to me having made a very good settlement on me and in every action he has evinced generosity and honor and I consider myself one of the most fortunate of women. The character of Mr. C. Twyford with all who know him is most [exceptional]. We went to London for a few days to order Wedding Clothes and to be introduced to Mrs. and Miss Twyford – they both received me very kindly and gave me a most friendly reception. Mary Twyford was at the same Hotel with us and returned to the Cottage with us – her Brother also for two days, he is very clever, very gentlemanlike and very agreeable. He comes to my Wedding the 7th of next month – also their relations Sir William and Lady Jolliffe (she was a Paget) with Mrs. G. Jolliffe. It is, I consider, a great compliment as they come between 70 and 80 miles for the express purpose of attending the Ceremony. . . . I am to be united to the best and most excellent of men about 10 o'clock – return to breakfast and then go off to Brighton for a fortnight. We have then promised to spend a little time with the Jolliffes who gave us a very early invitation, they are people of great fortune and respectability and relations of Mr. C. Twyford. The Barnards of Alverstoke claim a relationship to the Twyfords on the Beadon side – late Bishop of Bath and Wells. We meet them all at Commissioner Garrett's on Thursday. We afterwards go to Mrs. B. Goodrich for a short visit and shall certainly come on to see you – as I am anxious you should know Mr. C. T. in unprejudiced surroundings.

In describing the presents she had received, Georgina mentioned the items which had been the subject of Richard's postscript:

. . . Mr. C.T. a 30 [guineas] dressing box, a gold chain and cross and a handsome watch – he has also given me an elegant clock and 2 French vases for the chimney piece . . . I am to be married in a plain white [Gras de Naples] embroidered with flowers, a white satin hat with orange blossoms and [blond] – a [blond] lace veil and Pelerine – my Bride Maids in pink and blue dresses and white hats and feathers. . . . How is Ann – remember me to her. Simpson remains with me but Eames is in want of a situation as Mr. C. Twyford has a very good servant that remains and we shall not be stationary for some time as we go abroad in April or May. Is it true that H. Watson is to marry a widower with six children? Pray let me hear from you and say how you are – I began to think you had lost sight of me. – Accept my best love and good wishes for the return of many happy years; this is an eventful one for me, and believe me, my dear Aunt, Your affectionate niece, Georgina. †

Georgina was married to Revd. Charles Twyford at Fareham on 7th February 1828 and left Blackbrook for her husband's parish at Trotton. Blackbrook was not to be long without a mistress, however, as on the 10th June following, Georgina's brother George was married, at Chawton, Hampshire, to Mary-Jane Austen, daughter of Captain (later Admiral of the Fleet Sir) Francis Austen, and niece of Jane Austen the great novelist. Within nine months, Mary-Jane gave birth to a son who was christened the same as his father — George Thomas Maitland Purvis.

At Whitsbury on 6th July 1828, Richard's wife Bessy gave birth to another son who was also christened after his father — Fortescue Richard — with his first names transposed to avoid confusion.

In December, the Revd. Edwards returned to Portsmouth from Rio de Janeiro in the *Galatea*. He was grateful for the efforts which John and Richard had apparently made for his preferment while he had been away:

My dear Purvis, — Our stay in England in August last was so short and my own proceedings so extraordinary that I had no opportunity of hearing from or seeing either you or your brother. We returned from Rio on Sunday morning last and I called at Bury Hall yesterday. Mrs. Purvis was so unwell that I did not see her, but I was happy to hear a favourable account of my good friends at Whitsbury. I can hardly say whether I felt more surprised or gratified by the exertions you have made in my favour during my absence. I still remain entirely ignorant whether these exertions have been attended with success or not, but this does not in any degree diminish my sense of your kindness and that of your brother. I believe that no appointment has yet taken place at least no person in Portsmouth knows any thing about it. I cannot venture to make any further application until I ascertain whether the situation has been disposed of, but if it has not, Sir Charles has promised me his most strenuous support. I know of no place out of England where I should like to spend a few years of my life so much as Malta.

---

† A page of this letter is reproduced on page 17.

Edwards had been impressed with Rio de Janeiro and by the
growing status of Brazil among its Latin American neighbours:

Our trip to Rio so far as weather is concerned has been a very pleasant one. We
have never had more than a double reefed topsail breeze and have not I believe
carried away a single spar during the whole time. I found Brazil rather superior
to my whole expectations. The first thing a seafaring man generally looks at is the
harbour and that of Rio de Janeiro can hardly be surpassed for security, size or
beauty by any in the world. They have a great deal of trade the better portion of
which is in the hands of the English. The state is rapidly rising in civilisation,
wealth and importance, and was the Emperor, now that his hands are at liberty by
the peace with Buenos Ayres, to turn his attention to the improvement of his
subjects he would soon be more than a match for the republican states around
him, for, from the best accounts I could gather, they are all retrograding rather
than advancing.

He had brought back some seeds for Richard's wife but feared that
she might not be able to germinate them in English climatic
conditions. He had also brought a small tropical bird for little
Bessy:

. . . but am puzzled how to get it over to Whitsbury for Capt. Purvis objects to
taking charge of any living animal after his bad success with the fish. It is pretty
certain that we shall now be paid off but we are in great doubt whether we shall
remain here or be sent to the Eastward or Westward for that purpose.

P.S. We have just received orders to prepare to go up the harbour consequently
we shall be paid off here. I understand from your brother that the application for
the Chaplaincy was made to Dr. Cole of Greenwich Hospital this Sir George
Garrett and should it so happen that no appointment has taken place renew my
suite in that quarter, tho' I believe the disposal of the place rests entirely with the
Admiralty.

After spending so much of his earlier years in the constant struggle
for patronage, it must have been gratifying to Richard to be in a
position where he could assist a friend.

Also in 1828, Richard was delighted to receive as a guest at
Whitsbury his old friend from the 2/21st, James Cock, now a
Lieutenant-Colonel recently commanding the 12th Native Infantry,
and back in England on a long furlough. He took the lease on a
house near to Whitsbury — Fryern Court (more recently the home
of Augustus John) — and spent much time in Richard's company
recalling their time together in India. Richard introduced him to his

parents-in-law and their copious family in Norfolk and it soon became evident that Cock's legendary and unremitting search for a wife was at last nearing its end.

In June 1829 James Cock was promoted to full Colonel and on the 27th August, at Whitsbury, Richard conducted the service for the marriage of his old friend to his 17 year-old sister-in-law, Georgiana Mary Baker.

On 2nd January 1830, Bessy had another daughter, Emily Mary, and the godparents, James and Georgiana Cock, were present at the christening at Whitsbury. The Cocks were to remain in England on furlough for another six years during which time Georgiana was to bear four children. The second of these, Georgiana Rachel Cock, was born at Fryern Court on 30th March 1831.

On the death of King George IV in 1830, Prince William, Duke of Clarence, had acceded as King William IV. As a young Midshipman in 1778, the Prince had been placed in the care of Lieutenant John Child Purvis in the *Invincible* and had not forgotten him. Richard's brother John was invited to one of the new King's first levees and, when his name was called, the King came straight to him and, according to family tradition, said: "Ah Purvis, Purvis. How do you do? So the poor old Admiral your father is dead. Left you very well off, I understand — ah, very well off indeed".

# 7. Aunt Timms

*Colchester, Essex.*
*22nd May 1831.*

In the spring of 1831, John travelled to Colchester to visit Aunt Timms who was ill. Something was clearly troubling the old lady and, upon questioning her about it, John discovered she was in debt. She had led a drear life, nursing a chronically sick husband for many years and then, on his death, herself falling victim to ill health. It appeared that the allowance that her brother, the Admiral, had provided for her was insufficient to meet the ever-growing bills of Mr. Waylan, her doctor, and to support a new taste she had, perhaps not unsurprisingly, acquired. John wrote to Richard:

Entre nous I fear the old lady has found out <u>Brandy</u> is a more efficient cure than the supply of restoratives etc. she receives from Mr. Waylan. She certainly took it at all times of the day in such proportions as really to astonish me – and in a conversation I had with Mrs. Cross she certainly hinted at it, as being habitual. In fact Anne told me she had recently bought a Keg of the smuggled stuff, which is a compound of spirits of wine etc.

John paid all her debts and left instructions that any future shortfall would be settled immediately by Richard and himself. Aunt Timms also mentioned to John that she was very against the Twyfords, in spite of Georgina's attempts to impress her with the worth of "the best and most excellent of men".

John and Richard were also concerned about an intimation they had received from their stepmother that she, too, was not managing to live within her income and might not be able to afford to keep on Vicar's Hill. Already she was economising at the expense of essential repairs and decoration of the property and, on 11th May, Richard Smith, the butler, who had been in the family's service for twenty-eight years, wrote to John:

Sir, — This has been a painful day to me and which no doubt you will acquiesce with me in when I tell you that this day my Mistress has communicated to me it is not in her power to keep me any longer in her service, from the correspondence she has had with Sir A. Dickson at Woolwich which is to reduce her establishment from the pressure of the times; that may be! But to begin with me seems so very extraordinary after twenty eight years service to her and your ever to be lamented dear Father and the more so when she has so often apprised me that sooner than I should leave her she would part with every servant she had. I cannot in any way account for it. I have had two conversations with her today to know if I had any secret enemies who had given any insinuations against me that I might learn the same – however thank God I have served them both faithfully and honestly and latterly the place has been my pride to keep in order and I shall ever retain a grateful remembrance of the many favors I have received from you Sir and all the family and although it is not my intention to go into service again I shall ever be most proud to wait upon any one of the same. I have taken this liberty Sir with you as the Head of the Family and one who has ever been kind to me and I hope you will come over before I leave, as you can make an excuse on the plea of my Mistress being unwell and pray Sir do not name you have heard from me. I sincerely hope this will find you Sir your wife and family well and believe me to remain, Your most grateful and obedient very humble servant, Richard Smith.

Elizabeth Purvis obviously had second thoughts on the matter for the next day Richard Smith wrote again to John:

Sir, – Since I posted my letter to you this morning respecting my leaving Vicar's Hill, I have made an arrangement to stay. Should anything further occur I will let you know . . .

John sent these two letters to Richard as an illustration of what he suspected was going on at Vicar's Hill. He added the following postscript which gives an interesting insight into how John and Richard regarded their stepmother:

A curious coincidence my Mother sending for you and Smith for me — "When rogues fall out, etc". — <u>Pray burn this.</u>

Only nine days after John's visit to Aunt Timms, the old lady died and he was back in Colchester to settle her affairs. By the time her funeral expenses and local accounts had been paid there was a small deficit. Rather than sell off her pathetic little trinkets — pieces of family silver, lace, etc. — John met the deficit from his own pocket trusting on reimbursement to the estate from any member of the family who wished to have any of the trinkets as a keepsake. He also realised there were insufficient funds in the estate to make an adequate provision for their Aunt's old servant, Anne, and that it would be incumbent upon her heirs, Renira and Georgina, to make her an allowance — a matter in which John was not prepared to tolerate any parsimony on the part of Charles Twyford:

When I see Twyford we will arrange about the allowance we shall make her; if he does not agree, she shall enjoy it from me.

It would have distressed the old Admiral, who had always placed such value on maintaining good relations with the Blackbrookites, that the rift between his sons, particularly John, and their cousins had never healed. Indeed it had intensified and would get even worse as the years progressed. The distribution of Aunt Timms's trinkets, and the administration of her (almost non-existent) estate, caused more ill-feeling than their worth could ever merit. John, as a joint Executor with Richard, had wound up her affairs in an open and honourable way but his actions were, nevertheless, under suspicion from Blackbrook. He wrote to Richard on 15th July:

I have much to communicate relative to our joint executorship, which by the bye at the Cottage [Blackbrook] is to go through a regular audit, and I upon a hint of it from Mary-Jane immediately made out a list of articles composing residue, with what they sold for, together with every item augmenting the same so that George and his wife might at one view observe the change he had in distribution without the possibility of refunding, but this morning a letter arrived from the Stamp Office which will diminish the sum which I gave him as likely to be shared by some three or four Pounds – I have all bills, receipts etc. together with regular vouchers for disbursements . . .

Despite the fact that Aunt Timms had always promised her gold watch, engraved E.P., to Richard's daughter Bessy (who shared the same initials), its eventual transfer to her was heralded as an example of Charles Twyford's magnanimity:

The watch marked E.P. is a present from Twyford (or Georgina) to little Bessy and I am desired to charge its valuation to him. So I congratulate my little niece in the promise and she may be assured I will see it fulfilled.

The box of lace had also caused some bad blood:

I have been twice over to the Cottage, and all very friendly but George has never been near us. She [Mary-Jane] sent for the lace box, took what she wanted, and never sent me the money or said a word about payment although I particularly said it must be bought to make up the sums for closing the Executorships Accounts – bad taste!

Nor were the cousins invited to the christening of Mary-Jane's third child, Herbert Mark Garrett Purvis, who was born at Blackbrook Cottage on 23rd June 1831:

The Christening took place on Tuesday, Renira called the same Monday unintentionally not a word was said to her about the subject – the whole Austen family were there.

Although their stepmother had, by now, advised John and Richard that she could no longer afford to live at Vicar's Hill and would hand the place over to them, they were nevertheless surprised to see an announcement in the Salisbury newspaper on 15th July 1831 of a forthcoming auction of the entire contents. To avoid the damage and disruption of such an auction, John and Richard agreed to buy the contents of the house themselves at valuation. They also felt the house would be easier to dispose of if it were not stripped bare.

The estate was placed on the market at an asking price of £10,000 plus timber, furniture, etc. at valuation. A gardener's cottage, at nearby Pilley, John and Richard decided was not to be included with the estate so that they might sell it separately to cover their expenses. John and Renira spent much of their time sailing their yacht *Janette* in the Solent and Richard began to feel that too much of the work of finding a buyer was being left to him. He hinted at this to John who hastened to reassure his brother that he was doing all he could:

You appear to attribute to me a want of that interest in the sale of the property I do not deserve . . . I delivered notices at the Club House, Cowes, in London, Brighton etc. Under the circumstances what could I do more ?

As the price they were asking covered little more than what their father had paid for the property, John cautioned Richard against involving anyone in the sale who might expect a commission which would reduce their net proceeds. There had been an instance of this when part of the Blackbrook estate had recently been sold:

I advise a caution being used in giving a price to an Auctioneer or an Appraiser or any one likely to ask for per centage. The Blackbrook party put into Mr. Driver's hands the Estate for sale by Private Contract – and when Col. Le Blanc bought it, he sent us the Attorney General's opinion that he was entitled to the commission because we had neglected to take it out of his hands, although he had no more to do with the finding of a purchaser than you had.

On 23rd August John advised Richard that he was going to Cherbourg for a few days:

My Friend Captain Wyndham has given me a passage to Cherbourg to witness the sailing of the Yachts for the Frenchmen's Cups, and as we start tomorrow morning I think it right to apprise you of it, leaving the sale of Vicar's Hill to you, but in the meantime I will not fail in doing every thing I can with the Members of the Club. Any device you may judge necessary will meet my approbation, and I agree with you rather than lose a willing purchaser the Timbers might go in.

A friend of Captain Wyndham had intimated that he could be interested in buying Vicar's Hill so, on their return from Cherbourg, they sailed up to Lymington in Captain Wyndham's schooner where they were forced, by the onset of a gale, to anchor for a couple of days. The house felt damp so John ordered half a chaldron of coals and arranged for some fires to be lit. Down in the cellars beneath the house, he discovered his father's old papers — log books, order books and letter-books covering his entire career at sea. They had become very damp:

I had them up, dried them at the fire in the drawing room and locked them up in the drawers of the press in my mother's room. You will find in the secretary drawer a memo of it.

There were several prospective buyers for Vicar's Hill including several senior naval officers and Sir Thomas Bradford of Cowley Parsonage, near Uxbridge who wrote:

At this moment, I am, altho' not actually in treaty, about a place in Sussex, a county in which I should from early recollection prefer living to Hampshire but as I have heard much of the beauty of your part of the Country, and of the Society, should I not purchase the place to which I allude, it is still not improbable that I may vent my attention in your direction and, if it affords me an opportunity of making your acquaintance, it would give me much pleasure.

Lieutenant-Colonel James Bouchier of the 11th Light Dragoons, a veteran of Waterloo, also expressed interest:

A friend of mine who knows I am on the look out to purchase a residence, recommended me to go to see Vicar's Hill in the neighbourhood of Lymington. On reference to the Salisbury and Winchester Journal I observe an advertisement stating that it is to be sold with or without its furniture, and another giving notice of a sale at the place, at the same time stating that the furniture has been disposed of by private contract. I take the liberty in consequence, of applying to you to know if the place is still on sale, whether the furniture can still go with it, if approved of, and whether I can view the premises if I come to Lymington for the purpose.

The most serious enquiry seems to have been from a Mr. E.A. Greaves of Kenilworth Hall who wrote to John in October saying that, although he was primarily interested in a lease, he might be tempted to buy if the price was sufficiently attractive.

In addition to his worries about the disposal of Vicar's Hill, John, who was becoming increasingly political, had another matter of major importance on his mind. After years of public unrest, the *Reform Bill* which would redistribute voting power to include the new industrial centres and would effectively extend the franchise to the newly-prosperous middle classes, was about to go before the House of Lords. John, who saw its introduction as highly undesirable, wrote to Richard on 4th October 1831:

Last night was the commencement of I hope that which will finish the odious Reform Bill, God grant the Lords may be firm and shew the Country it is not threats can intimidate them; the Constitution is in their hands, and upon their decision rests the fate of this Country, the preservation of which matured as it has been for ages has caused us to be the envy of the world. I think Lord Brougham is inclined to throw in the apple of discord; glorious tidings from Dorsetshire – they appear to have had enough of Reform already.

He also asked if Richard knew of a good groom:

Can you assist me in getting a sort of man to take care of my horses, and go with them when employed on the farm; he must be a good groom, and drive occasionally, that is when we dine out, if possible neat in his person. You sometimes have persons of this description out of place in your neighbourhood, if so pray think of me; my wages – 18£ per Ann. and a suit of livery every nine months – I will pay coach hire from Southampton.

Georgina and her husband were in the area and John and Renira had been due to meet them the previous evening at the house of mutual friends — the Mansfields:

. . . but Charles had over eaten or over drank himself [the day before] at Sir [Edward] Taylor's; he was seized in the night and a Medical Man sent for.

By 9th December, Vicar's Hill was still unsold. John's third son, George, was intended for the Navy and the Captain of the *Revenge* had promised Captain Austen that he would apply for a position for him. The Blackbrook estate, except for the Cottage and its gardens, where George and Mary-Jane lived, had been divided into lots and put up for sale in a manner which John considered had been structured primarily for the enrichment of the solicitors involved:

> Blackbrook has been divided into Lots and disposed of. The buildings and all the bad land remaining with the Trustees, each purchaser requiring a Title for his Lot — nice work for Paddon, the exact thing for which and to effect it, he created the Trust. I begin to think George, who has been the prosecutor of this mode of sale, finds the difficulties he has to contend with [too great], and means to have his Wife and Twyford to wind up.

Then on 8th January 1832, John heard again from Mr. Greaves, their best prospect for Vicar's Hill, who was in Lymington and who had been up to the house the previous day:

> Sir, – I came here yesterday from Southampton and have been this morning to Vicar's Hill which I find is at present unoccupied, except by servants. The place would suit me well in most respects and the land is not more than I require. My object is to rent for the present, unless the price asked offered a temptation to purchase. If you can visit Vicar's Hill during my short stay here it will be satisfactory to me to converse with you on the subject of Terms as I am about to settle myself in a residence on the 25th of March next.

Recognising what at last looked like a serious prospect, John wrote immediately to Richard:

> . . . my intention is to leave in the evening for Southampton, sleep there and go on per Mail tomorrow morning to Lymington; if you can meet me there in the course of the day I should feel much obliged because I think it would be more satisfactory to both of us, being present at any thing like a negotiation and I do think it has the earnest appearance of one. . . . I shall be at The Angel; perhaps after your duty in the morning you would come over and return on the Monday again.

And so, within a few weeks, Mr. and Mrs. Greaves of Kenilworth Hall became the new proprietors of the Vicar's Hill estate.

**Above:** Vicar's Hill House, near Lymington, the home of Admiral of the Blue John Child Purvis. During the Second World War it became a U.S. Army Air Force Hospital and is today "Southlands School" a centre of excellence for boys suffering from Asperger Syndrome.

**Right:** Captain John Scott R.N. (1784-1867) was a shipmate of Richard's in H.M.S. *London*. As a fifteen year-old Midshipman during the Ferrol Expedition in 1800, Scott earned a Commendation for his part in the cutting out of the French Privateer *La Guepe*. In 1815, while serving in H.M.S. *Tonnant* during the American War, Lieutenant Scott showed great enterprise and gallantry during the storming of a strongly-defended American fort on the banks of the Mississippi which earned him promotion to Commander and the praise of Admirals Sir Edward Codrington and Sir Edward Thomas Troubridge. Despite his bravery and an exceptional record of service, he was relegated to the Half-Pay List in 1815 and never got another seagoing appointment. It is probable that John Scott was the natural son of Richard's father, Admiral John Child Purvis.

**Above:** St. Leonard's, Whitsbury, as it was in Richard's time *(from a sketch by Sophie Giddings, 22nd September 1865; Photo: Peter Letcher LRPS, Fordingbridge, Hants.).*

**Below:** The Church today showing the alterations to the tower undertaken by Richard's son, Revd. Fortescue Richard Purvis, who succeeded him on his death in 1868 and was vicar for seventeen years.

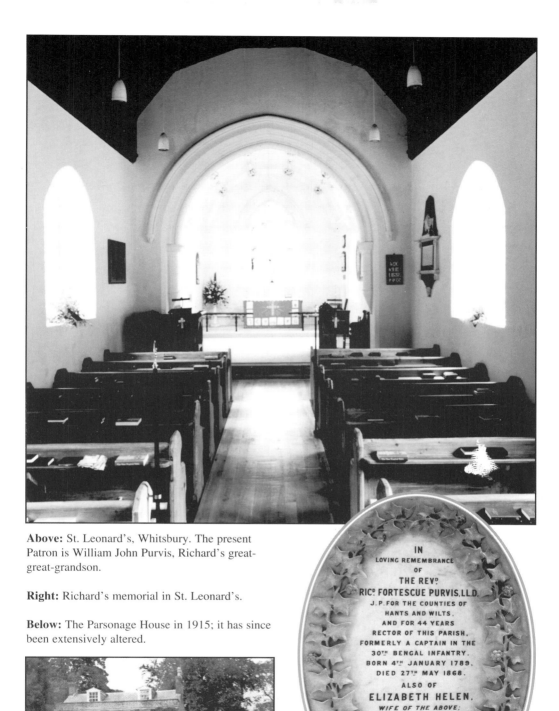

**Above:** St. Leonard's, Whitsbury. The present Patron is William John Purvis, Richard's great-great-grandson.

**Right:** Richard's memorial in St. Leonard's.

**Below:** The Parsonage House in 1915; it has since been extensively altered.

IN
LOVING REMEMBRANCE
OF
THE REVᴰ
RICᴰ FORTESCUE PURVIS, LL.D.
J.P. FOR THE COUNTIES OF
HANTS AND WILTS,
AND FOR 44 YEARS
RECTOR OF THIS PARISH,
FORMERLY A CAPTAIN IN THE
30ᵀᴴ BENGAL INFANTRY.
BORN 4ᵀᴴ JANUARY 1789.
DIED 27ᵀᴴ MAY 1868.
ALSO OF
ELIZABETH HELEN,
*WIFE OF THE ABOVE;*
BORN 8ᵀᴴ MARCH 1796,
DIED 8ᵀᴴ AUGUST 1885.

**Above:** "Purvis Pasha" — George Frederick Godfrey Purvis (1859-1936), Director-General Egyptian Coastguard Service.

**Right:** Herbert Mark Garrett Purvis (1831-1912), Major-General and Colonel-Commandant Royal Artillery.

**Below right:** Captain (later Rear-Admiral) Francis Reginald Purvis (1833-1895).

**Below:** Esther Frances Purvis (1852-1885). Born Fanny Pegler, daughter of an itinerant brush salesman, she married Captain F.R. Purvis at the age of sixteen and died from cirrhosis of the liver aged thirty-three.

# 8. Middle Years

*Whitsbury Parsonage. 1832.*

We must now move faster through the remainder of Richard's story as, from this point, records become more sparse. On 2nd October 1832 Bessy gave birth to another son at half past six o'clock in the morning. He was christened John Child Purvis in remembrance of his illustrious grandfather. Then the gloomy conjecture of the melancholy Revd. Edwards was realised with the death of little Bessy, aged nine, on 26th September 1834, at twelve minutes past 2 p.m. It is unlikely that her parents had curtailed their love for her in anticipation of such an event.

In August of the following year, Bessy had another son whom they, once again, christened Home. It was recorded in the family bible that this name was a second attempt to commemorate the sincere friendship previously described but, this time, there was an added poignancy to the gesture as Major John Home was present at the christening, as a godfather to his young namesake. He had returned from India on Sick Certificate in February and stayed with Richard at Whitsbury for some time. As James Cock was still nearby at Fryern Court, there were many convivial meetings between the three old friends. James Cock returned to India as Colonel of the 51st Native Infantry in January 1836 taking his wife, Georgiana, and their four children with him. John Home remained in England until December 1838.

Richard had for some time been serving as a Magistrate for the County of Wiltshire but, as the county boundary with Hampshire was "within a pistol shot" of his parlour windows, and the actual boundary had been the subject of recent political dispute, he considered he should also be appointed as a Magistrate for Hampshire. On 28th December 1836, he wrote to Mr. John Fleming asking that the position should be brought to the attention of the Duke of Wellington, Lord-Lieutenant of Hampshire, and pointing out that:

... the objections originated (but not maintained) by our political opponents, as to the actual boundary line, render me very diffident as to the true extent of my jurisdiction: thus the ends of justice might chance to be defeated on some future magisterial act of mine connected with this undefined restriction. †

Though the Duke was reluctant to recommend clergymen to the Lord Chancellor, he doubtless took account of Richard's law degree and military experience as he was duly appointed and remained a Justice of the Peace for both counties for the rest of his life.

The following day, on 29th December 1836, Mary-Jane, having borne two further children — Francis Reginald in 1833 and Helen Catherine in 1835 — died at Blackbrook Cottage after an illness of fifteen months. Her husband, George, was serving at the time as First Lieutenant in the *Sulphur*, 8, and was obliged to leave his ship. With four small motherless children, he married again on 10th January 1838 and Esther North Harrison, daughter of the Revd. W. Harrison, Vicar of Fareham and Canon of Winchester, became the new mistress of Blackbrook.

Three months later, on 24th April 1838, John Home, now a Lieutenant-Colonel, was married to Susan Batsford, eldest daughter of Charles Batsford of Weston, Somerset, and in December returned to India to command the 50th Native Infantry.

In June the same year, James Cock, always the career soldier, was promoted to Major-General. But his wife Georgiana, Richard's sister-in-law, did not take to the Indian climate and, the following year, James was obliged to send her back to England in the Indiaman *London*. Sadly, she did not survive the voyage and, as the memorial which James erected for her in the church at Rollesby records, she died at sea on 3rd April 1840 in lat. 27° north, long. 39° west. At twenty-eight, she was one year younger than Mary-Jane.

Richard's brother John, after twenty-two years ashore, was recalled to sea service on 20th October 1841 when he hoisted the broad pendant of Commodore 2nd Class aboard the *Alfred*, 50, in which, in the spring of 1842, he sailed for "The Brazils" as Commodore South American Coasts and Republics. Here, he played a major role

---

† *Wellington Lieutenancy Papers*, University of Southampton Library, 25M61, 8/2.
© Crown Copyright reproduced by permission of The Controller H.M.S.O.

in bringing peace and stability to the infant Republic of Uruguay. Having gained its independence from Spain during the Napoleonic Wars, the Banda Oriental, as it was then known, had been annexed in turn by the Argentine and Brazil and had thrown off the yoke of the latter in 1825 to declare itself, in 1830, the independent Oriental Republic of the Uruguay. Since then, the State had been racked by civil war and by 1843 the capital city, Montevideo, was under siege by an Argentine-backed rebel army which threatened British and French residents and trade interests. Commodore Purvis, together with the British Consul, encouraged the residents of Montevideo to resist the rebels while, at sea, the British Squadron prevented the Argentine Navy from bombarding the city from the sea and from blockading the River Plate. Among the city's defenders was one Giuseppe Garibaldi who would later use the military experience he gained at Montevideo in the struggle for Italian unification.

John and Renira's third son, George, died in January 1843 but their fourth and youngest son, Richard, was a Midshipman who had already seen action and been wounded while serving in the *Blonde*, 42, on the China Station, during the First Opium War. In May 1843, Richard sailed in the *Curacao* to join his father's Flagship, the *Alfred,* in which he returned to England the following year.

When the *Alfred* sailed from Montevideo in June 1844, the Government of Uruguay gave John a copy of a testimonial it had ordered to be lodged in the State Records:

The Government of the Oriental Republic of the Uruguay — Having ordered a Memorandum to the following effect to be invested in the Records of the State: Whereas John Brett Purvis, Esquire, Commodore and Commander-in-Chief of Her Britannic Majesty's Naval Forces in these waters is about to sail for Rio Janeiro, the Government of the Republic desirous of testifying in a solemn and lasting manner, those sentiments of Respect, Gratitude and Attachment which the noble, generous and magnanimous manner in which he has conducted himself during his lengthened sojourn in this country, at the most difficult and hazardous period of its existence, has excited in the mind of the Supreme Authority of the State, also to express its best wishes for the happiness of himself and of his amiable family, whose names in the Republic of the Uruguay will never be pronounced without the highest veneration and regard. And for this purpose the Government has commanded this memorandum to be drawn out and a copy delivered to Commodore Purvis under the sign manual of the Government.

The document was signed by the President, Joachim Suarez, and three leading members of the Government. John returned to England in the *Alfred* in August 1845 and on 9th November 1846 was promoted to Rear-Admiral.

In the same year, Richard received the additional appointment of Domestic Chaplain to the Earl of Limerick. By this time he and Bessy had a further two daughters — Elizabeth Helen, born in 1837, and Renira Anna, born in 1841. Their eldest surviving son, Fortescue, was destined for the Church and would, two years later, follow in his father's footsteps to Jesus College, Cambridge, to read Law. Their second son, John Child, had been sent to Eton for his basic education and was now, aged fourteen, in the Navy, serving aboard the *Endymion* in the West Indies.

There was quite a gathering of the Purvis family on the West Indies Station at the time: the Commander-in-Chief was Admiral Sir Francis Austen and aboard his Flagship, the *Vindictive*, he had his grandson, young George Thomas Maitland Purvis from Blackbrook, and John's son Richard, now aged twenty, who had just received his Lieutenant's Commission.

The *Endymion* was commanded by Captain George Lambert who, in response to a letter from Richard exhorting him to look after young John, replied in December 1846:

I will not fail to pay attention to your wishes respecting young Purvis who appears a very nice boy. Indeed I should think myself sadly wanting if I was not to pay attention to all those entrusted to my care. — He has several nice little companions.

On 8th May 1846, young John Child wrote home to his parents from Barbados mentioning the attention he had received from Admiral and Mrs. Austen and that he had met his Blackbrook cousin aboard the Flagship and at the Austens' house in Bermuda:

I have just received by the last mail three letters one directed to Falmouth another to Plymouth Sound and the third to Madeira which was rather provoking not having received them before and as well as having to pay one shilling a piece for the England letters and sixpence for the Madeira letter. The Captain desired me to tell you that he wished us to have five pounds more a year as it is not enough to pay all washing and mess money; as it is he does not allow us to have any ale or wine. I think we are the most unlucky ship in commission as on the passage from Bermuda here we lost another man over board which makes 8 men in 7 months commission. We have had some very good bathing here there is very nice bathing places. You say I forgot to mention my hand it is much better indeed you cannot tell it at a little distance. All my nails have come off and I have got as good ones as on the other hand I can go up the rigging as well as most of the other naval cadets. We made a very good passage from Bermuda, exactly a week. I stayed at Bermuda with the Admiral and Mrs. Austen and always they were very kind to me and I dined in the berth of the Flagship with my cousin Maitland. At the Admiral's we both slept in one room. I have also made some friends here some coloured gentlemen they live some way up in the country. . . I am writing in a great hurry with the great guns firing over my head so you must excuse the writing. Give my love to all at home and accept the same yourself. Believe me, Your affectionate son, Jhn. Child Purvis.

The following year, Captain Lambert handed over command of the *Endymion* to Captain Courtenay and wrote to Richard from Port Royal, Jamaica, to assure him that his son was well and that no change would be made to the method of funding his money account:

An arrangement was made with Captain Courtenay when I quitted the Endymion that no alteration was to be made respecting the youngsters' money accounts and that the parents who had hitherto paid the sum allowed into Chard's hands were to continue to do so. I mentioned this to your Son who I fear omitted to inform you of it. I have not heard from him but by letters I have recently received from the Endymion I hear he is quite well. I trust he continues to like his profession and I shall always be glad to hear of his well doing.

On 9th August 1847, Georgina died at Portsmouth, aged forty-six, having borne four sons and three daughters. Her husband, the Revd. Charles Twyford, died three years later.

In June 1851, thirty-five years after the event, Richard was awarded the India Medal and Clasp for his service in the Nepal War. Major-General James Cock was not so fortunate as to see his service recognised. In 1843 he had returned to England with his brother, Colonel Henry Cock C.B., and had bought Hopton Hall, near Lowestoft in Suffolk. During a visit to his brother, Henry died at Hopton Hall on 17th February 1851 and James died exactly one month later on 17th March. He therefore never saw the India Medal and Clasp which was awarded to him posthumously three months later; nor did he live to attend the marriage on 4th September of his daughter, Georgiana Rachel, to Richard's nephew, Commander Richard Purvis. The service was held at Whitsbury, by Richard, who four years later was to marry another of James Cock's

# The Attack on Fort Kinburn

## 17th October 1855

**SECONDARY FORCE**
Smaller ships under Rear Admiral Sir Houston Stewart and Rear Admiral Odet Pellion

3-gun Battery

5-gun Battery

Fort Nikolaev

Ochakov Point

KHERSON BAY

Kinburn Point

8 feet sounding line

Earth Battery

Earth Battery

4 French and 4 British gunboats to protect right flank of land force

DNEIPER OR KHERSON BAY

Fort Kinburn

**French Floating Batteries**
Tonnante, Lave and Dévastation (the first ever armoured warships)

**MAIN FORCE**
Ships of the Line under Admiral Sir Edmund Lyons and Admiral Bruat

**French and British Mortar Vessels**

Salt Lakes

**N**

**LAND FORCE**
Troops under General Bazaine and Brigadier General Hon. A A Spencer landed on 15th October to block enemy's retreat

0 miles   1   2   3   4

daughters, Elizabeth Mary, to Captain Edward Metcalfe Grain of the Royal Engineers.

In 1852, John was appointed Commander-in-Chief Ireland and hoisted his Flag in the *Ajax*. He held this position for two years during which time his cousin George, of Blackbrook, now a Commander, served as his Secretary. In 1853 John was promoted to Vice-Admiral.

Britain and France declared war against Russia in 1854, in support of the Turks, and what we know today as the Crimean War ensued. The Purvis family was again well represented: Georgina's eldest son, Samuel Twyford, was a Lieutenant R.N. serving ashore from the *London* in the Naval Brigade before Sebastopol. He was killed on the 10th April 1855 and his death was recorded by William Russell, the famous war correspondent of *The Times:*

In the Naval Brigade one most excellent and zealous young officer, Lieutenant Twyford, of the "London", lost his life. He was killed on the spot, and a piece of stone knocked up by the same shot struck Lord John Hay on the face, cut his mouth, and knocked two of his teeth down his throat, besides wounding him in the shoulder.

Samuel Twyford's death was also mentioned by Lord Raglan, the Commander-in-Chief, in a letter to Lord Panmure from Sebastopol dated 10th April 1855:

I have not yet received the return of the casualties beyond the 9th Instant, which are herewith enclosed; but the death of Lieut. Twyford of the Royal Navy, a most promising officer and greatly respected by all, has been notified to me; and Capt. Lord John Hay, who has taken a most active part in the gallant and distinguished services of the Naval Brigade, was wounded almost at the very moment, I believe by the same shot.

Richard's son, John, and his cousin George's son, Francis, were both now naval Lieutenants and both took part in the bombardment of Sebastopol, the former in the *Rodney* and the *Royal Albert* and the latter in the *Spiteful,* in which he was slightly wounded.

After the fall of Sebastopol on 11th September, both officers changed ship for the expedition to Kinburn. John transferred from the *Royal Albert,* a 121-gun, screw-driven battleship, to the

*Leopard,* an 18-gun, paddle-driven, frigate. Francis did it the other way round transferring from the *Spiteful,* a 6-gun, paddle-driven sloop, to the *Algiers,* a 91-gun, screw-driven battleship. Together with a huge Anglo-French fleet, comprising some ninety ships carrying 9,000 troops, commanded by Admiral Lyons and the French Admiral Bruat, they sailed for the rendezvous anchorage off Odessa on 6th October.

Kinburn was a heavily-defended Russian fort at the end of a long spit of sand commanding the estuaries of two rivers, the Boug and the Dneiper, up which were situated, respectively, the important Russian naval base of Nikolaev and the industrial city of Kherson. The Allied Command therefore considered it essential to gain control of the entrance from which they could deny the Russian Navy navigation of both rivers and thereby seriously weaken the lines of communication with their armies in the Crimea.

John's ship, the *Leopard,* carried 370 men of the 57th Regiment and reserve ammunition. Francis's *Algiers* had 500 men of the 20th Regiment and eighty Royal Marines. The troops were landed on the 15th October about four miles up the spit from the citadel to cut off the retreat of the Russian garrison. Lieutenant John Child Purvis was the first man ashore and, together with his boat's crew, hoisted the Union Flag on the spit.

Two days later the massive naval bombardment was launched. Three French "floating batteries", which had been specially built for this purpose, moored close inshore to the south of the fort and released their awesome power which was augmented by Admiral Lyons's ships of the line, including the *Algiers.* At the same time, a squadron of smaller ships under the command of Rear-Admiral Sir Houston Stewart, which included the *Leopard,* sailed through the entrance and engaged the fort from the north side. The enormous power of the bombardment soon had its effect, the Russian batteries fell silent and the Garrison Commander, General Kokonovitch, with 1,400 men, surrendered to the Allies.

Though it was not an action which would be remembered in the same way as the Siege of Sebastopol, the Charge of the Light Brigade, or the Thin Red Line at Balaklava, the action at Kinburn had a special significance in terms of naval warfare: it was the first time that armoured warships had been employed and the first major action undertaken by a fleet comprised entirely of steam-driven vessels. As such, it can be regarded as the point at which the Royal Navy changed from sail to steam and it is pleasingly symbolic that John and Francis Purvis, both grandsons of sailing Admirals and both destined to become steam Admirals themselves, should have taken part in the action.

Francis took home with him two Russian cannon-balls from the fort at Kinburn which he gave to his father who mounted them on the gate pillars at Blackbrook.

The following year, Richard's stepmother died at Clarence House, Southampton which brought to a head the question of the Whitsbury advowson. The codicil to the Admiral's Will had been ambiguously phrased leaving both John and Richard with the belief that it had been their father's intention that the advowson should pass to their heirs. Now, John's solicitors, Thomas F.W. Kelsall of Fareham, wrote to Richard asking him to withdraw his objection to the Deeds being handed over to John:

Do you not think that it will be best to bring all matters now to a close with Mrs. Purvis's Executors? but, unless the Whitsbury advowson deeds are handed over to your brother, these will remain a subject for discussion with them on a future day – and the deeds will not be so safe as in the charge of a party beneficially interested.

In consequence, we believe, of some objection raised by you, Messrs. Dunn & Co. hesitate to give up the deeds to your brother, and propose, at his and your expense, getting counsel's opinion – which we object to as an unnecessary expense as, whatever questions may be raised as to beneficial interests under the Will, we have not the slightest doubt but that your brother is strictly entitled to the custody of the deeds, being clearly the person to present at the first vacancy. The possession of the deeds, however desirable in itself and for all legitimate purposes, cannot entitle [the holder] to prejudice any body beneficially interested under the Will, the trusts of which will always be patent to the world. We should be glad therefore if you would enable us, without further contest with the executors, and without increased expense, to obtain the safe custody of these deeds for your brother by withdrawing any objection you may have formerly expressed to them. We assure you that we would not suggest such a step for your adoption, were we not satisfied that it had no prejudicial bearing whatever on the interests of yourself and children, and that it really is most desirable that the deeds should no longer be left in the hands of strangers, who have no concern in them whatever.

John and Richard had no wish to fall out over this issue but were nevertheless anxious to protect the rights of their individual families in the way in which each believed to have been their father's intention. Consequently, each obtained Counsel's Opinion. Kelsall wrote to Richard again on 10th October 1856:

Admiral Purvis was with me yesterday and showed me your letter of 30th and its enclosure: he saw also our recent correspondence and we had a long conference of the subject of the advowson – and finally he instructed me to communicate to you unreservedly his views and intentions in regard to it. In the first place, let me assure you, he responds most cordially to your feeling that whatever difference of opinion exists between you, as to the legal rights of your mutual families, need not and ought not disturb the fraternal relations. The Codicil is unfortunately worded loosely enough to justify very different constructions. In Mr. Everett's opinion, which we have attentively read, the argument on behalf of your sons, (which goes to the full extent of claiming, not merely the next presentation but the perpetual advowson) is very fairly presented: but on the other hand the at least equally decided opinion of Sir Anthony Hart (whose eminence as a legal authority must be well known to you,) negativing this claim to all but the next presentation, appears to your brother, and, I must own, myself, to be the more correct interpretation – and you cannot be surprised that, with this strong conviction, he feels not only justified, but called upon, from a proper regard to his own descendants to assert what he conceives to be his just legal right to a property which will yield a valuable provision to many a future generation. As you may not have a copy of Sir Anthony Hart's opinion at hand, I enclose a copy, in order that your sons, as well as self, may consider it attentively: and I would then submit to you whether it may not be judicious for both the families to accept it as the basis of arrangement between them, and put an end to all risk of future, I do not say hostility, but expense and annoyance, by now making it binding on all parties. It would afford me much pleasure if I could be the means of effecting an object, which I cannot but think most desirable, knowing as I do the general uncertainty of the law, and the particular perplexities of this question. During your brother's lifetime and yours, especially your brother's, great facilities exist for a satisfactory solution of it, which could not afterwards be met with. If ever the question goes before a Court, its very difficulties will be all in your brother's favour, as heir at law of the testator, and in that capacity he will take all interest in the advowson which cannot be clearly shown to pass elsewhere by the codicil. Nay, a very serious doubt cannot fail then to arise, whether the whole attempted testamentary disposal of the advowson is not void at law, and must now be judicially annulled. . . . This was the opinion offered a few years ago to your brother (not through me) from an eminent counsel, – the present Attorney General, I believe – having carefully inspected the legal authorities, I am myself constrained to adopt it. Were I writing to a lawyer, I would refer him to Mr. Fearne's essay on contingent [remedies] p. 509 where in a note of Mr. Butler's he will find the justification of this view. Your brother's sons have, each of them, a latent contingent right under the codicil, supposing it valid, which might possibly be made available, thus wholly superseding their cousins' claims.

Having emphasised how important it was that an amicable settlement should be reached during the brothers' lifetimes, particularly John's, Kelsall came up with a compromise offer to which he hoped Richard would agree:

> They would, however, now concur in an arrangement enabling Admiral Purvis to ensure to your eldest son the next presentation of the Living, you and your sons in return formally relinquishing to your brother all further claim whatever on the advowson. This proposal is well worth consideration on the part of yourself, your family and friendly legal advisers: for it seems to me to offer the only sure means of closing, with tolerable satisfaction to all parties, a fertile source of legal perplexities. After full deliberation you will perhaps communicate to me the result.

A copy of Sir Anthony Hart's Opinion, which had been obtained thirty years previously, was enclosed:

**Opinion of Anthony Hart Esquire, of Lincoln's Inn, as to the Living at Whitsbury dated 6th June 1825.**

I am of opinion that under the device in the codicil, Captn. Purvis took the fee in the Advowson, subject however to an obligation in the nature of a trust to present any son of his own who may be in Orders capable of taking the Living when a vacancy shall happen, and in case he shall not have any such son at such time, then subject to a similar obligation of presenting any son of the Revd. R. F. Purvis who shall be capable of taking it. Subject to this obligation, which any purchaser of Captn. Purvis would be subject to, it appears to me that Captn. Purvis has a right to the fee of this Advowson and may convey it to a purchaser – The terms of the device are obscure, but the above is the best opinion I can form on the title.

It seems that Richard agreed to this proposal and Kelsall was able to legalise the arrangement in time to avoid a family row. One year later, on 1st October 1857, with Richard in attendance at his bedside, Vice-Admiral of the Red John Brett Purvis died at Bury Hall, aged seventy, and was buried in his brother's churchyard at Whitsbury.

Earlier in the year, on 23rd January, Richard's son Home (the younger), a Lieutenant by purchase in H.M. 10th Regiment, died aged twenty-two and was also buried at Whitsbury. Poor Home had never been strong and his ill-health had been exacerbated by the fact that his entire service had been spent in India.

# 9. Eventide

*Whitsbury Parsonage. 1857.*

In May 1857, Northern India erupted in violence with the mutiny of the greater part of the Company's Bengal Army. Reports of the massacre of British servicemen, civilians and their families reached Britain and every household which had relatives and friends in India lived in daily expectation of bad news. Richard Comings, a friend of Richard's, wrote to him from London on 10th August, expressing the fears of many at the time:

Deep indeed is the general anxiety with which the approaching news from India is looked for, and we are not without our special cause for trembling, having many friends and some very near relations more or less involved in danger. Perhaps the most perilous case among the latter is that of my Brother in Law Charles Radcliffe of the 7th Bombay Light Cavalry at Lucknow. The last mail brought us no letters from him, and the last intelligence which we received spoke of the meeting of two troops of his Regiment and of his having just achieved a harassing and anxious march in search of missing treasure. He happily succeeded in his mission, bringing in 40,000£, but after a great amount of difficulty and exposure, the latter having given him a severe attack of Opthalmia. His wife, then daily expecting her confinement, had been sent with the children as also the other ladies and children from the Cantonments (six miles from Lucknow) to the City where they were lodged at the Resident's House. At the Cantonments they kept up the most vigilant lookout – guns loaded, gunners with lighted matches day and night, etc. But their reliable force was sadly scanty and their danger correspondingly great. God protect them! One cannot doubt the issue, but before it is attained there may be yet a fearful amount of suffering, public and private, to be encountered; and what a task must the reorganisation of such a Government be! – how urgent the need of master minds, civil and military.

The atrocities and appalling loss of life on both sides in this sad affair is extensively chronicled elsewhere. It is estimated that of 128,000 men of the Bengal Army, some 120,000 mutinied and it is worth recording here, though purely coincidental, that neither of Richard's old regiments — the 2/21st which in 1842 had become the 42nd Bengal Light Infantry, and the 1/30th which in 1824 had become the 59th Native Infantry — joined the mutineers.

Both John Home and his brother, Richard, were now Major-Generals. Richard Home and his wife had a son, Duncan Charles, and a daughter whom they had christened Caroline Purvis. Duncan was a Lieutenant in the Bengal Engineers and, on 14th September 1857, was Officer-in-Charge of the party tasked with breaching the Kashmir Gate at Delhi which was garrisoned by the mutineers. He was killed having exhibited astonishing bravery in placing the explosive charges in full daylight and under heavy and destructive musket fire from the enemy. He was posthumously awarded the Victoria Cross — the Sovereign's highest and most coveted recognition of heroism.

The horrors of the Mutiny focussed both parliamentary and public attention on the system of government in India and the long-overdue recognition of the fundamental flaw in a system which entrusted the government of a vast sub-continent to a commercial organisation which, no matter how well-intentioned and diligent, was ultimately motivated by profit.

During the first half of the year 1858, the Honourable East India Company pleaded its case with the Nation for the retention of its franchise but an overwhelming majority had been awakened to the need for radical reform and on 2nd August, *"An Act for the Better Government of India"* received Royal Assent, after an easy passage through both Houses of Parliament, and all the military and civil functions of the Company became the responsibility of the Crown.

The Court of Directors held its final "Solemn Assembly" at East India House in Leadenhall Street on 1st September 1858 and handed over their Empire to the Queen with the words:

Let Her Majesty appreciate the gift — let her take the vast country and the teeming millions of India under her direct control; but let her not forget the great corporation from which she has received them, nor the lessons to be learned from its success.

It is unlikely that Richard, with his pension of half-a-crown a day after seventeen years in their service, would have endorsed that part of the Directors' statement which claimed:

The Company has the great privilege of transferring to the service of Her Majesty such a body of civil and military officers as the world has never seen before. . . . To those services the Company has always been just, has always been generous.

On 1st November 1858, the transfer of government to the Crown was announced to the people of India by a Royal Proclamation which was read in public at all major centres and began:

Whereas for divers weighty reasons, we have resolved, by and with the advice and consent of the Lords Spiritual and Temporal, and Commons, in Parliament assembled, to take upon ourselves the government of the territories in India, heretofore administered in trust for us by the Honourable East India Company.

The text of the Proclamation, which was much influenced by the Queen's own suggestions, accepted previously-negotiated treaty obligations, renounced any further territorial ambitions, promised complete religious tolerance and offered conditional clemency to the vast majority of those involved in the uprising. It finished with a pledge:

. . . to stimulate the peaceful industry of India, to promote works of public utility and improvement, and to administer the government for the benefit of all our subjects resident therein . . .

— thereby laying the ground rules for the generations of civil servants, soldiers, engineers, doctors and educationalists who were to dedicate their lives to the fulfilment of this promise over the next ninety years.

In 1858, Richard's son, Lieutenant John Child Purvis R.N., and the crew of H.M.S. *Pylades* were in Fort William where they had been brigaded for its defence during the mutiny. When the Queen's Proclamation was read, Lieutenant Purvis with an escort of picked seamen from the *Pylades* had the signal honour of hoisting the Royal Standard for the first time upon the shores of India.

On 9th November 1858, George and Mary-Jane's second son, Herbert Mark Garrett Purvis, a Lieutenant in the Royal Artillery serving in Ireland, married fourteen year-old Elizabeth Jane Grogan, daughter of Captain J.E.K. Grogan of the 32nd Regiment. The following year, on 16th November 1859, at Ballincollig, County Cork, Elizabeth gave birth to a son who was christened George Frederick Godfrey.

Richard's eldest surviving son, Fortescue, had obtained a Second

Class Law degree at Jesus College, Cambridge, and had been ordained Priest in 1855 since when he had held curacies in Hollinfare, Milford and Ibsley. On 2nd February 1860, he was married to Louisa Harriet Eyre Matcham, youngest daughter of Harriet Eyre, the heiress of Newhouse, whom Renira had recommended as a bride for Richard so many years ago. As part of the young couple's Marriage Settlement, Richard passed on to his son the farms at Upminster, the tenant of which had failed so miserably to deliver Aunt Timms's goose on time.

Two months after this happy event, Richard was deeply saddened to learn of the death of his oldest and dearest friend, Major-General John Home, at his residence — The Retreat, Weston Lane, Bath, on 12th April 1860. His brother, Major-General Richard Home, died in Brighton two years later.

In 1861 Herbert was posted to India and on 2nd May 1863 his wife, Elizabeth, had a daughter who was named Mary-Jane Austen after her grandmother.

Two months later on 29th July, at Anglesea, Hampshire, Richard's daughter Elizabeth (the second) died aged twenty-six and was buried at Whitsbury. This was the fourth of Richard's eight children, two Homes and two Elizabeths, who had died prematurely. On 7th September 1865, his youngest daughter, Renira Anna, was married at Whitsbury to Captain Edward Lambert R.N.. Richard wrote to Herbert, in India, with the news but, with the improved communications which the age of steam had brought between Europe and India, Herbert had already read of the marriage in the newspapers. He replied from Kamptee on 5th November 1865:

My dear Uncle, — Your letter of the 12th September only arrived a few days ago having just missed the mail of the 12th from Southampton. The contents did not cause us any astonishment as we had seen the announcement of Ren's wedding in the papers. Both Lizzie and I offer our heartiest congratulations and best wishes for the happiness of the Bride and Bridegroom.

Richard's naval son, John Child Purvis, had been promoted to Commander on 11th September:

We must also congratulate you all on Jack having at last got his promotion. It
must be a great comfort to him after waiting so long for it. Pray convey the same
to him. I suppose he is with you long before this and I hope in time to assist his
cousin in knocking over the partridges, or at any rate having a shot at some of the
long tails. I was glad to hear the box had at last arrived and I am only sorry the
contents should have been such an insignificant present: but you must take the
will for the deed, as the Rajah of Nagpur is said to have answered when asked
what his country produced at the time of the Exhibition of 1851. – "My country
only produces oranges and paan", and as neither of these could have been an
acceptable present, I was compelled to resort to my cook, or rather to my butler,
who was celebrated for his art in making condiments of all sorts – I don't know
whether you know "paan" by that name. It is the beetle nut which the natives
chew (the beasts!). We are now enjoying the commencement of our cold weather
and it promises to be much colder than last year. Lizzie is in daily expectation of
her confinement. I hope to be able to announce it before I close this letter. Poor
girl, she has suffered very much for some time but I am happy to say is stronger
now than I almost dared to hope – after that attack of cholera at Nagpore in
August last. Her sister, Mrs. Finlay, lives a few hundred yards off, which is a
pleasant thing for them both.

The shortage of officers for duty, from which Richard and his
friends had suffered so grievously in the early part of the century,
was not apparently unique to the old Bengal Army:

I am in a nice state as regards officers, not having a single officer in my battery
for duty besides myself. One is gone home to get married and of the other three,
two have been invalided and the other is on the sick list and will very probably
be invalided – so you may imagine I have not much spare time. If I had had my
full complement, I could have gone home in a few months, in charge of invalids,
which would have given me a spell at home of about six months with a free
passage home and out again.
    Nov. 7th – no signs of the little stranger, so I can't keep this open any longer
but I hope before next mail leaves to be able to send good news.

In a postscript to his letter, Herbert added that he had just heard that
his sailor brother Francis, known by his second name Reginald, had
just arrived at Trincomalee and how much he was looking forward
to their reunion — a strange *déjà vu* for Richard from his own
situation nearly fifty years previously. The "little stranger" arrived
ten days later, on 18th November, and was christened Herbert John
Edwin.

In 1867, a strange slander came to light which seems to have further
widened the schism between Blackbrook and Bury Hall which had
been developing for some time. The victim was Reggie — Captain

Francis Reginald Purvis R.N. — and the perpetrator a Captain Heath R.N. apparently abetted by Reggie's cousin, Captain Richard Purvis R.N. The Revd. Richard, now very much the elder statesman of the family, whose arbitration was sought on all matters of dissension, must surely have had a special sympathy for Reggie, having himself been a victim of a similarly ill-founded slander before he left India. Reggie wrote to him from Blackbrook on 22nd July 1867:

My dear Uncle, — It has for a long time been a source of sorrow to me, that an estrangement for which I could not account has for some years taken place between us. I have felt this deeply as I always valued your good opinion and never knew until I received a letter from Herbert in April last what could have caused this coldness to exist.

He then quoted a paragraph from Richard's letter to Herbert:

"But the first and chief subject of your epistle is the enquiry about your Brother Reggie and that I will first reply to all that I can – I am precisely of the same mind as yourself upon that painful subject, more so to you than to me. I know nothing of any specific accusation against him and have long determined in my own mind not to know any thing. In short, your own letter expresses exactly my own feelings, I do not for myself want to know what it is – a report has only reached us here that Reggie's name is cancelled as a candidate for the Senior United Service Club. I give you my honor this is the sum total of the report that has reached Whitsbury. To make any enquiries among his Brother Officers I conceive might be fishing in troubled waters and I am got too old for the task of finding and proving even in cases connected with my own interest".

Reggie continued:

I dare say you recognise your own words. As soon as this reached me and on Capt. Richard Purvis's return from Ireland, I demanded an explanation, and he persuaded me to allow him to propose me, in December 1861, and got a friend of his to second me. I have copied out all my share of the correspondence, and I beg of you as a favour to me, to peruse it all – I shall send it by this night post, and if you will read it as ticketed together you will see how disgracefully I have been treated and a charge trumped up against me by a man who eventually eats dirt – i.e. denies his own statements which he has previously sent me in black and white. I of course refer to Capt. Heath and he was, I believe, my only enemy in H. M. Service. However, if you will read the correspondence you will be able to judge for yourself . . .

Reggie enclosed what he believed offered conclusive proof that the smear on his good character was entirely without foundation and the sole result of Captain Heath's unprincipled malice towards him.

My sole motive in sending all this correspondence to you, is to clear my character with you and regain your good opinion. I have felt most keenly the loss of it and most particularly as when poor darling Helen was taken from you, for I was deeply attached to Helen and felt her loss far more than if any of my own sisters had been taken. I felt deeply your silence when I wrote to you expressing my sorrow on that most painful and sorrowful occasion. I should like Fortescue to read all the correspondence of this case that he may see how I have been treated – I should like Emily also to read it if she is at home. I wish the letters kept as they are of importance to me and you will perhaps kindly send them back . . .

Reggie explained that the reason he had not visited his uncle recently was that he had been cut by his cousin John Child, on going up to speak to him, when he had been in Richard Purvis's company and had consequently assumed him to be party to the slander.

I often and often think of the happy days I spent at Whitsbury and of the great kindness you always showed us – of happy days past and gone and never to return. I now only wish for one thing of you and that is an acknowledgement I have still your good opinion. I know of no act of mine of which I am ashamed and I have, I must tell you, repeatedly begged members of your family to tell me what was said against me but as this malicious scandal was spread against me in confidence ? – I was not to be told. A mere accident, I may say, has at last given me a clue and I have been enabled to force the promulgation thereof – to prove himself what I always knew him to be, and hated and despised him for. Will you, my dear Uncle, therefore take the trouble to read my letters and tell me afterwards if I have regained your good opinion and believe me ever, Your very attached nephew, F. R. Purvis.

Richard suggested that he should submit the whole matter to arbitration by the members of the Senior United Service Club. This Reggie declined to do as he had not been "blackballed" and felt that the members would say it was a private concern between the parties involved. He now believed that the slander had been perpetrated "After Dinner!" i.e. when his enemy Captain Heath had drunk too much and Heath now refused to admit that he had made the allegations in the first place. Reggie decided that he must now, as a matter of principle, apply again for membership, this time proposed and seconded by officers of real standing who knew his character well. His father agreed with him and wrote the following letter to his cousin Richard which illustrates the low state to which relations between Blackbrook and Bury Hall had sunk. It seems that Richard Purvis had also blackened his uncle George's name causing an estrangement between him and his sister Renira:

My dear Cousin, — By desire of my Son "Reginald", I forward you a letter he
sent first for my perusal. I heartily concur in the sentiments therein expressed.
Did you know as much as I do of Captn. Richard Purvis, perhaps you would be
as shy of his society at Whitsbury as he seemingly is of mine at Bury Hall. Let
this hint suffice, you may yet find out to what I allude. Captn. Richard Purvis has
blackened me to his heart's content: and has attempted to bespatter my poor dear
Reginald. I can only denounce him as an unmitigated hypocrite: and though he
may subscribe £100 to build a church he will find to his cost that will not pay his
way to Heaven. I believe my poor Sister long ere this would have been on good
terms with her only Brother: but for the influence exercised over her by her
worthless Son. I am glad he is away: she (my Sister) will enjoy her liberty now.
I am, dear Cousin, Yours faithfully, Geo. Thos. M. Purvis.

Captain Reginald Purvis circulated several of the senior officers
under whom he had served with a full dossier on the case. Admiral
Montresor, his late Commander-in-Chief in India, came
immediately to his defence stating that it was obvious that the
charges against him were false and insisting that he, himself, should
now propose him for membership. Captain Gore Jones, late Flag-
Captain to Admiral King on the China Station, immediately passed
the matter to Admiral Ryder, a member of the Club's Committee,
who embraced Reggie's cause without reservation and referred the
matter to the Committee who were similarly outraged. Several
members of the Committee offered to propose and second him,
though Admiral Montresor and Captain Gore Jones had already
claimed this right, and his name was reinstated in the Candidates'
Book with his original *Locus Standi* as at December 1861. Captain
Heath was called to account for the mischief he had made.

Reggie wrote to his uncle with a blow-by-blow account of the
above on 25th November 1867 concluding:

It is quite impossible any case could have been taken up more warmly than this
was by all my Brother Officers who knew of it, and, as I imagined, anywhere but
amongst Captain Richard Purvis's own clique, the thing was not heard of. — So
ends as should always end such pieces of business as was this.

Richard appears to have been irritated by this further letter from
Reggie on the subject — probably because it showed up his nephew
Richard in a bad light, as an accomplice in the slander, and Richard,
now aged seventy-eight, had no wish to be involved. Reggie wrote,
for the last time upon the subject, on 29th November 1867:

My dear Uncle, — I am exceedingly sorry that my last letter to you should have caused annoyance relative to your ties of Kindred – pray forgive me – I did not intend to do it. I wished to let you know what the result had been of my carrying out your kind and good advice, and also the feelings of my Brother Officers. . . . I feel convinced in my own mind that Captain Heath made the false statements he did purely from vindictive motives and himself well knew it to be false and I consider it a proof he was ashamed and afraid to repeat his statement to and from the repeated attempts he made to get out of it and his ultimate denial of his own statement – which I have in his own writing. Had he never met Captain Richard Purvis, nothing of the kind would I believe have ever occurred.

Recognising that his uncle had had quite enough of it, he concluded:

I have now told you everything relative to this unpleasant business and will abstain from mentioning the subject to you any more.

Though the animosity between Blackbrook and Bury Hall had not abated, and would intensify, any breach which may have existed between Blackbrook and Whitsbury was now healed. Herbert, in India, had sent his two eldest children, George Frederick Godfrey and Mary-Jane Austen, to live with their Uncle Reggie and Aunt Mary at Blackbrook. Young George, aged nine and destined for the Navy, had just been sent to school at Titchfield and, in April 1868, Reggie and his sister took the two children over to Whitsbury to attend Divine Service at St. Leonard's and to spend the day with their aged and revered Uncle Richard.

The following month, on 27th May 1868, Richard died peacefully, aged seventy-nine, at the Parsonage House, Whitsbury and was buried in a vault in St. Leonard's Church where he had been Vicar for forty-four years. Richard Fortescue was succeeded by his son, Fortescue Richard, who was Vicar for seventeen years until his death in 1885. The Patronage of St. Leonard's, Whitsbury, is still in the hands of the Purvis family. The present Patron is William John Purvis, Richard's great-great-grandson, who also read Law at Jesus College, Cambridge.

# The Purvis Trail

# The Purvis Trail

The two sparring cousins both became distinguished Flag Officers. Rear-Admiral Richard Purvis died in 1875 leaving Bury Hall to his eldest son, Charles Hotham Purvis, (Richard had been Sir Charles Hotham's Flag-Lieutenant in the *Penelope* in the 1840s). Charles was educated at Wellington thereafter joining the 17th Lancers with whom he was present at the Battle of Ulundi, the final conflict in the Zulu War of 1879.

In 1878 the Bury Hall estate was divided into four lots and sold with the exception of the house, the farm and about forty-one acres of land. This was let to a succession of tenants, including a Mrs. Lane who is remembered for her endearing custom every Christmas of presenting a red flannel petticoat to each of the village maidens whom she believed to have retained her virtue. In 1905, Charles sold the house to an army doctor, Major C.E.G. Stalkartt, who was stationed at the naval hospital at Haslar, and the remainder of the estate was eventually broken up for development.

During the Second World War, Bury Hall was used as the Headquarters of the local Home Guard and the structure of the house was seriously weakened as a result of enemy bombing. After the war it stood empty and derelict for several years until it was demolished in the 1950s to make way for the Northcott House Old People's Home which now stands on its site.

The eldest Blackbrook brother, Captain George Thomas Maitland Purvis R.N. (the same name as his father), died at Yokohama, Japan, in 1880, aged fifty-one, "after an illness of four days only".

The second brother, Herbert, after a distinguished career in India, including the command of a brigade in the Afghan War of 1879/80, became a Major-General and Colonel-Commandant of the Royal Artillery. His first wife, Lizzie, whom he had married when she was fourteen and had borne his four children, died in 1885 and, later the same year, he married again, this time to Daisy Bickers, daughter of a Lucknow barrister. He retired to Weston House, Weston, a large, thatched house near Cullompton, in Devon, where he died in 1912. The house was later destroyed by fire.

The third brother, Rear-Admiral Reggie, served in the steam corvette *Highflyer* in the Second Opium War and, as a Lieutenant-Commander, commanded the *Highflyer's* boats in the gallant assault of the Taku Forts on the Peiho River in June 1859, in which action he was wounded and the British force severely mauled. With him in the *Highflyer,* was Midshipman John Arbuthnot Fisher, later to become the famous Admiral of the Fleet and First Sea Lord. Fisher was already showing signs of greatness and was entrusted by Admiral Hope with the temporary command of the *Coromandel,* a steam-driven paddle tender, as he mentioned in a letter to Mrs. Edmund Warden in April 1860:

I forgot to tell you that the Admiral gave me command of the Coromandel for four days, and I took her up to Canton and back. I was regular Captain of her. We passed close by the old Highflyer on our way up and down. Old Purvis and all the fellows up there could hardly believe their eyes. †

Reggie retired from the Navy in 1884 to a house in Highweek, near Newton Abbot, Devon, and it was at nearby Paignton that their father, George Thomas Maitland (the first) died, aged eighty-one, during a visit to his son in October 1883. His death heralded yet another amazing slander against the Blackbrook Purvises. An obituary notice in *"The Portsmouth Times and Naval Gazette"*, having given a full account of the late Captain Purvis's career, continued with the following extraordinary allegation:

He was a native of Fareham, having been born on the Blackbrook Estate, which was the property of the family and then very extensive. His father was an officer belonging to the Royal George, but happened to be ashore when the awful catastrophe of the sinking of the ship at Spithead occurred in 1782. When subsequently divers went down to the ship and brought up the books and records it was found that Mr. Purvis's accounts were in a state of confusion. He was obliged to make up large sums to the government, was compelled to sell a large part of the family property, and died in such pecuniary embarrassment that his body was seized by his creditors at the churchyard gates. However, the father of Mr. J.E. Paddon generously came forward and satisfied their claims and the funeral was allowed to proceed.

---

† *First Sea Lord — An authorised biography of Admiral Lord Fisher* by Richard Hough, George Allen & Unwin Ltd. 1969, P.41

Several correspondents rushed forward to countermand this gross libel of George Purvis pointing out that he had never served in the *Royal George* and, far from dying a pauper, had left:

To one daughter £5,000 Consols; to the other daughter and to his only son sufficient property to produce to each an income of £840 per annum. The property was valued, after Mr. Purvis's decease, at £34,500 cash . . . so much for the statement as to Mr. Purvis's embarrassment. If the body was seized, as stated, it must have been the body, not of a pauper, but of a wealthy man, who required no friends to pay his debts, supposing any existed on his decease.

Blackbrook Cottage was sold by the brothers some time after their father's death. It changed hands several times until in 1927, when the Diocese of Portsmouth was created, it was acquired by the Church Commissioners as the new Bishop's Palace. Its name was changed to Bishopswood and it remained the Bishop's Palace for seventy years until 1997 when the Church decided it could no longer afford to maintain so large a property and placed it on the market at an asking price of £800,000. It is now back in private ownership with its name changed, again, to Blackbrook Grove. The Purvis Arms, in stained glass, are still in the window of the room where Georgina danced her quadrille while the Marine band played and, in the garden, the weeping willow, grown from a cutting brought back by her brother, George, from Napoleon's grave on St. Helena, has reached appropriately imperial proportions. One of Reggie's cannon-balls from Kinburn can still be seen on its gatepost; the other has fallen. Blackbrook House, the gloomy mansion which George Purvis abandoned in favour of his pretty *cottage orné,* is now a maternity hospital.

Vicar's Hill also changed hands several times after John and Richard sold it. During the First World War, the owner installed a machine shop in the basements where 16,000 artillery shells were produced to aid the war effort. In the Second World War, the house became a United States Army Air Force hospital then, after a time as a private girls' school, was acquired by the London Borough of Brent as a school for boys with emotional and behavioural difficulties. Today it is known as Southlands and, since 1995, has earned a conspicuous reputation as a centre of excellence for boys with Asperger Syndrome. From the window of an upper room, the

Needles and the Isle of Wight can be seen in the distance. It was here that the dear old Admiral, who had served his country with such valour and fidelity, stood in his twilight years to watch the ships beating up the Solent. In another former bedroom, which today resounds with the clamour and vitality of youth, Richard had sat more quietly, on Christmas evening 1818, suffering from a severe headache, to write that critical letter to his father which would decide the whole course of his future life.

St. Leonard's Church and the Parsonage House at Whitsbury have both changed radically since Richard's time. Nine years after his death, his son, Revd. Fortescue Richard Purvis, obtained permission from the Bishop of Winchester for a programme of radical repairs and alterations to the church which included raising the walls and tower, changing the windows and doors, re-roofing, re-paving and the building of a vestry. The gallery which existed in Richard's day was removed and a new pulpit, reading desk, lectern and font were installed. Yet Richard's aura is still heavy within. Around the walls on stone tablets and in stained-glass panels at the foot of the windows, Richard, his father, his brother, his wife, his sons and his daughters are all commemorated and, outside in the churchyard, headstones on Purvis graves, right up to the present time, mark this peaceful place as the spiritual home of Richard's descendants.

So many of the protagonists in our story had worshipped in this little church — the old Admiral and Richard's stepmother, brother John and Renira, Georgina and Twyford, Mary-Jane Austen and the Blackbrook Georges, John and Richard Home, James and Georgiana Cock and, of course, little George Frederick Godfrey Purvis who had been brought here, aged eight, by his uncle Reggie and Aunt Mary in 1868.

The little village of Southwick, nestling behind Portsdown Hill at the end of the Meon Valley, has changed little since good Mr. Garrett resided there, lobbying for Letters of Introduction for Richard as he awaited Bonaparte's planned invasion. In 1944 the village became the Headquarters of the Supreme Allied Commander, General Eisenhower, as he planned another invasion — better constituted and enacted than that of Napoleon.

A visit to Portsmouth Dockyard is an essential part of the Purvis Trail. In 1800 it was the largest industrial complex in the world servicing the needs of the greater part of the Royal Navy's 684 warships. The position of Richard's grandfather, John Sowers, as Clerk of the Cheque, may therefore be regarded as something akin to that of the Financial Director of General Motors today. He probably occupied one of the Admiralty houses, now mainly used as offices, in the beautiful Georgian terrace known as Long Row. It was built in 1719 to house eight of the principal dockyard officials, each having servants' quarters and substantial gardens to the rear. Close by is the former Royal Naval Academy, now an Officers' Mess, attended by Richard in 1802-03 and later by his cousin George, of Blackbrook.

A tour of H.M.S. *Victory*, which is restored and preserved in the Dockyard, is an essential pilgrimage. Richard's brother, John, was carried on her books in 1795-96, though he never actually served in her. His uncle, George Purvis, did serve in her as Secretary to Admiral Sir John Jervis (later Lord St. Vincent) and was aboard in 1797, with his personal belongings in his little brass-bound, leather chest, at the momentous Battle of Cape St. Vincent. The *Victory* and the *London* were sister ships, both having been designed by the same naval architect and built at the same time in the same dockyard. *London* was marginally smaller having 90 guns as opposed to *Victory's* 100. The visitor can therefore get a good impression of the environment into which Richard was introduced at the age of eleven and of his father's quarters in the great galleried cabin in the stern.

Before leaving the *Victory*, stand on the quarterdeck for a while and view the power and complexity of this massive fighting ship; try and imagine her heeled over and pitching wildly in heavy seas, her canvas taut and every spar straining; try to envisage the teeming activity, above and below decks, as her crew of 800 clear the decks and prepare for action; and the mind-shattering, spine-jarring shock as the great guns thunder into a broadside. Even here, where it actually happened, one cannot come anywhere near to imagining the deafening violence of warfare in such ships as these; or of the raw courage and consummate skill of the men who sailed them and fought them — men like John Child Purvis.

Vernon Hill House, once the home of Admiral Vernon, can still be seen just outside Bishop's Waltham. It was leased by Captain John Child Purvis in the 1780s before he bought his house in Wickham. John was born here in 1787 and, years later, Admiral Villeneuve, commander of the Franco-Spanish Fleets at Trafalgar, was confined here after his defeat though he was permitted to travel to London to attend Nelson's funeral. Bishop's Waltham is also at the centre of another Purvis mystery — the origins of John Scott, the Admiral's special protégé.

John Scott was born on 9th December 1784, possibly at Bishop's Waltham, and was a boy under Captain Purvis's patronage in the *London* from 1797 to 1800, having served in the ship under a variety of captains since 28th August 1794. Though the Admiral took an ongoing interest in the careers of all the boys who had been in his charge, his special interest in Scott is apparent throughout his correspondence. John Scott was known to John and Richard, and to the Blackbrook family — even Barrington of the Beccles branch had met him in Madeira on his way out to India in 1809. We know that Richard corresponded with John Scott, though none of the letters has survived, and the relationship between him and the Purvis family as a whole seems to indicate something more closely allied to kinship than friendship. The proposition is, of course, that John Scott was an illegitimate son of John Child Purvis which is supported by the late codicil to the Admiral's Will leaving him a legacy of £2,000 — a very great deal of money in those days to leave to anyone other than a close relative.

The late Eric Duke Scott, a Canadian citizen and a great-grandson of Captain John Scott, went to considerable pains and expense in the 1970s and '80s to establish the truth, or otherwise, of the tradition which had always existed in his family that John Scott was Admiral Purvis's natural son. The professional genealogists he employed to search the relevant records were unable to establish anything positive. After his death, another great-grandson, Eric David Scott, a U.S. citizen from California, took up the crusade with a similar lack of success. However, during his retirement, Eric David Scott travelled to many parts of the world to locate and meet up with distant cousins also descended from Captain John Scott. Every branch of the family that he met — in England, Scotland, the

United States, Canada, South Africa, Zimbabwe and Australia – shared the same tradition that Admiral Purvis was their ancestor's father. It is probable that he was.

The next question is — who was John Scott's mother? There are two theories: the first is that she was a lady of the name of Scott which was widely extant in the Bishop's Waltham district at the time. All research has failed to identify her. The second theory is that Catherine Sowers was the mother and that she went to the altar with Captain Purvis, on 11th October 1784, seven months pregnant; but, so severe was the stigma attached to such a situation in those days, that she was hidden away at her father's house in the Dockyard until the birth of her firstborn son whose legitimacy was never acknowledged by his parents. This is unlikely as Catherine's first daughter, Catherine, was born only eight months after John Scott. Another tradition among John Scott's descendants is that he ran away to sea and assumed the name of Scott from another boy in the *London* who had died; but this merely muddies the waters further and we are unlikely ever to know the full story.

Whatever may have been the case, the enigma of John Scott in no way diminishes the character of the Admiral who led an otherwise exemplary life and, at the end of the day, whether or not he was Scott's father, was man enough to provide for him in a way which he knew would strengthen the supposition.

Just south of Alton is the village of Chawton. It was at the Parish Church here that Richard's cousin, George Thomas Maitland Purvis of Blackbrook Cottage, was married to Mary-Jane Austen in 1828. The cottage where her aunt, Jane Austen, lived is open to the public and contains some Purvis relics presented to the Jane Austen Memorial Trust by Purvis Pasha's widow. Among these are two miniatures of Richard's uncle George, of Blackbrook, and his beautiful wife Renira; Mary-Jane's little work table from Blackbrook; and a diamond-encircled miniature, by Smart, of Philadelphia Hancock, Jane Austen's exotic aunt who was the wife of Tysoe Saul Hancock, a surgeon in the Bengal Medical Service, and the mistress of Warren Hastings who was the father of her equally exotic daughter, Eliza, later Comtesse de Feuillide.

Young George Frederick Godfrey Purvis, who visited Richard at Whitsbury the month before his death, entered the Royal Navy on 17th July 1872. For his part in the Bombardment of Alexandria in July 1882, he received executive promotion to Lieutenant. He appears to have taken a liking to Egypt as, in 1890, he resigned his Commission in the Royal Navy and joined the Egyptian Coastguard Service of which he became Director-General in 1918 with the rank of Miralai and Pasha. During his service in Egypt, he met May Peel, daughter of William Felton Peel of Carnkerford Hall, Tamworth, a member of the great Peel cotton family many of whom had positions with the Company in Alexandria at the time. They were married in 1900 and on Purvis Pasha's retirement in 1922, they went to live at Burghfield Common, near Reading. His absorbing hobby was woodworking and he had a well-equipped carpentry workshop installed in his garden where he spent his retirement in carving chairs and making furniture. One project he undertook was to restore the little brass-bound wood and leather chest which had come from Blackbrook and had been with his great-grandfather, George Purvis, aboard the *Victory* at the Battle of Cape St. Vincent in 1797. In relacquering the edges, he was careful not to obscure the name of his grandfather's second wife, Esther North Purvis, which she had added in pencil with the date July 1846.

Purvis Pasha and his wife had no children. The elder of his two younger brothers, Herbert John Edwin Purvis, a Major in the 3rd Bombay Cavalry, died unmarried in Japan in 1901 having taken part in the Boxer Campaign of that year. The youngest brother, Major Eyre Walter Molyneux Purvis, was killed in an accident whilst on active service with his Regiment, the 16th Bengal Lancers, in Mesopotamia in 1915. Purvis Pasha died in 1936 thereby ending the direct male Blackbrook line of the family.

His younger sister, Mary-Jane Austen, however, married Captain Reginald Campbell of the 24th Regiment South Wales Borderers and presented him with a son, Spencer Bertie Cyril Campbell, in 1883. Captain Campbell took part in the Zulu War, in which his regiment featured with such distinction and, on his death, Mary-Jane married again to Captain Alfred Cotton Way D.S.O. of the same regiment. There was no issue.

And what of Richard's brother officers in the Bengal Army? Richard survived them all. We have recorded that the brothers John and Richard Home both became Major-Generals and that Richard's son won the V.C. in the Mutiny. We have also covered Major-General James Cock and his brother Colonel Henry Cock.

In 1820 Captain James Hales died in Calcutta and the friendless Colonel Tetley at Allahabad. Hales had been Adjutant of the 1/21st for six years before his death, aged thirty-five, and Tetley was Colonel of the 4th Native Infantry. Major Barré Latter died two years later at Kishnaganj never having completed his Tibetan dictionary.

Captain George Casement and Lieutenant George Gordon both died in 1823. Casement was serving as Brigade-Major at Mhow and Gordon as Fort Adjutant at Chunar. Casement's brother continued his distinguished career to become Major-General Sir William Casement K.C.B. He died of cholera at Kasipur in 1844.

The gallant John Swinton, three times wounded and having held the perilous job of Commanding Officer of the Pioneers for most of his service, was eventually invalided in January 1825 in the rank of Lieutenant-Colonel. Three years earlier he had attended the marriage of his sister, Mary, to Sir James Weir Hogg Bart. who, among many other distinctions, was to be twice elected Chairman of the Honourable East India Company. John Swinton died at Bhagalpur in December 1825.

Poor George Snodgrass, Richard's companion on the voyage back to England in the *Thomas Grenville,* was never to see the waters of the Forth again and also died in 1825, at Benares, where he was acting as Deputy Paymaster. He was aged forty and still a Captain. The 2/21st's trusted physician, Dr. Josiah Ridges, died the following year at Nasirabad but history does not relate whether or not he was survived by his sable venus, Lutchimar.

Captain John Neufville, the fainéant Old Etonian, eventually applied himself to his profession and was commanding the 1st Assam Light Infantry Battalion when he died at Jorhat, Assam, aged thirty-five, in 1830. Tetley's favourite, the blue-blooded Hugh Wrottesley, also died in 1830 as a Lieutenant-Colonel commanding the 1st Battalion Native Invalids at Allahabad.

Jeremiah Johnson, the officer who raised the 2/21st as "*J'ansin ki*

*Paltan"*, became Colonel of the 30th Native Infantry and died in France in 1833. Lieutenant-Colonel Hugh Ross, commanding the 2nd Native Infantry, died in Cawnpore in 1838.

William Price, the "damn'd lazy boy", having decimated the tiger population of Bengal, became a Major-General and died in retirement at Abergavenny in 1844, aged sixty-eight. Lieutenant-Colonel William Nichol, the revered C.O. of the 2/21st, never returned to India after his furlough in 1816, during which he visited Admiral Purvis at Vicar's Hill. He retired in 1818 and died at his home in Beaumont Street, Marylebone, in 1845 aged eighty-one. Captain John Johnson, who had also been a guest at Vicar's Hill, and had made such a good impression upon the Admiral, returned to England in 1817, having been at Makwanpur with the 1/30th. He is believed to have been the author of *"A Journey from India to England, through Persia, Georgia, Poland and Prussia in 1817"* which was published in 1818 with coloured and plain aquatint plates. Johnson did not return to India after his furlough and died in Bath in 1852.

Of all Richard's contemporaries, George Hunter reached the greatest heights. He received a serious sabre wound on his left arm during the capture of Bhurtpore in 1826, was honoured with a C.B. the following year and became a Lieutenant-General in 1851. He died three years later, of apoplexy, at his home in Stirling.

Charles Russell retired as a Captain in 1822 and had a distinguished civilian career thereafter, though it ended tragically. He entered politics and was Member of Parliament for Reading from 1830 to 1837, and then again from 1841 to 1847. He was also Chairman of Great Western Railways for sixteen years from 1839 to 1855. The following year he committed suicide, by shooting himself, at 9 Argyll Street, London.

Gilbert Watson, who had been Mentioned in Despatches as a Lieutenant in the 2/21st for "Conduct most conspicuous in transactions before Fort Beety in the Vizier's territory", retired as a Major in 1834 and died in 1859, aged sixty-nine.

Ironically, the one who, next to Richard, survived the longest was the stentorian Captain William Menzies who had twice won a lakh in the Lottery. He retired in 1818 and died in 1861, aged eighty-three. One wonders if his cries of "Ahm tellint yew" tormented his neighbours in Morningside as sorely as they had his brother officers in Mirzapur.

Of Richard's twenty closest contemporaries — fourteen (70%) died in India and fifteen (75%) were still in the Company's service. Only two (10%) were killed in action though it must be said it was a period of comparative calm in India. Their average age at death was forty-one years.

In 1824 the 2/21st Bengal Native Infantry was renumbered as the 42nd; then in 1842 it became the 42nd Bengal Light Infantry and in 1861 the 5th Bengal Light Infantry. In 1903 it had its final name change to the 5th Light Infantry before being disbanded in the 1922 reorganisation of the Indian Army.

The 1/30th became the 59th in 1824 and the 8th in 1861. In 1897 its largely Rajput strength was recognised with the title the 8th Rajput Native Infantry which in 1903 became the 8th Rajputs and in 1922 the 4th/7th Rajput Regiment. On Independence in 1947, the Regiment was handed over to the Indian Government and today carries forward its proud traditions as the 3rd Battalion of the Rajput Regiment of the Indian Army.

As has been previously mentioned, both Regiments remained loyal to their British officers in the Mutiny of 1857.

# Epilogue

# Epilogue

There comes a moment, as anyone who has been deeply involved in the research of historical characters will know, when those characters become so real that they actually stand at one's shoulder expressing censure or approval or, worse still, maintaining a contemplative silence which makes one want to scream at them: "Well, have I got this right or is there something else I ought to know about?"

So it has been that Richard has visited me regularly over the past four years to oversee my work. He is normally in his mid-twenties, a dashing young officer in the 2/21st Native Infantry, 5 feet 8 inches tall with dark, curly hair, a bushy moustache, thick black beard and with what remains visible of his face tanned mahogany brown by the relentless Indian sun. "Why on earth," I have frequently asked him while struggling with his handwriting, "could you not have written this more clearly"? His answers are always charming and well-reasoned but so endlessly grandiloquent that I seldom have the patience to hear him out; and it is this that has been one of my greatest problems in telling his story — deciding upon which of the letters to include and to what extent I should edit them. Part of me has said that I have no right to edit them at all — they express most perfectly, if discursively, what it is their intention to convey and to cut, or paraphrase, large sections of them might be to ruin their orchestration for those few enthusiasts who delight in the verbal construction of that period. Another part of me has warned that the majority of modern readers, accustomed to today's concise use of the language, would reach their boredom threshold within the first fifty pages of the book, start to skip the excerpts, and thereby miss out on the glorious pathos and humour they contain.

I consulted Richard, trying to explain to him the changes in the vernacular over the past two centuries, but he was clearly offended that I should suppose that anyone might be bored by his carefully crafted letters. We discussed the three most consequential of these — all to his father: the first explaining his reasons for being in debt;

the second his plea for assistance in transferring to the Civil Service; and the third, that momentous letter written on Christmas Day 1818 advising his father that he would not return to India.

"Could you state my case, on each of these occasions," he asked me, "with any greater clarity?" and I had to admit that it would be difficult. I was also aware that in presenting the story of his life, I was exposing him to the judgement of posterity who might perceive him as a vacillating and irresolute young man who had rejected a career in which his advancement was reasonably well assured by his father's interest and had then lacked the commitment to settle down in that which he had chosen for himself. In these circumstances, I felt that the least I owed him was the opportunity to present his case in his own, unabridged, words. I have therefore reproduced these letters in full and who, on reading them, can claim to be unmoved by his arguments?

There was then the question of what, in delicacy, I should omit. One day Richard visited me, not as a young officer, but as a deeply devout and universally respected clergyman in his twilight years. Was it really necessary, he asked me, to sully his character by divulging the fact that he and his brother John had consorted with prostitutes in their youth? This was a difficult one and I have to admit to a certain feeling of treachery in exposing to public scrutiny what had clearly been a confidential exchange between brothers. I thought about it long and hard and eventually decided that I would be doing him no favour in concealing anything I knew of him; a man's achievements are the greater, after all, when evaluated in the knowledge that he was subject to the same human weaknesses as the rest of us. I was also aware of the bitter loss to posterity caused by well-meaning executors having excised whole periods of a person's life, or whole facets of their character, by the destruction of material which, in their opinion, or by the standards of probity of the age, did them no credit. Cassandra Austen, who burned, or cut pieces out of, the greater part of her sister Jane's letters after her death, is a prime example. Richard's life, I decided, was quite sufficiently worthy to be judged on a "warts and all" basis and I have concealed nothing. Indeed, had I tried to present him as having remained celibate until the age of thirty, I might, in today's changed moral climate, have exposed him to charges of a graver nature.

Having read Richard's story, nobody can suppose that he received a "calling" to the ministry — he was quite prepared to consider any career which would prevent his return to India; but this is not to say that he undertook his duties as a priest with any less devotion. His final choice of career was undoubtedly the best founded — his personal qualities seemed ideally suited to those required in a country parson. He was a man of great intelligence who was capable of sustained mental effort, as witnessed by his achievement of a First at Cambridge having led an active and adventurous life for the previous nineteen years. He was a person to whom others tended to turn for guidance and arbitration and one in whose company men of widely differing backgrounds seem to have felt comfortable. He certainly had the "gift of the gab" and his early advocacy in his letters to his father must have been good schooling for later entreaties to his congregation. He was very conscious of the responsibilities and dignity of the cloth and, most importantly, if we are to believe in the sincerity of his letters, his faith was strong.

With regard to his early vacillations, it is worth considering that Richard was Vicar of Whitsbury for forty-four years — a period which, today, would often constitute a full career span. On this basis it is tempting to regard his time in the Navy and the Bengal Army as a youthful adventure, a warming up "gap" before his proper, grown-up job; yet this would be to trivialise the job he did and the responsibility he bore when little more than a child. We have no present-day parallel to a boy of sixteen being placed in command of 100 native grenadiers in an isolated fort a day's march from the nearest European.

When one reads of the value which Richard ascribed to his father's, and Mr. Garrett's, letters of "Good Advice", one is inclined at first to question his sincerity. Daniel Garrett's letters to Richard have not survived but were probably very similar to those from his father which, typically and inevitably, would contain passages such as:

I have not been so collected as I would wish to inforce on your mind the very great consequence it is to you to preserve through life a fair and unspoted Character, too much cannot possibly be said on so interesting a subject, and as Mr. Garrett will probably commit some of his thoughts to paper for your future guidance; I intreat you to pay every possible attention to them, preserve them, and read them over frequently and always keep in your mind the pleasure and satisfaction I shall derive from hearing as good accounts of you as I have of your Brother; . . . Remember Richard the strong admonitions I have so frequently and forceably given you in common with the other youngsters on board the London and Royal George, I think they can never be forgot unless the Heart should become so corrupted as not to retain a virtuous sentiment; this my dear Richard I trust will never be your case; God forbid it should; I only wish you clearly to understand how much I am interested in your doing well and always acting uprightly honourably Religiously and honest; never suffer yourself to be led out of the proper path, by any specious deceitful Characters, which you may [chance] to fall in with; civility is due to all, but do not hastily form friendships with those your scarcely [are] acquainted with, you will have the advantage of being recommended to some of the Principal Gentlemen in the Settlements, to them you should look for advice, and their reports of you will give me I hope all the satisfaction I can wish.

To which Richard responded:

Be assured, my dear Sir, I consider your letters and poor Mr. Garrett's, both, and all of which I have preserved with the greatest care, as treasure inestimable. I peruse them frequently, and I am certain, with the greatest attention; for although my thoughts were ever so instantly thrown upon any subject only the moment before, They never fail to fix my attention in the most firm and earnest manner; when this is the case, I leave you to judge whether it is not most probable that I profit by the good advice they contain.

Was it really possible, I wondered, that Richard should have read and re-read these repetitive homilies and drawn comfort from them? The letter of "Good Advice" seems to have followed a standard format which had changed little in 100 years. It would emphasise the importance of maintaining a good character, upon which the writer's continuing patronage and affection naturally depended, and would warn that, sooner or later, the writer would receive reports from third parties as to whether or not their advice had been heeded. This same construction can be noted in a letter received by the Admiral's grandmother, Mary English, from her aunt, Mrs. Elizabeth Howland (daughter of Sir Josiah Child, the famous Chairman of the East India Company after whom the Admiral received his middle name), when she first went out to India in January 1716:

. . . Mr. Lewis takes my word for it when he recomends you as a Modest Virtuous young woman that has had a religious education and I have recomended you as such to all I have writ to. I hope you will take care to maintain that character to your lives end to abstain not only from what is Criminal, but from the approaches of all vanity, from every thing leading to impurity and immodesty and while you are a shipboard never to be out of the sight of the Gentlewoman that goes in the ship with you if she be a woman of Vertu that she may be a wittness of your past conversation. Your salvation depend upon it and therefore tis nothing to say that your fortune depends entirely upon it, tis all you have to recomend you, and is yet less to say that your name will be pleasent or odious to me, as you answer the character I have given of you, of which I shall have a true account if I live to see the return of the ships. . . .

Anyone who was at boarding school or who has served or worked away from home, knows the intense joy of receiving mail from home; and how much greater must have been this joy when letters commonly took between six months and a year to arrive, and many never arrived at all. If, when they did arrive, they contained little more than a tedious, moralising harangue, it is probable that they were still read with pleasure as they represented the only point of contact with a far-distant parent or relative. There were no photographs; some fortunate people may have had a miniature or locket but, for the great majority, these letters were the only tangible reminder of parents they may not have seen for ten years or more and might, in all likelihood, never see again.

When Admiral Sir Francis Austen died, the letters of "Good Advice" he had received from his clergyman father were found among his private papers, stained and dog-eared from frequent re-reading. Richard also kept his father's letters all his life and passed them on to his heirs, well worn and tied up with pink ribbons. I am therefore inclined to think that his response to his father was rather more than a disingenuous attempt to "keep the old man happy". There were occasions when he did this: when telling his father of his close friendship with John Home, for example, he stated that they had met on the Indiaman on their voyage out to India. In reality, they came out on different ships; but who, having read the Admiral's "Good Advice" on the dangers of forming hasty friendships, can blame Richard for having elaborated a little on the length of time he had known John?

Nor, I feel, can we blame him for overplaying the effect of the Indian climate upon his health. The knowledge that, in the event, he outlived all his contemporaries, does tend to subvert the gloomy prognosis he presented to his employers in 1820. However, he was trying to justify his early retirement from their service and to secure their sympathetic consideration of his request for an enhanced pension and the health card was really the only one he had to play.

The slander against Richard which he was so anxious that his father should ignore and which was, apparently, the cause of his estrangement with his brother John after their meeting in Ceylon in 1816, must remain a mystery. There is little doubt in my mind that somebody "smeared" him, either from malice or, as often seems to have been the cause of otherwise unaccountable slanders, by confusing him with someone else. I have found no record in the India Office archives of any charge against Richard for an unpaid debt — indeed all the evidence we have shows him to have been punctilious in their settlement (remember how he pestered George Homer to submit his trivial mess bill from the *Thomas Grenville*). He was certainly not a gambler and there is every indication that he had his personal finances well under control by 1816. Having suffered from being in debt during his early years in India, and having got himself out of it by his own resolve, he was sufficiently intelligent not to get himself into financial difficulties again.

Some light may be thrown on this incident in a letter I have very recently come across in the National Maritime Museum. It is dated 22nd November 1817 from Rear-Admiral Sir Richard King at Admiralty House, Trincomalee, to Richard at Barrackpore. It is very long (seven sides) and strikes one as being surprisingly intimate and gossipy for a communication between the naval Commander-in-Chief and a junior army officer. It does, however, give some insight into the intrigues and scandals which were current in Ceylon at the time and suggests that Richard had already advised Admiral King of the slander against him and that the Admiral, for one, gave little heed to it. Having thanked Richard for having undertaken his commissions and advising him that he had arranged payment through his agent, he continues:

. . . I suppose you did not see Captain [L...] otherwise I think he could not have told to your face what you mention respecting old Reynolds (who to be sure is a nasty fellow and I am glad to get rid of him) but I am sure he was civil to you and you express yourself to me and the report you have heard was never in circulation here. I rather think Capt. L. scandal originated because R. giving a response to Miss Morris, Scott, a Major Davenport and Sharman went home with R. — one perfectly happy excepting the latter who R. took out of charity to save his life but he behaved so ill that R. would not carry him further than the Cape. This is saying a great deal for the Elephant Captain — I have no [...] person to annoy me, I am [glad] he is gone — a more deceitful man never existed, rather was he a friend to Trincomalee, I could tell you a <u>great deal</u>. One thing we never had any disagreement but all he said was not <u>gospel</u>. His tongue . . . was like a cow's — a rough and smooth side . . .†

This incident shows Brother John in a bad light; when Richard's character was impugned, he surely should have challenged him with it and asked for an explanation rather than embarking upon what seems to me a pretty shabby reprisal against his own brother. I am also surprised at Richard, having himself been a victim of this sort of character assassination, not having given more overt support to his nephew Reggie when he suffered the same thing some fifty years later. Rectitude, I suggested to Richard quite firmly, was surely of greater importance in this matter than the relative closeness of kinship of the combatants, or the need to keep his head down in an unpleasant family "broil". He replied that he was seventy-eight at the time, an age at which he had earned the right to divorce himself from such proceedings; and I must concur with this.

In reconstructing the story of Richard's abortive courtship of Georgina I have had to make certain assumptions as some of the key letters are missing — destroyed, I suspect, (and why not?), by Richard himself. It consequently appears to have been a clumsy and rather sad affair, which it very probably was, conducted within the framework of Richard's excessive propriety and Georgina's skittish frivolity. I make no apology for including some of her letters in full, in all their trivial, malicious, gossipy, glory — for me, and I hope for others, their Austenesque charm is quite irresistible.

And what of Admiral John Child Purvis? Here is a man for whom I have developed such a profound admiration and respect that I am tempted to rise to my feet when I feel him near at hand — a man who embodies every worthwhile British characteristic; upon whose character one could bend iron bars.

He may not have been a commander of genius, in the Nelson or St. Vincent league, but he was representative of that breed of

---

† N.M.M. PRV/101 *Loose Papers* MS.55/009

officer, few of whom are remembered by history, but without whose total dependability and professional competence the very great commanders could never have made their mark. Lord Collingwood knew his worth and it surprises me that the success of Admiral Purvis's command at Cadiz, the culmination of half a century of hard and devoted service to his country, was not recognised by his Sovereign with a Knighthood at the very least. Had Lord Collingwood survived his voyage home in 1810, I feel sure he would have insisted upon an honour for his old friend; yet such was the character of Admiral Purvis, that I have little doubt he considered virtue to have been its own, and adequate, reward for, as he told Richard in a letter in August 1816: ". . . even without such inducements there is a self satisfaction in knowing you have always deserved that which may not ultimately fall to your lot".

There is a touching tenderness beneath the veneer of severity in the Admiral's letters to Richard. He was an uncomplicated man of simple perceptions in an age where probity and success in one's career were the sole criteria of worth. He thus saw his duty to his sons as a twofold pursuance — to ensure their good character and to advance their prospects. Looked at closely, his "Good Advice", which, as we know, he offered at every available opportunity, is, in the main, as cogent today as it was then. Setting aside his exhortation to religion, which was in those days less of a personal determination than it is today, there is only one part of his advice which jars on modern views and this is the constant encouragement to Richard to ingratiate himself with his superiors. At the time, such behaviour was not only normal but was absolutely essential to any sort of progress in life. The civilised world ran on the system of patronage and, indeed, Richard's whole story can be seen as a constant quest for it — initially within and ultimately regardless of the constraints of his own pride. Today, of course, we must dismiss it as corrupt and yet, one feels, it had a certain behoof — it encouraged deference and respect to one's superiors and, given the integrity of those in a position to bestow their interest, really seems to have worked rather well in the 18th and 19th centuries.

The Admiral's frustration at having no contacts within the East India Company, through whom he could further Richard's career, is obvious. It clearly bothered him, particularly as he had done so well for his son John, and one rejoices for him when the opportunity at last arrives with the purchase of the Whitsbury advowson. It is also clear that he derived great satisfaction from being in a position to provide so handsomely for his sons and to implement his long-resolved, and regularly stated, intention of breaking with tradition and dividing his property equally between them. Though his principal concern was always the success of his sons, he took an ongoing interest in the careers of all the boys who had started life in his care and was a fair and indulgent master to his servants ashore some of whom, we know, stayed with him for the better part of their working lives.

The lot of women in the 18th and 19th centuries can only cause deep sadness to anyone who examines the period. Deprived of the franchise and any serious protection of their basic rights in law, their sole aspiration was marriage which, once achieved, with the coincident relinquishment to their husbands of whatever fortune they may previously have possessed, condemned them to a life of continual child bearing and the almost inevitable loss of some of their children in infancy. The strong, such as Richard's mother-in-law and his wife, Bessy, survived and raised enormous families; the weak, such as Catherine Sowers, Mary Garrett, Mary-Jane Austen, Georgiana Baker and Georgina Purvis, did their best before death at a tragically early age the sadness of which was often compounded by their husbands' early remarriage to start the breeding cycle again with younger, stronger wives. It was the way of the time, yet one cannot help but grieve for poor Catherine Sowers, the Admiral's first wife, who bore him four children in just over four years, lost two of them in infancy and died herself a month after Richard's birth aged just thirty-one. She is even denied a memorial as the headstones in the old Kingston Churchyard, where she is buried, were demolished when the new Victorian church was built. I have therefore dedicated this story of her son's life to her memory in the hope that it may, in some small way, serve as a memorial both to her and to the countless other women like her whose lives were so short and, seemingly, so inconsequential.

# Appendix 1

## Glossary of Indian terms used in the text.

| | |
|---|---|
| *Bahadur* | Moghul term meaning "hero". Added to the name of British officers to indicate gallantry — e.g. "Ochterlony Bahadur". |
| *Batta* | An allowance paid to officers and officials during active or detached service. |
| *Begum* | Muslim lady of high rank. |
| *Bildars* | Labourers. |
| *Brahmins* | Those of the highest Hindu caste. |
| *Bus!* | Enough! |
| *Butcha* | Child; baby. |
| *Chapplis* | (Pronounced chupplis), sandals. |
| *Chillum* | The bowl of the hookah which holds the tobacco. |
| Cantonment | (Pronounced cantoonment), the military area of a town or city. |
| "Curry & Rice" | Term meaning "India". |
| *Dak (Dawk)* | Network of covered litters between garrison towns carried by relays of dooley bearers on the post-coach principle. Later came to mean "mail". |
| *Doab* | The area of land between two river courses. |
| *Dooley* | Covered litter or palanquin. |
| "Griffin" | Recent arrival from Europe who has still to learn the ways of the country and is prone to "Griffish" behaviour. |
| *Hookah* | Tobacco pipe smoked through water. |

| | |
|---|---|
| *Jemadar* | Indian officer with the equivalent rank to Lieutenant. |
| *Keeledar* | Governor or commandant of a fort. |
| *Khitmaghar* | Butler or table waiter. |
| *Lakh* | 100,000 units — e.g. a lakh in the Lottery was 100,000 rupees (about £12,500). |
| *Lathi* | Iron-bound stick used as a club. |
| *Logue* | People; tribe. |
| *Machan* | A raised shooting platform. |
| *Marathas* | Warlike Hindu tribe. |
| *Munshi* | Writer or teacher (generally of languages). |
| *Nullah* | Stream or ditch. |
| *Paan* | A mixture of fragrant seeds and betel nut chewed by Indians. |
| *Paltan* | Regiment of native infantry. |
| *Rajputs* | Warlike Hindu tribe. |
| *Rupee* | Unit of Indian currency. At this period there were approximately 8 rupees to £1. |
| *Sepoy* | Private soldier of native infantry. |
| *Sirkar* | The government or, at this period, the Honourable East India Company. |
| *Zemindar* | Small landowner. |

# Appendix 2

## Sources and References.

All extracts from letters, unless otherwise acknowledged, are from the collection of private correspondence in the possession of the Purvis family (Whitsbury descent). Early genealogical data is based upon family records which were the property of the late George Frederick Godfrey Purvis (Blackbrook descent). Other principal sources consulted are as follows:

### Manuscript Sources:

*Establishment Records of the 2nd Battalion, 21st Bengal Native Infantry and 1st Battalion, 30th Bengal Native Infantry,* Archives of the Honourable East India Company, The British Library Oriental & India Office Collections, **L/MIL/8/16-26.**

*Logbooks of the Honourable Company's Ships "Sir William Bensley" for 1804 and "Thomas Grenville" for 1818,* Ibid. **L/MAR.**

*Biographical Notes etc.—Rear Admiral George Purvis—Capt. G.T.M. Purvis—Admiral Francis R. Purvis,* National Maritime Museum, Greenwich, **BGY/P/4.**

*Correspondence Admiral Orde—Lord Nelson—George Purvis,* Ibid. **ORD/11.**

*French Naval Maps of Cadiz and Mediterranean Ports,* collected by Admiral J.C. Purvis, Ibid. **PRV/36, MS55/029.**

*Letters Lord Nelson—George Purvis,* Ibid., **AGC/N/13 and 14.**

*Letters to Admiral Purvis—Duke of Wellington—Lord Collingwood—Sir John Jervis,* Ibid., **AGC/23/7.**

*Lieutenant's Log, H.M.S. "London" 1794-1802,* Ibid.
**ADM/L/L/192.**

*Log H.M.S. "London" 1797,* Ibid. **PRV/7.**

*Log H.M.S. "London" 1800,* Ibid. **PRV/9.**

*Loose Papers from Purvis Collection, Peninsular War,* Ibid.
**MSS/73/RS.**

*Official Letters Admiral John Child Purvis,* Ibid., **PRV/39.**

*Purvis Papers, Peninsular War Documents,* Ibid., **MSS/73/125.**

*Letterbook (1824-29) of Revd. R.F. Purvis, Vicar of Whitsbury,* in
private ownership.

*Duke of Wellington Lieutenancy Papers,* Hampshire Record
Office, **25M61, bundle 8/2.**


**Published Sources:**

*A Matter of Honour, an Account of the Indian Army, its Officers
and Men,* by Philip Mason, London, Jonathan Cape, 1974.

*An Historical Account of the Rise and Progress of the Bengal
Native Infantry from its First Formation in 1757 to 1796* by
Captain Williams, London, John Murray, 1817.

*Britannia Rules, the Classic Age of Naval History 1793-1815,* by
C. Northcote Parkinson, London, Weidenfeld & Nicolson,
1977.

*Correspondence and Memoir of Lord Collingwood,* edited by
G.L.N. Collingwood, 4th Edition, 1828.

*From Sepoy to Subedar,* by Sita Ram, First English edition 1873.
Reprinted by the Military Book Society 1970 by arrangement
with Routledge & Kegan Paul.

*History of the Organisation, Equipment and War Services of the Regiment of Bengal Artillery* by Major F.W. Stubbs, London, Henry S. King & Co., 1877, 3 vols.

*Medical Officers of the Indian Army,* compiled and edited by Messrs. Dodwell & Miles, East India Army Agents, Cornhill, London 1839.

*Memoirs of the Extraordinary Military Career of John Shipp, Late a Lieutenant in His Majesty's 87th Regiment,* by Himself, first published in 1829. 1890 edition, London, T. Fisher Unwin.

*Officers of the Bengal Army 1758-1834* by Major V.C.P. Hodson, London, Constable & Co. Ltd., 1927, 4 vols.

*Officers of the Indian Army 1760-1834,* compiled and edited by Messrs. Dodwell & Miles, East India Army Agents, Cornhill, London, Longman, Orme, Browne & Co., 1838.

*Old Oak, the life of John Jervis Earl of St. Vincent,* by Admiral Sir William James, London, Longmans, Green & Co. Ltd., 1950.

*Roll of the Indian Medical Services 1615-1930,* compiled by Lieutenant Colonel D.G. Crawford, Bengal Medical Service (Retd.), London, W. Thacker & Co., 1930.

*Sea Saga, being the Naval Diaries of four generations of the King-Hall Family,* edited by L. King-Hall, London, Victor Gollancz Ltd., 1935.

*Shipboard Life and Organisation 1731-1815,* edited by Brian Lavery, Navy Records Society Vol. 138, 1998.

*The British Expedition to the Crimea,* by William H. Russell, London, G. Routledge & Co., 1858.

*The Great Mutiny, India 1857,* by Christopher Hibbert, London, Allen Lane, 1978.

*The Honourable East India Company's Bengal Civil Servants 1780-1838,* compiled and edited by Messrs. Dodwell & Miles, East India Army Agents, Cornhill, London, Longman, Orme, Browne & Co.,1839.

*The Indian Army,* by Boris Mollo, Blandford Press Ltd., 1981.

*The "Londons" of the British Fleet,* by Edward Fraser, London, John Lane, The Bodley Head, 1908.

*The Oxford History of India,* by V.A. Smith (continued by S.M. Edwardes), Oxford, Clarendon Press, 1923.

*The Royal Navy, a History from the Earliest Times to the Present,* by William Laird Clowes, first published 1897 by Sampson, Lowe Marston & Co. 1996 paperback edition, London, Chatham Publishing, 7 vols.

*The Wooden World, an Anatomy of the Georgian Navy,* by N.A.M. Rodger, London, Collins, 1986.

Excerpts from the Purvis Papers in the National Maritime Museum are reproduced by kind permission of the Trustees.

**AUTHOR'S NOTE:**

I have tried very hard to contact the copyright holders of every excerpt I have quoted from previously published works. With the amalgamation of publishing houses in recent years this is not always easy and, if I have inadvertently breached anyone's copyright, I apologise and will, of course, pay the appropriate fee if the copyright holder will contact me.

# THE DESCENDANTS OF GEORGE PURVIS 1718-1773

**TABLE A**

**George Purvis (3)**

*Admiralty Official. Secretary to the Sick & Wounded Board*
*b. 25 Nov 1718 at Darsham d. 26 Mar 1773 at Donhead Hall, Wilts bur. in Donhead Churchyard*
*= 5 May 1742 at St. Ann's, Soho. **Mary Oadham***
*b. 26 Oct 1720 at Fort George E9 d. 4 Sep 1801 bur. St. Giles's, Colchester*
*dau. of Catesby Oadham. Member of the Council of Madras, HE9C*
*She inherited the estates of Porters, Essex, and Beckenden Grange, Warwicks, from her cousin Lady Clifton*

**Richard Purvis**

*Captain RN*
*of "The Porters and Beckenden Grange*
*b. 26 Aug 1743 at Stepney*
*d. 2 May 1802 at Beccles*
*= 3 Jun 1780 at Melton*
**Lucy Leman**
*b. 5 Nov 1747 at Kirkstead, Norfolk*
*d. 15 Jan 1825 bur. at Wenhaston*
*dau. of Revd. John Leman, Rector of Wenhaston*

**Mary Oadham Purvis**

*"Aunt Mop"*
*b. 2 Apr 1745 at Stepney*
*dsp. 29 Dec 1812 at Blackbrook Cottage, Fareham bur. Fareham*

**John Child Purvis**

*Admiral of the Blue*
*b. 13 Mar 1747 at Stepney*
*d. 23 Feb 1825 at Vicar's Hill House, nr. Lymington bur. Boldre*
*= 1.11 Oct 1784*
**Catherine Sowers**
*= 2.11 Mar 1790*
**Mary Garrett**
*= 3. 2 Aug 1804*
*Elizabeth Dickson*

**Elizabeth Purvis**

*b. 2 Dec 1748 at St. Olave's, Heart St., London*
*d. 28 Dec 1772 bur. Rochester*
*= 1.1 May 1768 Benjamin Good*
*= 2. at Minster, Isle of Sheppey*
**Andrew Long**

**Amy Elizabeth Long**

**George Purvis (4)**

*Secretary to Lords Howe and St. Vincent*
*b. 29 Jun 1751 at Allhallows, London*
*d. 2 May 1826 at Blackbrook Cottage, Fareham bur. Fareham*
*= 6 Jul 1791*
**Renira Charlotte Maitland**
*b. 30 Nov 1772 at Gosport*
*d. 29 May 1823 at Vicar's Hill, Boldre*
*dau. of Lieut. David Maitland RN*

**Lissey Anna Purvis**

*b. 27 Feb 1755 at Stepney*
*d. 28 Apr 1758 at Harwich and bur. in the church there*

**Emma Purvis**

*"Aunt Timms"*
*b. 12 Jul 1757 at Harwich*
*dsp. 31 May 1831 at Colchester and bur. with her mother in St. Giles's, Colchester*
*= 1 Jul 1789 at Great Hornsby, Essex*
*Capt. Richard Timms*

**The Beccles Family**

**CONTINUED AT TABLE B**

**The Vicar's Hill Family**

**CONTINUED AT TABLE C**

**The Blackbrook Family**

**CONTINUED AT TABLE D**

# THE DESCENDANTS OF CAPTAIN RICHARD PURVIS RN (1743-1802)

**TABLE B**

*The Beccles Family*

**Richard Purvis**

*Captain RN, of The Porters, Essex, and Beckenden Grange, Warwickshire*
b. 26 Aug 1743 at Stepney d. 2 May 1802 at Beccles

= 3 Jun 1780 at Melton, Suffolk. **Lucy Leman**

b. 5 Nov 1747 at Kirkstead, Norfolk d. 15 Jan 1825 bur. at Wenhaston
dau. of Revd. John Leman, Rector of Wenhaston

---

**Mary Anna Purvis**

b. 16 Jul 1781
at Beccles

d. 17 Aug 1781
at Beccles
bur. Wenhaston

---

**Lucy Anna Purvis**

b. 23 Aug 1783 at Beccles
d. 22 Jun 1817 in Edinburgh and
bur. New Calton Cemetery

= 1. 18 Nov 1806 at Colchester
**John Dudingston**
Capt. 28th Foot d. 28 Aug 1809

= 2. 7 Mar 1810
Chas. Dudingston, dsp. 7 Sep 1812

= 3. 11 Feb 1813, at Tongorra
**Archibald Kidd,** Capt. 21st Foot

---

**Richard Oadham Purvis**

"Cousin Oadham"
Lieutenant RN

b. 10 Feb 1785
at Beccles

dsp. 6 Jan 1804
on service in the
West Indies

Monument to him at
Port Royal, Jamaica

---

**John Leman Purvis**

"Cousin Leman"
Lieutenant Bengal
Native Infantry

b. 1 Mar 1786
at Beccles

dsp. 17 Mar 1805 at
Rangoon on service in
the East Indies

---

**George Thomas Purvis (5)**

Captain Bengal
Native Infantry

b. 7 Nov 1789
at Beccles

dsp. 28 Apr 1819
at Cape of Good Hope
aboard the Indiaman
"Sovereign" on
his passage home

---

**Barrington Oadham Purvis**

Lieutenant Bengal
Native Infantry

b. 21 Mar 1792, at Beccles

d. 4 Apr 1822, in London

= 11 Sep 1820
at Lawshall, Suffolk. his cousin
**Amy Laetitia Colville**
b. 13 Feb 1775 d. 9 Apr 1850

---

**Frances Laetitia Philippa Purvis**

b. 5 Oct 1821 at Beccles, Suffolk

d. 20 Feb 1873 at 26 Hyde Park
Square bur. at Lawhall Church

= 10 Jun 1841
**Edward John Francis Kelso**
Captain 72nd Highlanders,
Accidentally killed by a horse at
Slough 26 Oct 1857

3 sons, 2 daughters

---

[1]

**Lucy Frances Dudingston**

b. 11 Sep 1807 at
Burrtisland

= 23 Sep 1828
**Alexander Boyd**
Writer of the Signet
and JP for Edinburgh

1 daughter
who died in infancy

---

**John Charles Rainsford Dudingston**

b. 14 Dec 1808

= 26 Jun 1856 at
Crieff, Perthshire
**Mary Gavin Campbell**

1 son. 3 daughters

---

[3]

**Jean MacLean Kidd**

b. 16 Oct 1813
at Ponza, Naples

= 30 Aug 1831 at
Hillhousefield House
**Archibald Boyd**
Eldest son of
William Boyd

3 sons

# THE CHILDREN OF ADMIRAL JOHN CHILD PURVIS 1747-1825

## TABLE C

**The Vicar's Hill Family**

**John Child Purvis,** *Admiral of the Blue*

b. 13 Mar 1747 at Stepney. d. 23 Feb 1825 at Vicar's Hill House, near Lymington. bur. Boldre Churchyard

= 1. 11 Oct 1784. at Kingston. Hants.. **Catherine Sowers** b. 28 Dec 1757 at Deptford. d. 3 Feb 1789 at Wickham, Hants. bur. Kingston Churchyard. dau. and heiress of John Sowers, Clerk of the Cheque, Portsmouth Dockyard

= 2. 11 Mar 1790 **Mary Garrett** dau. of Daniel Garrett. She d. 1 Jul 1798

= 3. 2 Aug 1804 Elizabeth Dickson b. 6 May 1768. d. 27 Jul 1856 at Clarence House, Southampton bur. Boldre Churchyard
Only dau. of Admiral Sir Archibald Dickson Bart. and relict of her cousin Capt. William Dickson, 22nd Regt. who died at San Domingo in 1795

---

**[1]**

**[2]**

### John Scott
*Captain RN*

? Natural son by mother unknown ?

b. 9 Dec 1784

d. 8 Apr 1867

=1. 3 Jul 1815 **Mary Ann Cole**

=2. Nov 1840 Elizabeth Gibson

10 sons and 2 daus

---

### Catherine Purvis
b. 1 Aug 1785 at Havant

d. 10 Nov 1785 at Portsmouth bur. Kingston

---

### John Purvis
b. 24 Jun 1786 at Havant

d. 24 Jun 1786 bur. Havant

---

### John Brett Purvis
*Vice Admiral*

b. 12 Aug 1787 at Vernon Hill, Bishop's Waltham, Hants

d. 1 Oct 1857 at Bury Hall, Gosport bur. Whitsbury

= 24 Dec 1815 at Fareham, his cousin, **Renira Charlotte Purvis**

b. 28 Dec 1792 at Titchfield, Hants.

d. 21 Oct 1869 at Bury Hall bur. Whitsbury
Eldest dau. of George Purvis (4)

**Bury Hall**

**CONTINUED AT TABLE E**

---

### Richard Fortescue Purvis
*Capt. Bengal Native Infantry, Vicar of Whitsbury 1824-1868*

b. 4 Jan 1789 at Wickham, Hants.

d. 27 May 1868 at Whitsbury bur. Whitsbury

= 19 Jan 1824 at Rollesby, Norfolk **Elizabeth Helen Baker**

b. 8 Mar 1796

d. 8 Aug 1885
dau. of Revd. Thomas Baker, Rector of Rollesby, Norfolk

**Whitsbury**

**CONTINUED AT TABLE F**

---

### George Purvis
*died in infancy*

---

### Mary Emily Oadham Purvis
b. 26 May 1792 at Wickham, Hants.

d. 1796 bur. Kingston

# THE DESCENDANTS OF GEORGE PURVIS (4) 1751-1826

**The Blackbrook Family**

**George Purvis (4)**

Secretary to Admirals Lord Howe and Lord St. Vincent, Magistrate for the County of Southampton
b. 29 Jun 1751 at Allhallows, London d. 2 May 1826 at Blackbrook Cottage, Fareham bur. Fareham

= 6 Jul 1791 **Kenira Charlotte Maitland**

b. 30 Nov 1772 at Gosport d. 29 May 1823 at Vicar's Hill House, near Lymington bur. Fareham
dau. of Lieutenant David Maitland RN

---

**Kenira Charlotte Purvis**
b. 28 Dec 1792 at Titchfield, Hants.
d. 21 Oct 1869 at Bury Hall, Gosport
= 14 Dec 1815 at Fareham, her cousin
**John Brett Purvis**
Captain RN (later Vice Admiral of the Blue)

**Emma Purvis**
b. 28 Sep 1799
d. 12 Nov 1799

**Georgina Purvis**
b. 22 Dec 1800 at Blackbrook Cottage
d. 9 Aug 1847 at Portsmouth
= 7 Feb 1828
**Revd. Charles Twyford**
Rector of Trotton, Sussex who d. Aug 1850

**George Thomas Maitland Purvis (6)**
Captain RN
b. 10 Jun 1802 at Blackbrook Cottage
d. 7 Oct 1883 at Paignton, Devon
= 1. 10 Jan 1828 at Chawton, Hants.
**Mary Jane Austen**
b. 27 Apr 1807 d. 29 Dec 1836 bur. Fareham
dau. of Admiral of the Fleet
Sir Francis Austen KCB of Portsdown Lodge,
and niece of Jane Austen, the author
= 2. 10 Jan 1838 at Fareham, Hants.
**Esther North Harrison**
dau. of Revd. W. Harrison, Vicar of Fareham
and Canon of Winchester Cathedral

---

**Bury Hall** — Continued at TABLE E

**Blackbrook** — Continued at TABLE G

---

**Samuel Twyford**
Lieutenant RN
kia before Sebastopol
10 Apr 1855

**Dehaney Charles Twyford**
Lieutenant
Bombay Army
d.1858

**George William Twyford**
Lieutenant
23rd Fusiliers

**William Joliffe Twyford**
Lieutenant Colonel
23rd Fusiliers

**Edith Kenira Twyford**
= 17 Feb 1852
Capt. John Ormsby
Johnson RN

**Georgina Blanche Twyford**
d. 21 Dec 1851 aged
about 15 years

**Julia Elizabeth Twyford**
= George Walker

# THE DESCENDANTS OF VICE-ADMIRAL JOHN BRETT PURVIS 1787-1857

## TABLE E

**The Bury Hall Family**

**John Brett Purvis**
*Vice-Admiral of the Red*
b. 12 Aug 1787 at Vernon Hill House, Bishop's Waltham. d. 1 Oct 1857 at Bury Hall. Gosport bur. Whitsbury
= 24 Dec 1815 at Fareham, his cousin, **Renira Charlotte Purvis**
b. 28 Dec 1792 at Titchfield d. 21 Oct 1869 at Bury Hall. Gosport bur. Whitsbury
dau. of George Purvis (4)

**Richard Purvis**
*Rear-Admiral*
b. 12 Jun 1826 at Falmouth
d. 3 Dec 1875 at Bury Hall, Gosport
bur. Rowner, Hants.
= 4 Sep 1851 at Whitsbury
**Georgiana Rachel Cock**
b. 30 Mar 1831 at Fryern Court, Hants.
dau. of Major-General James Cock,
Bengal Army, of Hopton Hall, Suffolk

**George Henry Garrett Purvis**
b. 29 Apr 1820 at Titchfield
d. 29 Jan 1843 at Anglesea, Hants.
bur. in Alverstoke Churchyard

**Robert Brownrigg Arthur Purvis**
*Captain 78th Highlanders*
b. 29 Dec 1817 at Port Louis,
Isle of France, East Indies
disp. 13 Dec 1856 at Pau, Bas Pyrenees,
France and bur. there

**John Richard King Purvis**
b. 29 Oct 1816 in Ceylon
d. 20 Nov 1822 at Titchfield
bur. Titchfield Churchyard

**John Allen Ramsay Purvis**
*Lieut. 3rd King's Own Hussars*
b. 2 Nov 1866
= 5 Jan 1892 Ysabelle Schreiber

**Richard Brett Purvis**
b. 8 Nov 1862
= c.1869

**Rachel Louise Purvis**
b. 25 Apr 1859

**Arthur Dennis Molyneaux Purvis**
b. 7 Jun 1857

**Charles Hotham Purvis**
*Captain 17th Lancers*
b. 4 Oct 1852 at Queenstown
= **Mary Seton**

*One daughter in Canada*

**Ronald Montague Purvis**
b. 18 May 1891

**Charles Brett Purvis**
b. 15 Jan 1889

**Renira Elizabeth Frances Purvis**
b. 30 Jul 1866

# THE DESCENDANTS OF REVD. RICHARD FORTESCUE PURVIS 1789-1868

## TABLE F

**The Whitsbury Family**

**Revd. Richard Fortescue Purvis**

Captain Bengal Native Infantry. Retired 1820, then Vicar of Whitsbury 1824-1868
b. 4 Jan 1789 at Wickham d. 27 May 1868 at Whitsbury bur. Whitsbury

= 19 Jan 1824 at Rollesby, Norfolk **Elizabeth Helen Baker**

b. 8 Mar 1796 d. 8 Aug 1885

dau. of Revd. Thomas Baker, Rector of Rollesby, Norfolk

---

**Elizabeth Purvis**

b. 25 Mar 1825
at Whitsbury
d. 26 Sep 1834
bur. Whitsbury

---

**Home Purvis (1)**

b. 21 Nov 1826
at Whitsbury
d. 28 Sep 1827
bur Whitsbury

---

**Revd. Fortescue Richard Purvis**

Vicar of Whitsbury
1868-1885
b. 6 Jul 1828
at Whitsbury
d. 18 Aug 1885
bur. Whitsbury

= 2 Feb 1860
his cousin
**Louisa Harriet Eyre Matcham**

b. 13 Dec 1827
dau. of William George Matcham of Newhouse

---

**Emily Mary Purvis**

b. 29 Jun 1831
at Whitsbury
d. Jul 1891

= 2 Oct 1872 at
Rockbourne Church
J. R. Harman of
Sindlesham House,
Berks

---

**John Child Purvis (2)**

Vice-Admiral
b. 2 Oct 1832
at Whitsbury
d. 1 Sep 1904 at
Wildungen,
Germany

---

**Home Purvis (2)**

Lieutenant
10th Regiment
b. 28 Aug 1835
at Whitsbury
d. 23 Jan 1857
bur. Whitsbury

---

**Elizabeth Helen Purvis**

b. 29 Aug 1837
at Whitsbury
d. 29 Jul 1863 at
Anglesea, Hants.
bur. Whitsbury

---

**Renira Anna Purvis**

b. 1 Apr 1841
at Whitsbury
= 1. 7 Sep 1865 at
Whitsbury
**Edward Henry Gage Lambert**

Captain RN
who d. 16 Nov 1872
3rd son of Sir
Henry Lambert
Bart. of Aston
House, Oxon.

= 2. 21 Jul 1874
The Hon. Fitzgerald
Algernon Foley
Rear-Admiral
son of Thomas,
3rd Lord Foley

2 sons and
1 daughter by her
first marriage
(Lambert)

---

**Louisa Helen Harriet Purvis**

b. 30 Apr 1861 at
Wickford Rectory, Essex

---

**Alan Richard Fortescue Purvis**

b. 22 Apr 1864 at
Calstone Rectory, Wilts.
dsp. 26 Jan 1886

---

**Archibald Bellenden Purvis**

Captain RN b. 19 Nov 1865
d. 22 Dec 1926
= 13 Aug 1898
**Elona Maria Edwards**

2 sons, 1 daughter

---

**Charles Hugh Purvis**

b. 18 Sep 1867
d. 22 Jul 1917
= 14 Jul 1904
**Constance Augusta Burlton Allen**

2 sons, 3 daughters

---

**John William Malcolm Purvis**

b. 5 Oct 1869 d. c.1960
= 1892
**Isla Marie Leighton**

1 son

# THE DESCENDANTS OF GEORGE THOMAS MAITLAND PURVIS (6) 1802-1883

## TABLE G

The *Blackbrook Family* (continued)

This table shows the descent from George Thomas Maitland Purvis's first wife, Mary-Jane Austen. The descent from his second wife, Esther North Harrison, is shown on **TABLE H.**

**George Thomas Maitland Purvis (6)**

Captain RN b. 10 Jun 1802 at Blackbrook Cottage d. 7 Oct 1883 at Paignton, Devon

= 1. 10 Jun 1828 at Chawton, Hants. **Mary Jane Austen**

b. 27 Apr 1807 d. 29 Dec 1836 bur. Fareham

dau. of Admiral of the Fleet Sir Francis Austen KCB of Portsdown Lodge, and niece of Jane Austen, the author

= 2. 10 Jan 1838 at Fareham, Hants. **Esther North Harrison**

dau. of Revd. W. Harrison, Vicar of Fareham and Canon of Winchester Cathedral

---

**Helen Catherine Purvis**

b. 13 Jul 1835 at Blackbrook Cottage d. 26 Apr 1929

= 1. 1855 at Queenstown **John George Valentine Rickord RN**

eldest son of Thomas Pink Rickord of Malta

= 2. Edward MacDonald

*2 sons — Herbert and Maitland James Rickord*

---

**Francis Reginald Purvis**

Rear-Admiral, "Reggie"

b. 18 Jan 1833 at Blackbrook Cottage

d. 10 Jan 1895 at Newton Abbot, Devon

= 21 Jun 1869 in London **Esther Frances Pegler**

dau. of Alfred Pegler of Minchampton, Glos.

---

**Emily Florence Purvis**

b. 5 Oct 1872

**Francis George Herbert Purvis**

b. 30 Sep 1871 d. 15 Jun 1910

**Frances Mary Helen Purvis**

b. 10 Jun 1870

---

**Herbert Mark Garrett Purvis**

Major-General and Colonel-Commandant Royal Artillery

b. 23 Jan 1831 at Blackbrook Cottage, Fareham

d. 8 Oct 1912 at Westcott House, Cullompton, Devon

= 1. 9 Nov 1858 Co. Tipperary, Ireland **Elizabeth Jane Grogan**

b. 1844 d. Apr 1885

dau. of Capt. J E K Grogan, 32nd Regiment

= 2. 28 Dec 1885 at Lucknow, India

**Daisy Bickers** dau. of E Bickers, Barrister-at-Law, Lucknow

---

**Eyre Walter Molyneux Purvis**

Major, 16th Bengal Lancers

b. 13 Jul 1871

Killed on active service in Mesopotamia 4. Mar 1915 (dsp)

**Herbert John Edwin Purvis**

Major 2nd Bombay Cavalry, Governor of Bombay's Bodyguard

b. 18 Nov 1865

dsp. 15 Aug 1901 in Japan

---

**Mary-Jane Austen Purvis**

b. 2 May 1863 in India

= 1. 9 Mar 1882 **Reginald Campbell**

Capt. 24th Regt. S. Wales Borderers

d. 30 Aug 1901

Alfred Cotton Way DSO

Capt. 24th Regt. S. Wales Borderers

**Spencer Bertie Cyril Campbell**

b. 17 Jun 1883

---

**Mary Renira Purvis**

b. 31 Mar 1830 at Blackbrook Cottage

= Dec 1874 **J Paine** of Springfield, Taunton

**Maitland Francis Austen Paine**

b. 7 Jun 1876

---

**George Thomas Maitland Purvis (7)**

Captain RN

b. 21 Feb 1829 at Blackbrook Cottage

dsp. 11 Feb 1880 at Yokohama, Japan

= 21 Jul 1855 **Jane Pragnell**

---

**George Frederick Godfrey Purvis (8)**

Miralai, "Purvis Pasha"

Lieutenant RN Retd 1890 then Dir. Gen. Egyptian Coastguard

b. 16 Nov 1859 at Ballincollig, Co. Cork, Ireland

dsp. 1936 at Burghfield Common, Berks

= 18 Sep 1900 May Peel dsp. 1964 5th dau. of William Felton Peel of Carrikerford Hall, Tamworth

# THE DESCENDANTS OF GEORGE THOMAS MAITLAND PURVIS (6) 1802-1883

**TABLE H**

The
*Blackbrook
Family
(continued)*

This table shows the descent from George Thomas Maitland Purvis's second wife Esther North Harrison. The descent from his first wife, Mary-Jane Austen, is shown on **TABLE G.**

**George Thomas Maitland Purvis (6)**

*Captain RN  b. 10 Jun 1802 at Blackbrook Cottage  d. 7 Oct 1883 at Paignton, Devon*
*= 1. 10 Jun 1828 at Chawton, Hants.* **Mary Jane Austen**
*b. 27 Apr 1807  d. 29 Dec 1836  bur. Fareham*
*dau. of Admiral of the Fleet Sir Francis Austen KCB of Portsdown Lodge, and niece of Jane Austen, the author*
*= 2. 10 Jan 1838 at Fareham, Hants.* **Esther North Harrison**
*dau. of Revd. W. Harrison, Vicar of Fareham and Canon of Winchester Cathedral*

**Esther Elizabeth Cambria Purvis**

*b. 5 Dec 1841*
*d. 4 Feb 1879 at Langhorne, Carmarthenshire*

**Kathleen Leak Purvis**

*b. 3 Jan 1846*
*= 16 Feb 1867*
*Thomas Moultree Kelsall Solicitor, Fareham*
*dsp*

**William George Purvis**

*b. 31 Jul 1848*
*d. 1907 at Walton-on-Thames*
*= 17 Mar 1874,*
**Charlotte Finlay**
*dau. of Frederick Finlay*

**Madeline Sophia Purvis**

*b. 30 Oct 1849*
*= Dec 1894,*
*Reginald Beadon*
*Lieutenant Colonel, late of 60th Regiment of Foot*

**Eva Charlotte Purvis**

*b. 24 Jun 1852*

**Henry George Purvis**

*b. 2 Feb 1875*

**William Edward Purvis**

*b. 12 Oct 1876*

**Kathleen Charlotte Elizabeth Purvis**

*b. 31 Jan 1878*

# Index

| | |
|---|---|
| B.C.S. | Bengal Civil Service |
| B.M.S. | Bengal Medical Service |
| B.N.I. | Bengal Native Infantry |
| H.E.I.C. | Honourable East India Company |
| H.M. | His Majesty's |
| H.M.S. | His Majesty's Ship |
| R.N. | Royal Navy |

| | |
|---|---|
| B.&O. | Bihar & Orissa |
| C.I. | Central India (Madhya Pradesh) |
| C.P. | Central Provinces (Madhya Pradesh) |
| U.P. | United Provinces (Uttar Pradesh) |

[Table]    Refers to genealogical tables at pages 290-297

320

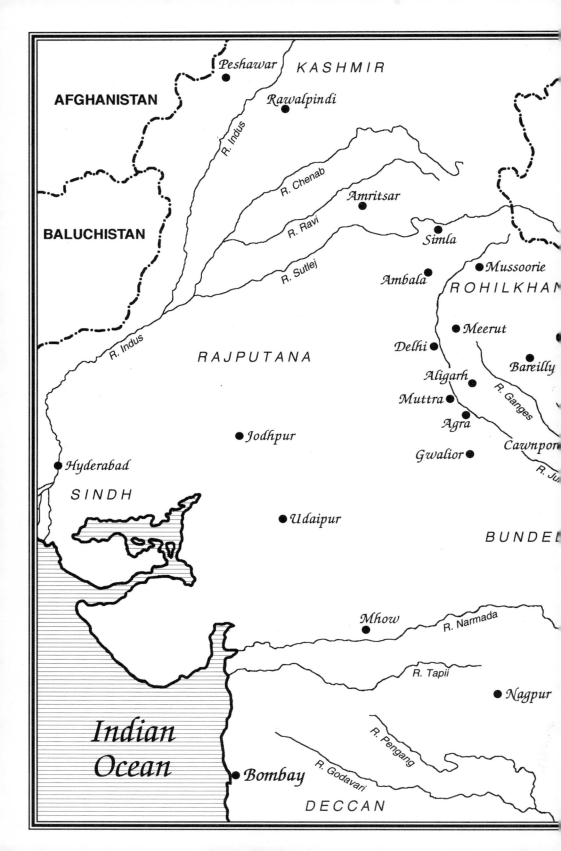